W9-BEA-677

LATIN AMERICAN DEBT

The Twentieth Century Fund is a research foundation undertaking timely analyses of economic, political, and social issues. Not-for-profit and nonpartisan, the Fund was founded in 1919 and endowed by Edward A. Filene.

BOARD OF TRUSTEES OF THE TWENTIETH CENTURY FUND

Morris B. Abram
H. Brandt Ayers
Peter A. A. Berle
José A. Cabranes
Joseph A. Califano, Jr.
Alexander Morgan Capron
Edward E. David, Jr.
Brewster C. Denny, *Chairman*
Charles V. Hamilton
August Heckscher, Emeritus
Matina S. Horner
James A. Leach

Georges-Henri Martin, Emeritus
Lawrence K. Miller, Emeritus
P. Michael Pitfield
Don K. Price, Emeritus
Richard Ravitch
Arthur M. Schlesinger, Jr.
Albert Shanker
Harvey I. Sloane, M.D.
Theodore C. Sorensen
James Tobin
David B. Truman, Emeritus
Shirley Williams

M. J. Rossant, *Director*

LATIN AMERICAN DEBT

Pedro-Pablo Kuczynski

A Twentieth Century Fund Book

The Johns Hopkins University Press
Baltimore and London

© 1988 Twentieth Century Fund
All rights reserved
Printed in the United States of America

The Johns Hopkins University Press,
701 West 40th Street, Baltimore, Maryland 21211
The Johns Hopkins Press Ltd., London

Library of Congress Cataloging-in-Publication Data

Kuczynski Godard, Pedro-Pablo, 1938–
 Latin American debt.

 Bibliography: p.
 Includes index.
 1. Debts, External—Latin America. I. Twentieth
Century Fund. II. Title.
HJ8514.5.K83 1988   336.3′435′098   88-1218
ISBN 0-8018-3659-X (alk. paper)
ISBN 0-8018-3660-3 (pbk.: alk. paper)

The paper used in this publication meets the minimum requirements of American National Standard for Information Sciences—Permanence of Paper for Printed Library Materials, ANSI Z39.48-1984.

Contents

Tables

Appendix Tables

Appendix Charts

Foreword

The international debt crisis is now entering its seventh year with no resolution in sight. To be sure, we have managed to avoid a global debacle, which some observers had predicted when the crisis first emerged. But that does not mean that things have improved. In some respects they have gotten much worse. Until now, it has been the debtor countries, especially in Latin America, that have borne most of the burden of their own excessive indebtedness. To ask them to do more than they have been doing is to run the risk of political instability, which so far at least they have been fortunate enough to avoid. Indeed, most countries in Latin America have turned to democratic governments in their efforts to grope their way out of the crisis. But if they fail, we could easily see a return to the authoritarian regimes that were the fashion only a few years ago.

The Twentieth Century Fund has devoted a considerable part of its research to the debt crisis. From the first, we did not think that it was a transient phenomenon. To the contrary, we have always believed that it would take the combined efforts of the public and private sectors of both the developed and developing countries to find a solution to the crisis brought about by the great borrowing and lending spree of the previous decade. And those efforts have not yet been made.

Our interest in the crisis naturally led us to Pedro-Pablo Kuczynski, who is perhaps the most knowledgeable individual on Latin American debt. A former official of the World Bank and a former cabinet minister in Peru who is now an investment banker with First Boston Corporation, he combines theoretical understanding with practical experience. He also has a sophisticated grasp of international politics. For these reasons, we invited him to write a book on Latin American debt and what should be done to arrive at a realistic solution, one that could bring an end to the crisis and enable the developing countries to resume their economic growth, which of course would do much to ensure political stability.

In his study he makes it plain that cooperation between debtors and creditors is essential to resolving the debt crisis. Unless that cooperation takes place, he warns, the debt problem will grow worse, endangering the economic and political well-being of the entire world. By the same token, once the debt problem becomes manageable, the prospect is that we will enjoy a quickening of economic growth in the First World as well as the Third.

The Fund is grateful to Kuczynski for his exposition of the problem and how best to deal with it. I believe his study will be of interest and use to political leaders, to bankers, and to the public at large. To put it succinctly, and with no pun intended, we are in his debt.

M. J. ROSSANT, DIRECTOR
The Twentieth Century Fund
December 1987

Preface and Acknowledgments

This book is intended for a broad audience. In the past six years, while giving talks about the debt problem in Latin America, I have found much interest in an explanation of how this problem arose and what might be done about it. Audiences have not been as curious about the drama of international financial negotiations and its main characters—a subject that has mesmerized much of the international press—as about the relationship between the political and economic aspects of the problem.

The debt problem first became clear to many of us in 1981. At that time, I was the energy and mines minister of Peru. My deputy and eventual successor, Fernando Montero, and I were frequently visited by foreign bankers. Quite suddenly, in late 1981, the visits of the bankers stopped. Developing countries, especially in Latin America, had been caught between rising interest rates on their external debts on the one hand and falling export income caused by plummeting commodity prices on the other. In April 1982, the South Atlantic conflict between Argentina and Britain further discouraged new lending. After that it was only a matter of time. The banks, which had financed most large Latin American economies at an almost dizzying pace during the previous decade, now sharply curtailed new lending. By August 1982, Mexico could no longer meet its scheduled obligations. Brazil followed in December. Although signs of the crisis had been clear for at least a year, little had been done by lenders, borrowers, or international financial institutions to forestall damage.

It is risky to write about current events. Much information has yet to come to light. And while the debt crisis has receded somewhat, the final outcome is still uncertain. At the time of the first oil shock in 1973–74, many analysts greatly underestimated the capacity of markets to adjust. Large energy price increases eventually brought about large cuts in energy consumption. In the same way, Latin American economies are likely in time to adjust to the loss of the stimulus that kept many of them euphoric during the 1970s and very early 1980s. However, given the fragility and social disparities of the countries in question, there is a valid question about the costs of this process. With some doubt as to the wisdom of my attempt, this book will try to shed some light on this question.

Even riskier than writing about current events is projecting the future without a solid footing in the past. My emphasis in the first six chapters is, therefore, on assessing what happened. In the last two chapters I examine what went wrong with the debt strategy envisaged in 1982 and what might be done about it. And given the evolution of the debt question and the uncertainties ushered in by the U.S. stock market crash in October 1987, I have added a postscript—an overall view of the question as of the end of 1987.

Clearly, the most urgent priority for the majority of debtor countries is the renewal of economic growth. Without it there will not be a favorable setting for the economic reforms necessary for long-term sustained growth, and thus growth will only come in short-lived spurts as happened in Mexico in 1984 and Brazil in 1985–86. The international financial situation, which has been highly adverse to commodity producers in the 1980s, needs to improve and has to be accompanied by greater official capital inflows to give economies the initial push toward growth. Such moves would start a virtuous circle of growth and reform; otherwise, the vicious cycle of depression, capital flight, and unrest is likely to continue.

I am grateful to the Twentieth Century Fund and most especially to its director, Murray Rossant, for supporting this book and for wise counsel and patience during its preparation and publication. My very special thanks go to Dr. Elizabeth Rabitsch, of First Boston, for her invaluable help in the preparation of material for the book, her many comments, and her review of the whole manuscript. My special appreciation also to Albert Verme, of First Boston, who helped with Chapter 3; to Dr. Miguel Urrutia and Joseph V. Hinshaw, and to their economics colleagues at the Inter-American Development Bank; to Dr. Emmanuel Melichar of the Federal Reserve Board, Washington, D.C., for his material on U.S. agriculture; and to Rinaldo M. Pecchioli of the Organization for Economic Cooperation and Development, Paris, for his valuable statistical assistance.

Many friends have given me useful comments. I would in particular like to thank Jesus Silva Herzog of Mexico, Rodrigo Botero of Colombia, Adalbert Krieger Vasena of Argentina, and Guy P. Pfeffermann of the World Bank, as well as my brother, M. G. Kuczynski, Fellow of Pembroke College, Cambridge. I am entirely responsible for the final product and for any errors it may contain. It does not in any way reflect the opinions that my employer may have on the subjects discussed.

Chapter 3 is based to a large degree on the chapter about the same subject, which I prepared for *Towards Renewed Economic Growth in Latin America,* by Bela Balassa, Gerardo Bueno, Mario Henrique Simonsen, and the author (Washington, D.C., Institute for International Economics, 1986). My special thanks to Bela Balassa and to Fred Bergsten, who made that book possible, as well as to many in the United States and in Latin America who supported the effort.

Chapter 8 follows the argument and presentation that I used in an article, "The Outlook for Latin American Debt," which appeared in *Foreign Affairs* (Fall 1987). My special appreciation to the editor, William Hyland, and the associate editor, Linda Robinson. The postscript appeared in modified form in *The International Economy* (January 1988); my thanks to its editor, Art Pine.

A word of special gratitude to my family, and especially my wife, who were most tolerant of the use of my time during the preparation of the book, and to my friends, who generously gave me time to discuss the subject.

In 1986, Raúl Prebisch, the leading international economic thinker from Latin America in the postwar period and also a friend, died. I discussed several of the ideas in this book with him, both privately and also publicly (I particularly remember a joint conference a few years ago at a Washington, D.C., book fair where we were supposed to debate our ideas on the debt question but ended up in a large measure of agreement). As of the mid- and late 1980s, the terms-of-trade question, which Prebisch brought to the forefront of economic literature almost forty years ago, continues to be a central one for developing countries. No book on the economic problems of Latin America can be complete without acknowledging a debt of gratitude and offering a special tribute to Raúl Prebisch.

LATIN AMERICAN DEBT

(1)

A Latin American Problem

The Setting

In August 1982, Mexico announced that it was unable to continue its scheduled external debt service. The big international banks immediately and drastically cut back new lending to most Latin American countries. Since then, one of the most visible and persistent international financial problems has been the "debt crisis" in Latin America. To be sure, there have been other, perhaps larger international financial problems, including high interest rates in the United States, the overvalued U.S. dollar until 1985, and the persistent U.S. trade deficit, but few issues have seemed as intractable as the external debt problem of most of Latin America and the Caribbean, as well as of the Philippines. Constant refinancings and well-publicized cliff-hanger deadlines (the latest of which have been a second Mexican crisis in mid-1986 and a major Brazilian crisis in early 1987), doubts about the safety of some of the larger international banks, and misery and turmoil in a number of the debtor countries are some of the ramifications of the problem which have contributed to its apparent complexity.

The debt issue is, to a large extent although not exclusively, concentrated in Latin America. The same problems occurred during the depression of the early 1930s, when most Latin American countries defaulted on their external debt payments; earlier, in the nineteenth century, frequent defaults occurred when the first external debts were incurred to finance the wars of independence against Spain. As in the past, the reason for these debt problems today is simple: Latin American countries have been the largest group of developing countries which have been able to borrow from commercial sources.

Why has the Latin American debt crisis attracted so much attention, especially in the financial press? First, it has involved large countries—for instance, Brazil (population 135 million) and Mexico (population 80 million)—which are among the leading emerging nations. And Mexico, with its long border with the United States and permanent immigration pressure, commands special attention in the United States. Second, the protracted length of the crisis has focused attention on the large amounts that leading international banks have lent to Latin American and other developing countries. The strict financial disclosure rules in the United States created fears, largely unfounded, that the safety of leading U.S. banks was at stake, even though other financial centers were also heavily exposed.

It is the international financial implications of the debt of Latin America which have received the most attention. Yet, in discussions about the threat to the international banking system, it has never been quite clear who stands at the end of the creditor line. Is it ordinary depositors, who account for the largest part of bank resources? Perhaps, but in the United States at least, small depositors are insured. Is it then the large corporate and government depositors, who in theory are not covered by deposit insurance but who in practice have been bailed out of all large bank failures in industrial countries during the last twenty or thirty years? Is it the taxpayer, who in the end finances the cost of the deposit insurance and the bank failures? Or is it the threat, diluted throughout the world by some degree of inflation, that follows central bank money expansion to refloat moribund banking institutions, as happened with Continental Illinois in 1984? So far, there are no clear answers to this important question, although, in the end, the effect of an unhealthy banking system spreads throughout an economy.

In any case, the emphasis here is on the developing country debtors. When the financial press and leading bankers talk about the crisis being over, they refer to the perceived threat to the international banking system. Much less attention has been placed on the real economic costs of the crisis for the debtor countries and their populations. In May 1987, as Citicorp created additional reserves of 22 percent of its outstanding loans for developing countries, the attention shifted away from the debtor countries again to the banks. The chairman of another large New York bank, which set aside similar reserves, told his staff that such an action "puts the problem behind us." Such an outcome remains quite unlikely.

The combination of international debt and the perceived threat to giant banks (the stuff of which novels are and have been made) also explains why the international debt crisis—magnified in name though still largely a Latin American affair—has received perhaps more attention in the United States than comparable problems closer to home, such as the farm debt crisis or the banking losses triggered by the unwise oil drilling loans assembled by one obscure Oklahoma bank, the Penn Square Bank. The losses caused by this last crisis, including the $4.5 billion federal government rescue of the Continental Illinois Bank in 1984, were comparable until 1986 to the write-offs for banks in the United States caused by the economic problems of Latin American countries. Still more important, the steadily growing farm debt crisis in the United States until 1985 was a comparatively silent affair.

As in the case of Latin America, the farm debt crisis in the United States is not without precedent. It is a typical case of the boom-and-bust cycle that has traditionally affected commodity producers. In Latin America, governments were the borrowers, whereas in the United States farm economy, they were the individual farmers. Hundreds of small rural banks and thousands of farmers have been hurt, but there have been no big international meetings, no Concorde dashes across the Atlantic, no all-night sessions at law offices and banks in New York. Not only have the troubled individual borrowers been relatively small debtors with no compelling media interest, but the economic problems on the farm have not materially affected big banks, although there have been some regional exceptions, especially in California.

Yet, the amount of U.S. commercial bank loans affected by the farm debt crisis, around $100 billion, is about the same as that involved in the Latin American debt crisis; the growth of debt over the 1973–83 decade has also been rapid; and the origins of the problem are also comparable: low real interest rates in the 1970s, rapid growth of debt based on the continued expectation of inflation of land prices in the case of U.S. farmers and of commodity prices in the case of several Latin American debtors, and then a collapse when inflation stopped and the terms of trade turned against the borrowers. In the case of U.S. farmers, where subsidized government lending is important and where the population is in constant decline, the size of the downward economic adjustment has been less brutal. Yet the story remained broadly the same in the early 1980s. The difference appeared later, in the 1986 data in table 1-1, as the U.S. farm debt, and hence the interest due, started to go down sharply as a result of write-offs of debt and farm acquisitions by new owners at lower prices.

The Euromarket

The Eurocurrency market, or Euromarket for short, has been the vehicle for most international bank lending over the past fifteen years. Since it took off in the late 1960s, and until 1982, most of this lending

Table 1-1   Debt Comparison of Latin America and the U.S. Farm Sector

		Latin America (External Debt Only)	U.S. Farm Sector (Excludes Household Farms)
Total debt outstanding	1973	48	60
(billions of dollars	1983	351	202
current prices)	1986	395	155
Of which owed to U.S.			
banks		100	90[a]
		(income from merchandise exports)	(gross income)
Debt as a proportion of			
income (percentage)	1973	188	67
	1983	394	145
	1986	494	104
Interest paid as a	1973	11	5
proportion of gross	1983	45	15
income (percentage)	1986	40	6
1980–84 change in:			
Per capita income		−13	+ 1
Terms of trade		−22	−10
(percentage)		(excluding effect of interest)	(including effect of interest)

Sources: Latin America: see Chapter 2. U.S. Farm Sector: E. Melichar, "A Financial Perspective on Agriculture," *Federal Reserve Bulletin* (January 1984), and "Turning the Corner on Troubled Farm Debt," *Federal Reserve Bulletin* (July 1987). I am also most grateful to Dr. Melichar for providing additional materials.

[a]Includes cooperative farm credit system.

was done by commercial banks at rates that vary or "float" with the cost of money to the lenders. The Euromarket is funded by a pool of currencies deposited outside the national banking systems of the currencies in question, mainly U.S. dollars deposited outside the U.S. domestic banking system. The supply of funds into the Euromarket grew especially rapidly during the 1970s, at an annual compounded rate of about 26 percent, stimulated by world inflation. In addition, the freedom from regulation in the Euromarket enabled banks to attract funds by paying higher interest rates than they could in their own countries. The funds of the oil-exporting, capital-surplus countries in the Organization of Petroleum Exporting Countries (OPEC) were in particular attracted to this offshore market. On the lending side, the fact that banks were able to pass on to the borrower the risk of the cost of funds going up, by lending at floating interest rates, also encouraged lending through the Euromarket.

During the 1970s, the supply of funds into the Euromarket grew at a pace far faster than the demand for international financing from traditional users of such funds, namely, large international corporations and the governments of the industrialized countries themselves. World inflation combined with economic stagnation—itself the result of the oil shock, and in turn the consequence of inflation—generated the loanable funds. Even though the large supply of funds served to drive down real interest rates, large international banks and even the not-so-large were forced to find an outlet for their new resources, whether they liked it or not. The most logical targets for lending were the emerging industrial nations among the developing countries, relatively unsophisticated borrowers who were willing to pay more for money than their industrial country counterparts and were thus attractive to lenders.

The task of lending to developing countries was made easier by the fact that for the most part governments constituted the borrowers, and therefore credit judgments were much simpler to make than for a corporation, which might disappear in bankruptcy. Countries do not disappear. This is the meaning of Walter Wriston's famous dictum that countries never go bankrupt.[1] They may not be able to pay, but their debts do not disappear.

The imperative of the market, namely, an excess of money with few places to go, was labeled "recycling"; the surpluses of oil-exporting countries were invested in oil-importing countries, or at least some of the main ones, thus helping to maintain growth despite the crushing burden of skyrocketing oil import bills. All of this took place to more or less universal applause. Necessity, driven by world inflation, became a virtue.

The upper tier of developing countries was a tempting target for this new lending because these borrowers were willing to pay significantly higher margins over the base interest rate than borrowers from the industrialized countries. Governments of developing countries were not especially worried about interest rates floating upward, since those rates were then low, and in some years even lower than inflation. The developing countries were eager to borrow in order to avoid cutting back their economies as a result of the increase in oil prices from 1973 onward. For the oil-importing countries of Latin America, the initial impact of oil price increases was equivalent to a one-time increase in the value of imports of about 30 percent, or roughly a cutback in growth of 5 percent. In the case of Brazil, the value of imports almost doubled in 1974. Without additional capital inflows, severe belt-tightening, probably under the auspices of the International Monetary Fund (IMF), would have had to take place and economic growth would have been curtailed. The banks provided a far more palatable alternative.

Put differently, rising oil prices stimulated the flow of both lending and borrowing at the same time. Monetary expansion and inflation in the Western industrialized countries, especially in the United States, pushed up the growth of credit. Meanwhile, the larger developing countries, most of them oil importers, were eager to borrow their way out of recessions brought on by higher oil prices. At first, dramatically higher oil prices created the need for external borrowing by major oil-importing countries, especially Brazil, and even to some degree Mexico, which was still a small oil importer at the time. Later, however, it was the availability of external credit, more than anything else, which led to the growth of debt. By then Mexico was exporting oil, but its external debt grew even faster than before. Together, Brazil and Mexico absorbed about half of all Euromarket lending to developing countries in the 1970s. Total bank lending to developing countries in turn accounted for between one-third and two-fifths of the total net flow of resources from the Euromarket, the rest going to corporations and the governments of industrialized countries.

The political orientation of the borrowing governments was not a key influence upon the lending decisions of banks. The resources of borrowing countries and their prospects for growth were the criteria for credit decisions, as indeed they should have been. However, the lack of timely statistics plus the economic pressure of surplus funds led banks to lend far more than they would have had all the facts been known. Hungary and Poland, centralized and socialist economies, were magnets for lenders just as much as Argentina and Brazil, with military regimes strongly espousing capitalism, or Peru, with a nationalistic and statist military regime under General Velasco, or Venezuela, with a traditional democracy. True, there was no bank lending to the Allende government, which was overthrown in a bloody coup in September 1973, but large-scale international bank lending was just beginning to expand sharply at about that time so that it is hard to judge whether banks would have lent to a longer-lived and economically more stable Allende regime, as they did to the Velasco regime in Peru. Profit rather than political orientation was the main motivator of lending during the 1970s. In every case, regardless of politics, banks preferred to lend to the public sector, not for any ideological reasons but because government guarantees eliminated commercial risk. And it was only in cases where the enthusiasm of the lenders for the economic policies of governments proved uncontainable, as in Argentina and Chile in the late 1970s, when liberalization of domestic financial systems was undertaken on a large scale—inducing the commercial bank lenders to set up shop locally—that the banks were willing to lend substantial sums to the private sector.

By 1982, when the Mexican debt crisis burst onto the international financial scene, about $360 billion of the approximately $1 trillion in Euromarket deposits, after netting out borrowing between banks within the market, was in loans to developing countries, and two-thirds of that was in Latin America.

The large-scale lending and borrowing of the 1970s and very early 1980s in Latin America was based on a critical but seldom discussed assumption, namely, that the world economy would continue to expand and that nothing much would change in the pattern of growth of the Western industrialized nations. It was expected that these nations would continue to be large importers of raw materials, boosting traditional exports of developing countries. They would also funnel to the developing world a large amount of capital in the form of government aid, commercial loans, and private investment. In fact, that comfortable pattern had already begun to change in the wake of the oil price increases of 1973–74, which hit industry in the advanced economies very hard. For a time, nevertheless, most governments of developing countries, cushioned by the large flow of commercial bank loans and by relatively high commodity prices, continued to think that the change was temporary. Talk of a commodity "shortage," fueled by inflation, helped to maintain the illusion, and ambitious development plans continued to be made.

Past Debt Cases

During the 1970s and early 1980s, as in the past, a number of countries ran into serious debt problems. Six in particular stand out: Indonesia, Zaire, Peru, Turkey, Poland, and Costa Rica.[2] None of these cases, however, were large enough by themselves to have been a material influence on international finance. They did not lead commercial banks to cut off international lending to a whole region or to slow down lending sharply elsewhere, as was the case after Mexico suspended repayments in August 1982. Nonetheless, an examination of these initial cases is instructive.

Indonesia encountered a difficult period after the first big oil price increases of 1973–74, largely as a result of loose and excessive borrowing by the state oil company, Pertamina. When Sukarno fell in 1966, a major external debt refinancing had already been arranged. The trouble in the 1970s was quickly corrected by the central government, however, and no large-scale debt refinancing was required. The troika of investment bank advisers to troubled countries—Kuhn Loeb Lehman Brothers, Lazard Frères, and S. G. Warburg—got its start in Indonesia.

Next came Zaire, viewed as a resource-rich country by eager international lenders, especially in Europe. For a time, they showered medium-term commercial loans upon this very poor country and its state-run industry in copper, a commodity for which there was declining world demand. When copper collapsed in the mid-1970s, Zaire began to wilt in the international financial wind, unable to grow or to service its debt. At the time, a committee of commercial banks under the leadership of Citibank made various attempts to monitor Zaire's finances. The colonialist overtones of this effort, as well as the lack of an impartial multilateral official arbiter such as the IMF, doomed this attempt to failure.

The same scenario took place in Peru in 1976. A new financial team straightened out public finances in 1978, partly by cutting the growth of public expenditures but mostly by imposing high taxes on the benefits of a commodity export boom that resulted from higher export prices and the start of petroleum exports. The Peruvian economy progressed through the transition from a military to an elected government in 1980 until natural catastrophes, the collapse of export prices in 1982, terrorism, and government indecision put the country back into the economic emergency room.

The most significant debt refinancings occurred in Turkey and Poland. The Turkish debt to commercial banks rose rapidly in the mid-1970s to somewhere around three times the annual value of exports through a device known as the "Convertible Turkish Lira Deposits," in effect deposits by foreign banks in Turkish banks. Since these loans were officially in the form of deposits, convertible into foreign exchange, they were not counted as debts and therefore were not subject to withholding taxes on the interest paid abroad. For a while, everyone, including the international agencies, was fooled; then, in early 1977, Turkish foreign exchange reserves ran out. The debt had allowed difficult economic decisions to be postponed. It was not until the arrival of Turgut Ozal, appointed finance minister in 1980 and elected prime minister in 1983, that real progress was made by overhauling the tax system and liberalizing the economy. Even though the Turkish external debt is still high, major progress has been made in strengthening the economy and expanding exports.

In Poland, the debt to Western banks and export agencies rose steadily from the early 1970s, under the growth-oriented policies of the Gierek regime, until it reached $26 billion in 1981, or four times its annual export earnings to the West. The economy and the investment projects for which the money had been borrowed were not productive enough to sustain rising growth expectations, and in early 1981 Poland defaulted. It has since slowly worked itself out of the crunch, with major internal strife and turmoil along the way.

Costa Rica also went into effective default in 1981. Beginning in 1976, large-scale borrowing from banks to finance a growing budget deficit, as well as the creation of state enterprises in sugar, cement, and other industries, created an external debt almost five times the annual value of exports. With the rise of international interest rates in 1981, it became impossible to service the debt, especially since the state investments did not generate profits or exports. Since 1982, the standard combination of public austerity and devaluation has begun to show results, although movement was quite slow at first. The interesting point about Costa Rica is that this has been its third debt crisis in twenty years; in all three cases, commercial bank lending played a major part, yet the bankers returned for more lending each time.

If there is a lesson to be learned from these events, it is that easy financing has a tendency to lead to uneconomic investments and the postponement of difficult austerity measures. As long as the future looks rosy, lending and borrowing go on. When prospects cloud, the cutoff in lending is apt to be sudden and the reversal in prospects dramatic.[3]

By 1981, the underlying world economic change became much clearer. In the aftermath of the second round of large oil price increases in 1979, the United States, along with many other countries, was forced to tighten its belt. The full force of the recession that began in 1980 then combined with the determination of the incoming Reagan administration in 1981 to root out inflation. A wrenching restructuring of old industries, such as steel and cars, began in earnest in North America and Europe. The recession deepened and raw material prices plummeted, affecting all developing countries plus many sectors of the industrialized countries, such as farming and the oil industry. Meanwhile, interest rates soared as the burden of cutting back inflation fell on U.S. monetary policy. Highly indebted corporations had been affected first, including such major ones as Chrysler, Dome Petroleum, and International Harvester. The effect on big debtor countries took longer because they were able to continue borrowing, albeit with increasing difficulty, until the first half of 1982. But when the consequences finally hit later that year, they were especially devastating in Latin America, which was both highly indebted and also dependent on a limited volume of commodity exports.

Why Latin America?

The story of the international debt crisis is largely about Latin America.[4] A few numbers make clear why the problem, even though it affected all developing countries and many debtors of all kinds, was concentrated in a particular regional group of highly indebted countries, regardless of whether they were oil importers or exporters. Moreover, special cultural, historical, and geographical features came into play rather than simply particular levels of income and industrial development, elements that some international organizations have focused on in discussing economic development and debt.[5] Only the Philippines has a comparable level of debt, making it a sort of "cousin" of the Latin American countries with high debt, high economic expectations, and limited savings and export earnings.

Table 1-2 compares three groups of countries—Latin America and

Table 1-2   External Debt Comparisons, 1983–1984

Totals (in Billions of Dollars)	Latin America and Caribbean	Other Developing Countries[a]	Selected Centrally Planned Economies[b]
Outstanding gross external debt, including short-term at end of 1983	351	383	61
Owed to commercial banks	232	130	42
Owed to official lenders and bondholders	119	250	19
Estimated interest payments on external debt, 1984	45	43	8
Estimated merchandise exports, f.o.b. 1984	98	270	23
Ratios (in Percentages)			
Total debt to exports	352	142	265
Floating rate debt to total debt	67	34	60 (est.)
U.S. dollar portion of debt	79	57	50 (est.)
Interest payments to exports, 1984	46	16	35

Sources: Author's estimates derived from debt data of the Bank for International Settlements (BIS), Annual Reports, *Maturity Distribution of International Bank Lending,* and International Monetary Fund, *International Financial Statistics;* data for Eastern Europe from the Vienna Institute for Comparative Economic Studies as well as BIS, and *Maturity Distribution of International Bank Lending* (July 1984).

[a]All other developing countries, excluding centrally planned economies and Arab capital surplus countries (Saudi Arabia, Libya, United Arab Emirates, Qatar, and Kuwait).

[b]Bulgaria, Czechoslovakia, German Democratic Republic, Hungary, Poland, and Rumania. In the case of these countries, only the debt and the exports to the Western countries have been included. Debt and exports from these countries to the Soviet Union are governed by special arrangements and are therefore not included.

the Caribbean, other developing countries, and the Eastern Bloc European countries—on four scores in 1983, the first full year after the Mexican crisis: (1) the ratio of external debt to merchandise exports—the income out of which debt gets serviced; (2) the proportion of debt which is at floating interest rates; (3) the U.S. dollar-denominated portion of the debt; and (4) the proportion of export income which is needed to pay interest on the debt—the most critical measure. It is obvious that there are many oversimplifications in these numbers. On the one hand, not all Latin American and Caribbean countries are highly indebted: Central American countries, Colombia, and Trinidad and Tobago have relatively moderate external debts. On the other hand, some of the other developing countries, especially in Africa, do have very serious long-term debt-servicing problems, although their debts are not large relative to the debt of all developing countries and their problem stems largely from the rise in oil prices and a shortage of managerial and natural resources for development.

Nonetheless, the numbers in table 1-2 make it clear why the debt crisis had been concentrated in Latin America, especially in the largest borrowing countries—Argentina, Brazil, Chile, Mexico, Peru, and Venezuela. These six countries alone account for 85 percent of the external debt of the region, heavily concentrated in commercial bank loans, and for about the same proportion of its gross national product. As income has fallen in these countries since 1981, depression has spread throughout the region. The debt problem affects only some countries, but the ensuing economic crisis involves the whole of Latin America and the Caribbean.

It may seem a tautology to say that the debt problem is a problem of too much lending and too much borrowing. But to a large degree, that is the central fact. The problem goes beyond oil-importing and oil-exporting countries. The former—such as Brazil—borrowed to pay oil bills without slowing growth too much. Some countries, such as Brazil, Mexico, and Venezuela, borrowed because they had large public investment programs, while others, such as Argentina and Chile, did so because of overambitious financial liberalization programs. It was a match seemingly predestined: commercial bank lenders eager to open up profitable new markets and large emerging economies eager for funds at low real costs, not because they were or were not oil importers but because their governments wanted these economies to grow at a substantially higher rate than their resources allowed. In the end, the main cause of the debt problem was simple: on one side, a set of eager borrowers; on the other side, its mirror image, aggressive lenders; and, in the end—after 1981—the collapse of the assumption on which they both operated.

Comparisons between Latin America and the other groups of debtors are telling. First, as of 1983 the region as a whole had an outstanding debt of three-and-one-half times (350 percent) its annual merchandise export earnings; only the Philippines was higher at close to 500 percent. By 1986, the Latin American ratio was close to 500 percent, because of falling commodity export prices and earnings. Even if such a measure is oversimplified,[6] it tells us that an interest rate of 10 percent in 1983 on the outstanding debt would be equivalent to 35 percent of export earnings; if the rate were 15 percent, the ratio would be 52.5 percent, and so on. In the case of the other developing countries, the ratio of debt outstanding to annual exports was only 1.4 (140 percent), reflecting the relatively low external debt of India and of most of the East Asian countries together with the high export earnings of most of the latter. Altogether, non-Latin American countries have about the same external debt as Latin American countries but three times more export earnings. Even the group of the most indebted Eastern European countries, Poland being the most publicized case, has a debt ratio that is on average much lower than that of the Latin American countries.

Second, the fact that the major Latin American debtors have borrowed abroad largely from commercial banks at commercial rates of interest, which vary with the cost of money to the lenders, means that two-thirds of the external debt of the region is at interest rates that have periodically floated to unusually high levels, especially in the period 1980–82.

Third, these rates are payable in U.S. dollars, which at the end of 1984 were worth about 60 to 70 percent more, in nominal terms compared to other major currencies, than in 1980, the peak year of external borrowing. Meanwhile, international recession and the strong dollar kept commodity export prices low in dollars, creating a "scissors effect" upon borrowing countries: high-cost debt service obligations and weak export earnings that still relied overwhelmingly on commodities. By 1986 the dollar had weakened sharply, but so had commodity markets, so that, even though some commodity prices improved marginally in dollar terms, they did so by much less than the relative fall of the dollar.

The combination of a large debt, denominated in dollars and at floating interest rates, with relatively low export earnings gives us the fourth and critical measure: in 1984 Latin America was paying out in interest on its external debt the equivalent of nearly half of its merchandise export earnings. Although the burden fell somewhat in 1985 and 1986, it was still in the 35 percent range.

In contrast, other developing countries borrowed largely from official sources at fixed rates that did not rise after 1981 and in a variety of currencies. Most East Asian countries, moreover, concentrated on dynamic industrial exports that were not dependent on depressed commodity prices. Even a country such as South Korea, which has the fourth largest external debt of developing countries ($46.8 billion at the end of 1985 but declining rapidly in 1986 and 1987), nonetheless has exports high enough so that its debt-to-export ratio is less than half the average for Latin America.

The scissors effect is the main immediate external cause of the debt problem in Latin America. As shown in table 1-3, only the Philippines, among other developing countries, is in a similar position of having a very large debt burden. The few African countries that borrowed from

Table 1-3 Estimated External Debt of Selected Developing Countries

	Total Outstanding External Debt, Including Short-Term at End of Year (in Billions of Dollars)		Debt as Percentage of Merchandise Exports	
	1983	*Est. 1986*	*1983*	*1986*
Argentina	$ 45.1	$ 49.2	578	703
Brazil	97.8	110.6	447	494
Chile	18.2	20.7	479	505
Mexico	93.0	104.0	417	650
Peru	12.4	14.4	413	576
Venezuela	32.3	33.6	221	386
Total	$298.8	$332.5	407	548
Nigeria	$ 18.2	$ 23.0	173	183
Philippines	26.5	28.3	530[a]	593[a]
Indonesia	29.2	43.0	156	230
South Korea	40.1	44.5	173	128
Turkey	23.9	32.2	419[a]	431[a]
Zaire	4.5 (est.)	4.6	250	422
Total	$142.1	$175.6	219	221

Sources: Debt as estimated by Morgan Guaranty Trust, *World Financial Markets* (November 1984), and Inter-American Development Bank, *Economic and Social Progress in Latin America, 1987 Report.* Exports shown in International Monetary Fund, *International Financial Statistics* (September 1987).

[a]The Philippines and Turkey are clear cases where service exports from factors such as labor should also be counted, because of the importance of worker remittances from abroad. If that is done, the ratios fall approximately to 400 and 250 percent, respectively.

commercial banks were not able to do so on a large scale. Their problem resulted mainly from the effects of having to devote, from 1973–74 onward, a very large part of their meager foreign exchange earnings to payments for imported oil, without at the same time benefiting from sufficiently large offsetting inflows of capital. Their pain, of course, eased substantially after the oil price drop in 1986.

Part of the debt problem for Latin America may lie in its being a commodity-exporting region. Growth in the advanced Western countries is today less dependent on raw materials, including oil; as cars and houses get smaller, more emphasis is placed on high technology products that use sophisticated systems rather than a lot of metal and other raw materials. For example, the consumption of nonferrous metals—such as copper, nickel, and zinc—per unit of gross national product (GNP) in the advanced Western economies is today about one-third less than it was ten years ago. This trend, largely resulting from energy conservation, higher real interest rates, and the gradual slowdown of growth in the industrialized countries in the last two decades, may not bode well for the long-term economic fortunes of commodity producers. Paradoxically, the inflation of oil prices, which began in 1973 and lasted until 1981, may have ushered in a long period of depressed commodity prices, quite the opposite result of what was originally heralded as a major triumph for the producers of the most important internationally traded commodity, oil.[7]

Lenders and Borrowers

No one can objectively claim that the economic problems of Latin America have resulted only from external conditions. The fact that the outstanding external debt of the region rose from about $48 billion at the end of 1973 to about $350 billion ten years later (or, from 21 to 58 percent of the GNP) was the result mainly of two factors: on one hand, the relative ease of external commercial bank credit and, on the other, the type of economic development pursued by the larger countries in the region.

The rapid growth of international commercial bank lending began around 1971–72, before the first oil shock, fueled by inflation in the United States. After the first oil shock and ensuing recession, and partly because of the development of new means of finance that bypassed the commercial banks, especially the issuance of commercial paper by corporations among themselves,[8] banks began to look for new customers. These included the so-called newly industrializing countries of Latin America and Asia—such as Argentina, Brazil, South Korea, Mexico, the Philippines, Turkey, and Taiwan—plus a few resource-rich countries—such as Algeria, Chile, Indonesia, Morocco, Peru, Zaire, and Zambia.

These borrowers were eager for cheap dollars. Not only was the dollar weak in comparison with other currencies, but, because of a rapid monetary expansion in the United States, real interest rates were low. A weak dollar, caused by U.S. inflation, was accompanied by relatively high dollar commodity prices. This helped the exports of Latin America, 80 percent of which came in the mid-1970s from raw materials or commodities. Because dollar interest rates were at or barely above inflation, borrowing dollars was cheap in relation to the ability to earn them through exports. Borrowing helped countries to avoid the painful transition away from protected, import-substituting industries toward exports, and thus it thrived. Whereas the official international lending agencies, such as the World Bank and the Inter-American Development Bank, were lending mostly expensive nondollar currencies, such as the yen, the Deutsche mark and the Swiss franc, commercial banks, with a surplus of "petrodollars," were lending these dollars at low nominal interest rates. The commercial banks were thus crucial in closing the circle started by high oil prices and a weak dollar. This recycling of money received by oil exporters was widely seen as a good way for the marketplace to offset the ravages of post-1973 oil prices. Recycling was widely praised by international institutions and private commercial bankers alike.[9]

But, as the saying goes, it takes two to tango; not only were there eager lenders, there were also eager borrowers. For Latin America in particular, as well as for some other developing countries, cheap interest rates were not the only motivation for massive external borrowing. Because of low domestic savings and relatively high incomes, the pattern of development in Latin America was already predisposed to a large infusion of external funds. That pattern became evident in the 1960s and even earlier; as a result of easy external borrowing, it simply became more pronounced in the 1970s.

It is obviously risky to generalize about a Latin American pattern of development. The ideas below are meant to provoke further inquiry; they are not meant as definitive conclusions based on careful study. Yet, the fact that all the large economies of the region, except for Colombia, succumbed to the burden of debt gives a few clues to the possible pattern of development. Two features of the pattern stand out, and they are unrelated to a country's imports or exports of oil.

First, the large economies—Argentina, Brazil, and Mexico—provide relatively large internal markets for the push to industrialize. Moreover, the needs for basic infrastructure, such as roads, electricity, and schools, are substantial. The incentive to look outward, as in the export-oriented economies of East Asia, is limited; instead, the push to industrialize essentially looks inward because that is where the market is. Yet, industry finds it hard to prosper without substantial protection from imports. The pattern in Latin America is much the same as it was in the United States a century ago. With only modest earnings of foreign exchange from exports and big demands for investment capital for a large domestic market, there is a need to import capital on a large scale.

The second apparent feature of the development pattern is that political power increasingly gravitates to the urban middle class—people who want their own homes, cars, and other requisites of modern living. Because Latin American cultures are less well insulated from the demonstration effect of U.S. culture upon consumption patterns than the lower-income countries of Asia, there is a rising trend of trips abroad and a strong bias toward electronic gadgets, whiskey, and so forth; thus the desire to keep exchange rates overvalued so that imports remain cheap. Cheap imports benefit the consuming middle class as well as the lower-income groups in urban areas who depend on imported food, especially wheat. Agriculture tends to be neglected because of state-controlled low farm prices, thus reducing the market for domestic industry.

Paradoxically, therefore, policies to strengthen domestic industry against imports are stymied by the slow growth of the internal market, because of the weakness of agriculture and by overvalued exchange rates, which make imports attractive. Industries that tend to do well are often based on cheap imported materials and products, such as cars and appliances, which are directed at upper-income groups. Brazil has been the notable exception to this tendency, as it has built up an efficient car industry, for example, based on its large domestic market.

At the same time, despite clear exceptions, industry is not particularly competitive on an international scale because total labor costs are relatively high in relation to productivity. There are substantial social benefits for the limited number of workers employed in modern manufacturing enterprises, while investment has only modest productivity because of technology lags and a tendency toward overvalued exchange rates. Since industry cannot supply enough jobs for a rapidly growing labor force, there is great pressure on the government to provide employment either directly or through state enterprises. In either case, the result tends to be large public sector deficits and rapid domestic inflation. Houses and cars are purchased only if interest rates are below inflation because of the risk that wages might lag. Negative real interest rates discourage savings, encourage consumption, and exacerbate the need to import capital and borrow abroad.

It is, of course, a vast oversimplification to attempt to describe Latin American and Caribbean economies in such terms. Some major countries, Colombia in particular, exercised caution in their external borrowing; the memory of recent balance-of-payments crises contributed to the conservative attitude that fostered export-oriented economic policies. But in most countries, pressures to borrow could not be resisted. Some governments have managed to deflect these pressures from time to time, as they are doing now in the mid-1980s; however, in general, geographical, cultural, and social forces—factors often overlooked by economic analysts—have tended to influence the patterns of economic development in Latin America. Whether these patterns will change in the future remains to be seen.

Obstacles to a Way Out

At the start of the 1982 crisis, there was a consensus among observers from the outside regarding the steps necessary to deal with the immediate problem: (1) renew growth in the world economy, especially in the United States and other Western industrialized countries; (2) implement austerity measures in the debtor countries; and (3) continue capital flows into the highly indebted countries.[10]

At the time, few analysts foresaw the depth and length of the economic depression that enveloped debtors. Income per inhabitant for Latin America and the Caribbean fell in real terms by about 14 percent from 1982 to 1985. While Brazil resumed strong growth in 1985, its slump had begun in 1980, earlier than other countries in the region. As of 1986, no major economies in Latin America, other than Colombia, traditionally a cautious borrower, appeared to have resumed reasonably sustained economic growth.

The social and economic consequences for debtor countries were serious enough by themselves, but there were also important side effects for the world economy. Latin America's share of world trade fell from 6 percent in 1981 to 3.5 percent in 1986; the sharp decline in its imports from the rest of the world affected world trade and depressed important activities in the Western industrialized countries such as farm and machinery exports. In addition, pressure felt by debtors to generate trade surpluses large enough to pay for the interest on their debt, in the absence of capital inflows, has led to a growing supply of commodity exports. These exports have intensified the long-term worldwide depression of most commodity prices in the 1980s.

World economic growth, one of the essential ingredients for a resolution of the debt crisis, has been less than projected, and its effects upon debtors have been less beneficial than in previous recoveries. As a result, even though their volume increased by about 25 percent since 1981, the nominal value of Latin American exports has hardly changed; in fact, it declined sharply in 1986 because of the collapse of world oil prices. It thus seems fairly clear that growth in the industrialized countries today does not have the same pulling power for developing country exports as it did in the past. Long-term reasons for this include the decline of smokestack industries, which means that industrialized economies are using fewer basic materials, such as copper and steel, per unit of output. The average car or light truck made in America today, for example, uses 2,500 pounds of metal, compared to 3,500 pounds in 1973, and the number of cars being produced has barely increased. Also, the growing service economies in the advanced Western countries are not particularly helpful for commodity producers. And until 1985 the strong dollar kept dollar-denominated commodity prices low. Thus, the terms of trade, calculated in dollars, of developing countries in 1985 were still about 20 percent below their level in 1980. In 1986, international commodity prices reached their lowest point in real terms since World War II. While it is true that the U.S. economy absorbed a large increase in imports in the 1982–86 period, these were not primarily commodity imports—the type that accounts for the largest part of merchandise exports from Latin America, Africa, and much of Asia.

As for austerity measures, not every country complied, but the performance of Latin America as a whole surprised many analysts after 1982: budget deficits were cut drastically and in some cases down to recessionary surpluses; merchandise imports fell 45 percent in dollar terms between 1981 and 1983 and have more or less stayed at that level since; and the current account balance-of-payments deficit of the region fell from about $40 billion in 1981 to $7 billion in 1983 and was almost nil in 1984. But the cost of these improvements was that per capita income fell dramatically and by 1985 was about 14 percent lower than it had been in 1982. Despite a strong recovery in Brazil in 1985 and 1986, partly but not only stimulated by lower oil import prices, overall per capita income in Latin America has stayed at this depressed level. There is, therefore, no question about the impact of austerity measures, only about who has borne the burden. Political leaders in a number of countries have been willing to face great unpopularity in supporting these measures. Only elections, the return to democracy, national pride, and the hope for a better future have kept the social pot from boiling over.

Regarding capital inflows, the trend has been disappointing and well below the expectations of 1983: Latin America is now systematically transferring to commercial banks more money than it receives from them, a sharp reversal of the trend that prevailed until 1980. Of course, the pace of lending during the late 1970s could not possibly be sustained over time; Latin American loans from major international commercial banks, especially in the United States, were rising by 20–25 percent a year, compared to a 10 percent annual growth, as measured by bank capital, in the banks' capacity to lend. Lending by official international agencies has been insufficient to offset the sharp decline in commercial bank lending.

As of the mid-1980s, the economic outlook is clouded by the depression of most raw material prices around the world. Except for Brazil, where the surpluses of a large manufacturing base account for about half of its exports, depressed commodities account for four-fifths of export earnings in Latin America. This is why, even though the volume of Latin American exports has increased in a world environment of relatively slow growth, their value has stayed flat. The worldwide commodity depression, despite a strengthening of prices in 1987, is unlikely to end for some time, as declining world economic growth combines with stagnant consumption of many commodities in developing countries that attempt to make ends meet only by producing even more raw materials.

The commodity depression has combined with a high relative level of external debt to keep the real burden of interest payments high, even though nominal interest rates fell sharply in 1985–86. Real interest rates are particularly high for commodity exporters. The "real" interest rate is usually understood to be the rate paid less inflation, since it is assumed that on average the income of debtors goes up at the same rate as inflation. However, the income of each particular debtor country affects its own ability to pay. In the case of developing countries, this ability depends on how much foreign exchange income rises. If export prices fall, this has the effect of inflation in reverse: the burden of paying interest on the external debt gets heavier for the debtor country.

Thus, the "purchasing power" interest rate for Latin American countries on their debt to commercial banks was about 17 percent in mid-1984, namely, the nominal rate of about 14–15 percent adjusted for the decline in the terms of trade since the peak period of borrowing in 1980. While the real interest rate adjusted for world inflation was about 8 to 10 percent, the interest rate adjusted for the export prices in developing countries was in effect much higher; hence, the problem of meeting interest service on the debt. By 1985 interest rates had fallen sharply, but commodity prices also continued to decline, so that the effective interest burden fell far less than it appeared to at first sight.

In the United States, a number of economists argued in the period of high interest rates from 1979 to 1984 that, in fact, after allowing for inflation and the deductibility of interest in the calculation of taxable income, rates were not unusually high. In broad terms, this was true, although there had still been a substantial percentage increase from the near-zero or negative real after-tax interest rates during much of the 1970s. The problem arises for those who cannot deduct interest in calculating their taxes, either because they have no income, such as the money-losing steel mills in the United States, or because they are the government itself, such as the financially hard-pressed governments of developing countries. For them, every dollar of interest paid is a dollar taken away from another purpose.

Each percentage point increase in nominal interest rates on an annual basis represents 0.3 percent of the GNP of Brazil and 0.5 percent of the GNP of Mexico. The 4 percent difference between the expectations and the reality of 1984 interest rates thus meant the difference between some growth and no growth at all in income per head. Mexico faced major difficulties in 1984 and 1985, well before the plummeting oil prices of 1986. As long as the risk exists that international interest rates can rise to high levels, as they did in mid-1984, the prospect for an orderly resolution of the Latin American debt crisis recedes.

A final critical obstacle concerns the dearth of capital inflows. Economic theory and experience show that developing countries cannot break out of the poverty cycle without additional external capital to supplement inadequate savings. Clearly, capital can be used more efficiently than in the days of frantic external borrowing during the late 1970s and very early 1980s. More growth can be obtained from fewer capital imports, especially if governments get out of commerce and industry and devote their investments to basic physical and social infrastructure and services. But since 1982 the problem has been the dearth of capital inflows after the initial emergency loans of 1983. Whether international public institutions can fill part of this gap remains an open question. Other sources, such as investment from abroad, are also uncertain. Some of the capital which fled, especially in the years of peak external borrowing, has to come back. At best, that is likely to be a slow process because stagnant economies are not strong magnets for the repatriation of capital. Given these prospects, recovery is likely to take time for most countries.

The oil price drop of 1986 gave a boost to a number of oil-importing countries, notably Brazil, akin to a capital inflow, but this was based on a fragile foundation and was in any case very costly to other debtors, such as Mexico and Venezuela. Only the rising tide of world economic growth, a most uncertain prospect, can safely lift all boats off the bottom.

The Political Dimensions

There is no doubt that the debt problem will in time fade from the international economic scene. But there is also little doubt that this time has not come. The debt crisis of the last six years is not the first nor probably the last in the long history of debt problems in most of the countries of Latin America and the Caribbean. The problem seems to transcend political systems. Cuba, with a centrally planned economy, has longstanding debt problems as serious as those of the majority of the free-market Latin American countries.

Apparently, the inward-looking economic policies of the region and a relatively high dependence on foreign capital, whether in the form of loans or investment from abroad, are to blame. For reasons that are probably as much historical and cultural as they are economic, the motivation to export and to save, which is strong in the rapidly industrializing economies of East Asia, is not present to the same degree in Latin America; hence, the more limited exports and the tendency to borrow abroad. This is, of course, not a black-and-white distinction. Developing countries are by definition importers of capital; because their investment needs are large while their own savings are modest, growth cannot take place without an inflow of foreign savings.[11] The question is how long this inflow needs to continue and whether it relies too much on borrowing instead of on risk-taking investment capital, as clearly it did in Latin America in the 1970s and early 1980s.

The gradual resolution of the debt problem is likely to take several years at best. The most immediate obstacles are the relatively high level of real interest rates for commodity exporters, the dearth of capital inflows, and the tenuous prospects for political and social stability in debtor countries. Without some alleviation of these obstacles, it will be extremely difficult to achieve the kind of political climate necessary for internal economic reform to flourish, particularly the restructuring—"el redimensionamiento"—of the economic role of the state.

To be sure, every day that goes by without the social upheaval one might expect from the sharp impoverishment that has taken place in the region contradicts the expectations of those who foresee turmoil and upheaval. So far, upheavals have probably been held back by the cushion remaining from the high economic growth of the three decades up to 1980. And the return to democracy in major countries such as Argentina and Brazil, as well as elections in Ecuador, Peru, Mexico, and Venezuela, also has some beneficial and restraining effect.

Still, drastic income readjustment has undoubtedly affected the urban masses far more than the average income decline suggests, and it is bound to lead in time to major political and social consequences, unpredictable as they may be today. Furthermore, the longer it takes for economic growth and progress to resume, the more difficult and dangerous those consequences will be.

The resumption of growth is itself dependent on internal economic reform, including the promotion of competition and exports and the reorganization of the role of the state away from commercial activities. But these changes are less likely to occur in an atmosphere of stagnation than in one of growth. There has to be a proper balance between what must be done from inside, particularly reform, and what has to come from the outside, namely capital and a more buoyant international economy. The idea of some officials in the industrialized countries that it is essential to starve debtors of capital until they reform is too one-sided and contradicts the notion of worldwide economic interdependence—interdependence between reform and growth, and interdependence between the economic fortunes of the debtors and those of the industrialized countries themselves.

In the meantime, it should be obvious that the high level of external debt in most of Latin America, reflected in the burden of interest on that debt, is by itself the single most important economic obstacle to the resumption of growth and the orderly resolution of the debt problem. Countries, like individuals, simply cannot pay a third to a half of their current (foreign exchange) income just to service interest without at the same time drastically reducing their standard of living. In the five years after the Mexican crisis of August 1982, herculean efforts were made by debtors and bankers to refinance amortization payments. These refinancings offset the fact that new lending had virtually stopped; instead of new loans to refinance the old, refinancings of the old debt took place. Even though some new net lending has been added, these refinancings do not deal with the critical issue of interest payments. Western governments, the United States in particular, have not wanted to get directly involved, although they know full well that it is the payment of interest, not of principal, which is vital to the solidity of their banking systems.

The natural unwillingness of the United States government to get too involved in the debt question—although it has gradually got in deeper—stems largely from domestic political reasons against bailing out the banks or the spendthrift Latin American countries, both of which are unpopular in domestic politics. It is clear, however, that if high interest rates return, Western industrialized country governments will of necessity have to get involved, preferably before a major debtor suspends interest payments. A precipitous and unexpected drop in oil prices had in 1986 already put Mexico on the doorstep of a second debt crisis in four years. The outcome is still highly uncertain, as is that of the second Brazilian suspension of debt service in four years in early 1987.

Clearly, an ounce of prevention is worth a pound of cure, and the best prevention, of course, would be lower interest rates in world markets, especially in dollar capital markets, and a stronger world economy. But that requires a mix of policies in the industrial countries that may be quite difficult to achieve.

At the end of this book, I shall look at some possible measures to ease the debt crisis, none of which are simple or easy. In the chapters that follow, I shall examine how the crisis arose, its dimensions, and also its domestic and international consequences. My objective is not to present a comprehensive and chronological account of events, but instead to try to understand and analyze the main forces at work. And my emphasis remains deliberately upon understanding what happened in the past, since that is the only way to plan for the future.

(2)

Setting the Stage:
Development in the 1960s and 1970s

The pattern of growth and development in most of Latin America in the 1960s, and especially the 1970s, set the stage for the debt problems of the 1980s. The actual crisis was triggered by the recession and high interest rates in the United States and Europe in 1981–82, but its seeds had been sown in Latin America during the previous decades. Patterns of development that were protective of foreign goods but reliant on foreign capital had much to do with this vulnerability.

Economic Growth

Most of the economies in Latin America and the Caribbean have grown rapidly since the beginning of World War II. That growth continued into the 1970s but slackened off noticeably toward the end of the decade. Production and income statistics for the 1970s show that economic growth, with the GNP expanding an average of 6 percent per year, was a little faster than it was in the 1960s, and that decade in turn showed some improvement over the 1950s. Only some countries in East Asia and a few underpopulated capital-exporting oil producers of the Middle East expanded as quickly as Latin America in the 1970s. By 1980 the average income per person in Latin America and the Caribbean had reached $2,000, up $550 in real terms in ten years and four times the combined average income per person in Africa, Asia, and the Middle East (other than oil exporters). However, much of the economic expansion in Latin America was concentrated in Brazil; with about one-third of the total population of the region, Brazil accounted for two-thirds of its output and income growth.[1] The fast-paced economic expansion did not run its course evenly among the different countries, or within them. Argentina and Chile grew very slowly, although the Chilean economy gradually picked up steam after the Allende years of 1970–73 and ended up in a boom fueled by foreign borrowing between 1979 and 1981. Peru had the opposite experience, and in the second half of the decade faced almost total stagnation—the price for nationalistic excesses, in part financed by foreign bank loans, of the military government in the initial years after the 1968 coup. Brazil had been bruised by the first big oil price increases of 1973–74 but still managed to average 6 to 7 percent annual economic growth for the decade, or more than double its population growth. Mexico, Colombia, and, to a lesser extent, Venezuela had comparable rates of growth for most of the decade.

The smaller countries fared unevenly. The five nations of Central America suffered from the loss of stimulus of the Central American Common Market, which in the 1960s had given their industry and exports an important incentive. In the Caribbean, prospects varied from strong growth in Barbados, the Dominican Republic, and Trinidad and Tobago to a major decline of income in Jamaica, in part the result of strongly nationalistic economic policies. Other countries fared well, such as Panama and Paraguay, while Bolivia had a spurt of growth cut short by the demise of orderly government in the mid-1970s.

The Distribution of Income

How evenly the benefits of growth have been distributed among sectors of the Latin American and Caribbean economies has been a highly debated question.[2] By its nature, the shift from an agricultural to an industrial and urbanized society, which has been the major direction of change in most of Latin America since the 1930s, creates tension and inequalities; such a change was common at the end of the last century in several nations that are today among the most advanced. In Latin America the inevitable tension arising from rapid change has been sharpened by the inability of industry to provide jobs on a large enough scale. This has brought about pressure on governments to create jobs, while the labor force continues to grow at close to 3 percent a year in most countries.

As industrialization proceeds, the gap widens between those employed in organized enterprises, who represent a privileged labor class, and those at work either in the countryside or in the "informal sector"—anything from sweatshops to street vending on downtown streets.

Only when population and labor force growth have begun to decline, and when industry and modern services have spread more widely, does it become possible to have a more even distribution of income.

Scarce as the evidence is on income distribution, available rough statistics show that, in general, most Latin American economies tend to have a high proportion of income concentrated in a small proportion of the population—more so than other developing countries at about the same state of development (table 2-1). The statistics are not reliable enough to judge whether distribution has changed much in the last decade or so.

A key reason for this state of affairs is the long-term neglect of agriculture. With the exception of Brazil and Colombia, and more recently Argentina, few of the major economies of the region have made a sustained and effective effort to boost farm output. The natural tendency for rural incomes to lag behind those in the cities has thus been made more acute. During the 1970s the farm output of Latin

Table 2-1   Estimates of Household Income Distribution

Country	Year of Data	Percentage Share of Pretax Income Received by Households			Population Mid-1982 (Millions)
		Lowest 40% of Households	Middle 40%	Top 20%	
Argentina	1970	14.1	35.6	50.3	28.4
Brazil	1972	7.0	26.4	66.6	126.8
Chile	1968	13.4	35.2	51.4	11.5
Colombia	1972	6.5 9	27.4 30	66.1 61	27.0
Mexico	1977	9.9	32.4	57.7	73.1
Peru	1972	7.0	32.0	61.0	17.4
Venezuela	1970	10.3	35.7	54.0	16.7
					300.9
Hong Kong	1980	16.2	36.8	47.0	5.2
Indonesia	1976	14.4	36.2	49.4	152.6
South Korea	1976	16.9 14	37.8 36	45.3 50	39.3
Malaysia	1973	11.2	32.7	56.1	14.5
Thailand	1975–76	15.2	35.0	49.8	48.5
Turkey	1973	11.5	32.0	56.5	46.5
					306.6

Sources: World Bank, *World Development Report 1984* (1984), pp. 272–73. (See cautionary comments on p. 285 of the same report.) Income distribution data for Colombia from *Statistical Abstract of Latin America,* UCLA Latin American Center Publications, vol. 21 (1982). The weighted averages for each group are estimated by the author.

America and the Caribbean rose at an annual rate of 3.5 percent, or slightly above the growth of population. However, much of that growth in farm output was concentrated in commercial agriculture in Brazil; performance elsewhere ranged from dynamism in Colombia to no growth at all in Peru and some of the Caribbean countries.

A deliberate policy to support rural incomes and farm output might have alleviated a situation in which rural populations account for as much as 40 percent of the total, but farm production is only about one-fifth of GNP. More supportive policies have been pursued in several industrializing Asian economies, such as South Korea and Taiwan, which have prosperous rural areas. The paradox contained in policies that fail to promote agriculture is that on balance they also hinder industrial development: overvalued exchange rates, which make foreign currency cheap, are designed to keep the price of imported staples, such as wheat, low for the urban consumer. Such policies not only encourage food imports and imports in general but also, by keeping agriculture depressed, limit the market for local manufacturing industry.

There is no direct relationship between income inequality and the rapid growth of external debt. A skewed income distribution, however, does create fear at the top of the income spectrum. A perception that the status quo is unstable tends to create pressures toward capital flight. Thus, when policies that are intended to maintain overvalued exchange rates are combined with a concentration of income, savings, and borrowing power, there is a motivation to invest abroad. Clearly, capital flight is not directly caused by external borrowing, but external borrowing makes possible the continuation of the policies that encourage capital flight. This is what happened in a number of Latin American economies, as well as in the Philippines, in the late 1970s and early 1980s.

Despite the unflattering picture of high-income concentration, it would be wrong to conclude that economic growth in the 1960s and 1970s did not affect a wide spectrum of the population. Table 2-2 shows indicators for the major economies in Latin America and the most dynamic ones in Asia and provides clear evidence of the improving prosperity of the average Latin American, despite the faster growth of the most dynamic East Asian economies. Again, however, much of the improvement was concentrated in Brazil, and especially in its urban middle-income groups.

At the end of the 1970s, most countries in Latin America and the Caribbean had healthier, longer-living, better-educated populations than twenty years earlier. The amenities of modern living were within reach of a large and growing group of the population, albeit probably a

Table 2-2   Selected Development Indicators

	Selected Latin American Countries (Weighted Average of 7 Countries)	Selected Other Developing Countries (Weighted Average of 6 Countries)
Life expectancy at birth (years)		
1960	57	47
1982	65	59
Adult literacy rate (percentage of adult population)		
1960	66	49
1980	81	70
Population growth rate (annual percentage)		
1960–1970	2.8	2.4
1970–1982	2.5	2.3
1980–2000 (projected)	2.0	1.8
Energy consumption per capita (thousands of kg of oil equivalent)		
1960	512	113
1981	1,031	422
Manufacturing as a percentage of GDP		
1960	24	11
1982	25	18
Percentage of families owning cars[a]		
1960	6.0	0.9
1980	28.0	4.1

Sources: World Bank, *World Development Report 1984,* Statistical Annex (1984); United Nations, *Statistical Yearbook 1981* (1983), and various earlier issues.

Note: The weighted averages for each group are estimated by the author. The countries are the same as in table 2-1. Weights by population.

[a]Assumes average family of five.

minority. Economies were becoming more sophisticated, especially the larger ones. Brazil and Argentina, for example, were increasingly self-sufficient in capital equipment and exported such equipment as well as complex services—such as construction of large projects—to the rest of Latin America and elsewhere in the developing world. Trade within the region, despite the roadblocks of distance, bureaucracy, and protectionism, had risen somewhat from 8 percent of total exports in the early 1960s to about 15 percent at the end of the 1970s.[3] A demographic transition was in process, with population growth rates falling because of urbanization, high incomes, and provision of birth control devices by private groups and some governments. Slowly, the gap between the incomes of the Latin American and the industrialized countries was closing, but again, much of the improvement was concentrated in Brazil (table 2-3).

The Pattern and Slowdown of Growth

Except in the case of Mexico, economic growth slowed down in Latin America during the course of the 1970s. This deterioration was the result of swollen oil import bills after 1973, which reduced national savings, and of the "stagflation"—or quasi-recession with inflation—in the industrialized countries, which gradually slowed the growth of commodity-exporting developing countries. Economic momentum could only be sustained through a higher proportion of foreign financing, mainly from commercial banks at floating interest rates and relatively short maturities. By the end of the decade, foreign financing accounted for about 25 percent of gross investment, versus 15 percent at the beginning of the 1970s. It is therefore fairly obvious that foreign fi-

Table 2-3   Gross Domestic Product per Capita: Cumulative Growth, 1960–1980

Countries That Narrowed the Relative Gap with the United States	Percentage Change	Countries That Fell Behind	Percentage Change
United States	60		
Brazil	170	Bolivia	49
Ecuador	130	Argentina	48
Paraguay	99	Chile	40
Dominican Republic	91	El Salvador	35
Colombia	88	Uruguay	32
Panama	84	Peru	24
Trinidad & Tobago	80	Honduras	24
Costa Rica	80	Jamaica	17
Mexico	67	Nicaragua	13
Guatemala	67	Haiti	10
Venezuela	64	Guyana	2
Total 1980 population 255 million		100 million	

Source: Data derived by the author from World Bank, *World Development Reports,* various issues.

nancing helped to maintain the rate of growth above where it would have been otherwise, making a difference of perhaps 0.5 to 1 percent per year in the gross domestic product (GDP) in the second half of the 1970s, up to 1980.

Two major changes occurred in the growing reliance on external financing. First, the composition of the foreign financing changed: there was now an increasing and eventually predominant proportion of loans from international banks, at floating interest rates and generally medium and short maturities; a declining proportion of official loans—from institutions such as the World Bank, the Inter-American Development Bank, and bilateral government lenders—which are generally at fixed interest rates and relatively long maturities; and also a decline in the importance of private investment from abroad, which depends on the outlook for profitable undertakings. Second, domestic investment, including the foreign financing component, lost its effectiveness so that a given amount of investment generated less growth than earlier. Among the many reasons for this weakening of growth, combined with the rapid growth of external debt, three in particular stand out: the push to industrialize; growing public sector deficits; and often-erratic exchange rate and interest rate policies.

To some extent, of course, the push to industrialize reflects the stage of development at which the larger Latin American economies find themselves, with large internal markets in comparison with other developing countries and with a per capita income level (especially among upper-income groups) that creates a demand for high-income goods found in industrialized countries, such as cars and appliances. The industries associated with this type of consumption generally require large amounts of capital and create a need for equipment imports and the loans to finance them.

The pattern of industrialization in the large Latin American economies has thus been different in emphasis from that in the East Asian developing countries.[4] The latter has been export-oriented, reflecting in most cases the relatively small size of domestic markets at the time industrialization began, and has relied on relatively low wages. In the larger Latin American economies, the orientation to exports, although growing in importance, has been a secondary consideration.

In general, Asian countries have tended to save more and to export a larger share of their domestic output than Latin American countries (table 2-4). But success in economic growth is not necessarily tied to a high proportion of savings or exports. For example, in 1983 Brazil continued to export about 8 percent of its domestic output, the same proportion as in 1965; but a buoyant domestic market kept its economic expansion going at a very rapid rate up to 1980. The export orientation

Table 2-4   Latin America and East Asia: Savings and Exports, 1965 and
1983 (Percentages of Gross Domestic Product)

	Gross Domestic Savings		Exports of Goods and Nonfactor Services	
	1965	1983	1965	1983
Indonesia	6	20	5	25
South Korea	8	26	9	37
Malaysia	23	29	44	54
Hong Kong	29	25	71	95
Thailand	19	20	28	22
Weighted average	16	23	25	39
Philippines	21	21	17	20
Turkey	13	16	6	16
Argentina	22	18	8	13
Brazil	27	21	8	8
Chile	16	11	14	24
Colombia	17	15	11	10
Peru	19	14	16	21
Mexico	21	28	9	20
Venezuela	34	23	31	26
Weighted average	23	22	12	13

Source: World Bank, *World Development Report 1985* (1985). Averages based on
GDP weights.

and relatively high growth of the savings rate of most of the East Asian
countries have meant that even those among them that were significant
external borrowers in the 1970s and 1980s were better able to withstand the international shock of the world recession and high interest
rates of 1980–82. Even though their external debts were almost as high
as those in Latin America in relation to GNP, they were much lower in
relation to their ability to service their debts, namely, their capacity to
generate savings and to export.

History is important in understanding the pattern of development in
Latin America. World War II, which cut off Latin American economies
from their traditional suppliers in Europe and the United States,
strongly stimulated the growth of domestic industry. Import tariffs and
restrictions, which had proliferated during the depression of the 1930s,
were intensified after the war in order to keep industry competitive in
the face of new competition from abroad. The economic circumstances
of the postwar period thus provided the practical background for the
influential views of the United Nations Economic Commission for Latin
America (ECLA, or CEPAL in Spanish), under the well-known Argen-

tine economist Raúl Prebisch. ECLA became the forum for the major economic debates in the region in the 1950s. It argued that there was a long-run tendency for the price of commodities to fall behind those of industrial goods. Latin American countries, as exporters of gradually depreciating raw materials, should therefore concentrate on substituting increasingly costly industrial products. Otherwise, economies would become increasingly dependent on outside capital. Protection against imports would thus be needed as a long-term instrument of economic policy and not just temporarily to protect recently established or "infant" industries, as classical economists had argued.[5]

These policies were eagerly embraced by most Latin American countries. After the first stages of industrialization, however, which in many cases were stimulated both by government protection and by the natural protection of the cost of transport, protectionist policies became costly. Basic industrial imports became expensive by world standards, holding back the growth of agriculture and of industry itself. By the late 1970s, the combination of overvalued exchange rates with high protectionism in Argentina, Mexico, and Venezuela, among others, led to a gradual exhaustion of industrial expansion.[6] The peak periods of overvaluation, especially in 1979, went with the peak periods of external borrowing. External borrowing made possible currency overvaluation, which in turn made necessary more external borrowing, which made possible increasing budget deficits in most countries (table 2-5).

These features of industrialization in the region, although very broadly and perhaps unfairly generalized, have been accentuated by another feature, the importance of state enterprises. Functioning under the umbrella of implicit or formal government guarantees, and often lacking sufficient capital, state enterprises in industry and related productive activities have tended to finance a very high proportion of investment with borrowing, largely external. As we shall see in the next chapter, state enterprises have been the most important vehicle for external borrowing after the government itself.

The losses suffered by state enterprises are often the result of low product prices mandated by governments in order to subsidize various groups, especially in the urban areas. Some governments in the late 1970s and early 1980s faced the problem of subsidies squarely—Brazil, Chile, and, at various times, Peru, for example—and, sometimes at considerable political cost, eliminated or reduced subsidies and substantially raised the price of basic services and staples. Such moves inevitably cause noticeable increases in the cost-of-living index, since it is heavily weighted by these basic items. In other cases, adjustments were delayed, at substantial fiscal cost, and perhaps even greater political cost, when large increases eventually had to be imposed. Even

Table 2-5 External Debt of Latin American and Caribbean Countries, 1973–1986 (Gross Outstanding Debt, Including Short-term, at End of Years Shown, in Billions of Current U.S. Dollars)

	1973[a]	1975	1979	1980	1981	1982	1983	1984	1985	1986[a]
Gross outstanding	48.0	75.4	196.8	241.5	293.5	331.3	355.0	374.1	383.9	395.0
Of which Argentina	4.5	6.0	20.9	27.3	33.7	43.6	45.1	46.8	48.4	49.2
Brazil	12.0	25.0	60.1	70.0	79.9	91.3	97.8	103.5	106.7	110.6
Mexico	9.5	16.9	42.8	57.1	77.9	86.1	93.0	97.4	97.4	104.0
Of which short-term	6.5	11.1	30.3	55.1	67.0	69.0	72.0	79.0	80.5	81.0
Interest paid	2.7	5.9	16.7	21.1	32.5	42.3	36.9	46.3	38.4	33.4
Merchandise exports, f.o.b.	24.6	38.7	71.2	93.9	100.7	86.3	91.5	100.9	95.3	80.1
Average maturity of debt, in years (excl. short-term)	13.4	10.4	10.3	10.8	10.5	9.9	10.2	11.4	12.7	13.0
Percentages										
Current acct. deficit/GNP	1.4	3.9	4.1	4.8	6.3	6.4	1.4	0.3	0.6	2.1
Debt/exports	195	195	276	257	291	384	388	371	403	488
Short-term debt/exports	26	29	43	59	67	80	79	78	84	101
Debt/GNP	24	26	38	45	51	54	55	56	55	56
Interest/exports	11	15	24	23	32	49	40	46	40	42
Interest/gross national savings	6	8	16	17	28	39	40	39	31	29
External debt/international reserves	366	428	477	621	768	1,227	1,262	942	954	1,236

Sources: Derived by author, with adjustments and estimates for 1973, 1982–1986, from United Nations, CEPAL, *Balance Preliminar de la Economía Latinoamericana 1986* (December 18, 1986); Inter-American Development Bank, *La Deuda Externa y El Desarrollo Económico de América Latina* (January 1984); and Annual Reports of the bank as well as its annual published surveys, *Economic and Social Progress in Latin America*; also Morgan Guaranty Trust, *World Financial Markets*, various issues, 1983–1987.

Note: Cuba, which has an outstanding debt of about US$13 billion and exports of $5 billion (1982), is excluded.
ᵃEstimate.

where the political conviction and courage exist, selling off state enterprises is not easy, given their size, and such a move may not solve
anything in the case of activities properly considered public services,
where the basic issue is price regulation.

A third area of concern has been the perennial conflict between
populism and orthodoxy in monetary and exchange policy. It is understandable that chiefs of state and others should dislike high interest
rates and devaluations, which are seen to raise domestic prices and the
cost of living, especially when large-scale adjustments have to be made
in the midst of inflationary expectations and after periods of substantial
overvaluation of the currency and negative interest rates. The economic records of Argentina, Chile, and Mexico in the late 1970s and
early 1980s illustrate once again the proclivity, even under sophisticated economic management, to repeat history.

In the Southern Cone countries in the late 1970s, an economic
theory took root that was peculiar in the inflationary setting of those
countries. The economy was to be made to adjust so as to maintain a
fixed exchange rate. In other words, employment rather than the exchange rate would vary. At least the theory had the unusual merit of
reconciling economic technocrats, who tended to be of liberal political
persuasion, with their autocratic rulers.

In the case of Chile, where the public sector had no deficit and
inflation was falling rapidly, the policy came close to succeeding. However, the momentum of prior inflation, after the exchange rate was
fixed in 1979, quickly led to an overvalued exchange rate. With a cheap
dollar, an apparently guaranteed exchange rate, and high domestic
interest rates, the private sector, and especially the commercial banks,
borrowed large amounts abroad—about $10 billion. Meanwhile, pro-
duction for the domestic market and for export languished as imports
flooded the domestic economy—artificially holding down the cost of
living—and the profitability of exports eroded. The collapse of copper
prices in 1981–82 completed the deterioration of the balance of payments, and in mid-1982 the authorities devalued the currency by about
60 percent, landing most of those who had borrowed abroad in virtual
bankruptcy. A critical factor in the large-scale foreign borrowing by
the private sector, and in the lending by foreign banks, had been an
informal although often-repeated assurance by the government that the
exchange rate would remain fixed. Although the government itself was
not a major borrower abroad, its policies led to the sharp and un-
checked increase in external borrowing between 1979 and 1981. According to official estimates, GNP in 1982 fell by over 10 percent while
the unemployment rate rose above 20 percent.

In Argentina, where the public sector deficit continued to be high, the policy of a slow and predictable devaluation, announced in a "little table," or *tablita,* in the face of still very rapid inflation never had a chance and instead contributed to the build-up of both private and public sector debt. Interestingly, the Chilean and Argentine experiments were widely praised by bankers and international financial journalists. The return to market economics was, of course, praiseworthy, but few noticed the major exchange and capital movement distortions that were introduced at the same time because of unrealistic exchange rates and large capital inflows, which for a time kept up the illusion that the exchange rates could be maintained.

The case of Mexico, where economic theory was not the main driving force, was more classically related to increasing public sector deficits, augmented in 1981–82 by the fall in the price of oil to a level well below budget projections. The resulting large-scale borrowing by the private and public sectors occurred paradoxically at the time that Mexico needed the money least—when the value of its own exports boomed in the period 1979–81—and eventually led to the large devaluations of 1982 and the introduction of exchange controls in September of that year. Exchange controls proved unmanageable in a country with no recent experience in the management of controls and with a long border and a very large trade with the United States.

Finally, political resistance to foreign investment continued in the 1970s. Few countries encouraged investment from the outside in an economically meaningful way. In the five years from 1978 to 1982, direct foreign investment in Latin America accounted for less than one-fifth of capital inflows and was heavily concentrated in Brazil and Mexico. It is even less than that today. In the 1950s the idea arose among politicians of various tendencies that foreign loans create less "dependency" than foreign investment. This theory became widespread in the 1960s and was clearly expressed in the 1971 report by Raúl Prebisch, *Transformación y Desarrollo,* issued in English as *Change and Development.*[7] In fact, the attitude of foreign investors had by then become much more flexible and accommodating than it had been twenty or even ten years earlier, but in the host countries government perceptions of the past inflexible attitude of many multinational companies continued. Seldom was the obvious argument made in favor of foreign investment—that profit remittance payments, which require the availability of profits and do not carry the same level of international obligation as the service on government debts, can be a much less problematic burden than debt service.

The emerging industrial economies of Latin America are in some ways at the same stage as was the economy of the United States in the period from the 1840s to the 1880s. There is a rapid expansion of the infrastructure and basic industry for the domestic market, based in part on a large inflow of foreign loans. The high rate of population growth, at that time in the United States augmented by migration, was comparable to that of Brazil and Mexico today. Bankruptcies, financial panics, and balance-of-payments crises were rampant in the United States as late as the 1890s. Today, however, we live in a more orderly world, with clearer rules of international financial behavior; while international borrowing followed by default was a relatively painless affair in the nineteenth century, it is much more difficult today.

Because of the gradual exhaustion of the pattern of development and, of course, because of the second round of large oil price increases in 1979, by 1979–80 growth was slowing down in most countries of the region. By 1981 the output of the region was rising by less than 1 percent annually, or hardly at all.

The Growth of Commercial Bank Debt

The total gross outstanding external debt of Latin America and the Caribbean grew at a compounded annual rate of 25 percent in the decade from 1973 to 1982, or at almost twice the rate of growth of export earnings and about four times that of the gross national product. The growth of debt was concentrated in the large- and medium-sized economies, except for Colombia, which was a modest borrower. Among the smaller countries, Costa Rica, Ecuador, Jamaica, and Panama expanded their external borrowing rapidly. Altogether, the total outstanding external debt rose from approximately $35 billion at the end of 1972 to $330 billion ten years later, $351 billion at the end of 1983, and approximately $425 billion today. Commercial bank lending, almost all of it at floating rates of interest, accounted for three-quarters of that increase, while funding from official sources and some publicly issued bonds—a broad category largely at fixed rates of interest—accounted for the remaining quarter.

Contrary to general impressions, the external debt rose steadily and rapidly throughout the period, not just in the aftermath of the oil price increase of 1973–74 and 1979. Those were indeed the periods of fastest growth of the external debt of Brazil, but Mexico increased its debt rapidly at other times, particularly in 1976 and 1980–81, reflecting the budget deficits and foreign exchange crises that are sometimes found as the Mexican six-year presidential term of office draws to a close.

Much has been made of the fact that *net* debt is the correct measure of debt. It involves deducting from the total debt the debtor's foreign assets, which could be used to pay off debt. The idea is the same as estimating the net worth of an individual after deducting debts from assets. The quality and liquidity of those assets lead to a judgment of creditworthiness. Clearly, foreign exchange and other liquid international reserves of borrowing countries could be used to service debt and should be deducted in order to arrive at the net external debt of countries. But focusing on net debt, which is simply a way of saying that part of the debt can be covered by existing assets, changes the analysis very little. In fact, since the foreign reserves of Latin American countries increased much more slowly than their external debt, the growth of net debt was faster than that of gross debt. In other words, the borrowing was spent rather than saved. From about \$15 billion in 1973, official foreign reserves rose to a plateau of about \$40 billion in 1979–81, from which they plummeted in 1982. The proportion of debt covered by reserves fell from about one-half in the early 1970s to one-eighth in the peak years of borrowing, a deterioration that should by itself have been warning enough (see table 2-5).

The proponents of the idea that the growth of debt was not as fast as it looked sometimes go a step farther and argue that *all* foreign assets of residents of the borrowing countries should be netted from the debt. Professor Larry A. Sjaastad of the University of Chicago has estimated that the foreign assets acquired by Latin Americans from 1973 to 1983 were worth nearly \$100 billion.[8] The implication is that the real debt burden of Latin America would be much smaller if governments of debtor countries could somehow get their hands on the capital that has fled their economies. The argument is logical but, as its proponents recognize, impractical. The fact that Argentinians, Mexicans, Venezuelans, and others bought cheap dollars, predominantly in the period from 1979 to 1982, and invested them abroad because of overvalued exchange rates does not give a claim to the lenders upon those resources and probably not to the borrowing governments either.

Clearly, much of the money was misused in countries with large capital flight—especially Argentina, Mexico, and Venezuela in the late 1970s and early 1980s—because of the combination of unrealistic economic policies with totally free exchange systems. It is doubtful if exchange controls could by themselves have prevented the outflow while overvalued rates were being maintained. If the cleaning lady likes alcohol, it is probably a good idea to keep the liquor closet locked (exchange controls), but it is certainly a very bad idea to encourage an increasing craving for liquor (overvalued exchange rates). Brazil and Colombia no doubt had some capital flight, but it was modest; both countries maintained the essential ingredients to keep savings at home from the mid-1960s onward: a continuing and predictable policy of reasonably realistic exchange rates and domestic interest rates, combined with moderate exchange controls as well as, of course, political and economic stability.

A careful reading of the data in table 2-5 shows that the external debt of the region was growing rapidly throughout the 1970s and early 1980s. However, signs of deterioration were already clear by the end of the 1970s in such measures as debt-to-GNP, debt-to-export earnings, debt-to-reserves, the rising proportion of short-term debt, and the growing burden of interest payments. At the same time, it is equally true that the really dramatic deterioration came in the early 1980s as a result of the interrelated growth of debt and interest payments with falling export earnings.

The Drive to Lend and to Borrow

Not all lenders were eager, nor were all borrowers. Yet enough features were common to the majority of large international commercial bank lenders and most of the Latin American borrowing countries. The drive to lend, on the part of large international banks, stemmed from a combination of rapid deposit growth—in the first instance from OPEC governments in the periods 1973–76 and 1979–81, but also basically as the result of world inflation—with slack economic growth in the industrialized countries, itself the result of the drain on savings and spending power caused by much higher oil prices. New outlets for the funds had to be found. The more advanced developing countries, especially those rich in resources, were a natural outlet. During the inflation of the 1970s, with its accompanying fears of the eventual exhaustion of key raw materials, resource-rich countries were considered attractive risks, especially if they also had a reasonable standard of living. This was the case for several of the major Latin American countries.

For the potential borrowers, the supply of loans offered a relatively easy way to maintain growth, if they were oil importers—such as Brazil, which otherwise faced the prospect of massive economic retrenchment in order to pay for its imported oil—or to accelerate it, if they were oil or commodity exporters. Until the mid-1970s, Brazil was a substantially larger borrower than Mexico (see table 2-5), largely because of its oil import bill. The government was virtually the sole borrower, mostly through its state enterprises. The inflow of funds allowed these enterprises to fund ambitious investment programs, while foreign exchange cushioned the impact of the huge increase in the oil import bill.

Mexico, on the other hand, which was still a minor oil importer but whose new oil reserves were discovered in 1971–73, was a more attractive borrower. Its rapid expansion of borrowing, however, did not begin until the last two years of the Echeverría administration, in 1975 and 1976, when the usual end-of-term expansion in public expenditures was combined with the need to fund the growing development program of Pemex, the state oil monopoly. Mexico had been given its start in large-scale international borrowing in 1972–73, when New York investment banks, especially Kuhn Loeb and First Boston, which had a long relationship with the Mexican government, started to seek surplus funds from a number of banks (especially Japanese banks) inexperienced in lending to developing countries and placed them at much lower spreads over the cost of funds than the U.S. banks were willing to entertain at the time. In due course, however, U.S. commercial banks, which were the largest recipients of surplus oil money and the most traditionally knowledgeable about Latin America, took over the leadership of the syndicated loan market.

In Latin America during the mid-1970s, there were only two parliamentary democracies among the larger countries, Colombia and Venezuela. Everywhere else there were either military regimes or strong centralized governments. Although there is no absolute correlation between military government and external borrowing—two substantial borrowers, Costa Rica and Venezuela, were parliamentary democracies—the bulk of the borrowing was done by highly centralized governments where parliamentary dissent and public criticism were muted. Even in Venezuela, the borrowing took place mostly during the short period 1978–81, under cover of a recognized arrangement to officially conceal the borrowing from Congress. Major lenders felt comfortable with centralized governments, where a few officials could speak authoritatively, as opposed to socialist regimes such as Allende's in Chile. The military coup against Allende in September 1973 brought a sigh of relief not only in Washington but among all commercial bankers concerned with Latin America. Even a radical nationalist regime such as General Velasco's in Peru was perceived for a time as an orderly yet reformist government.[9]

Resistance to the blandishments of easy borrowing was limited to a few countries: Colombia, where the memory of the foreign exchange crisis of 1965–66 was still fresh and Finance Minister Rodrigo Botero (1974–76) took a strong stand against borrowing from commercial banks; Guatemala, where the central bank had traditionally been conservative; and Chile in the initial Pinochet years, when Finance Minister Jorge Cauas, a former World Bank director of economic research, promoted export growth through a policy of a realistic exchange rate. Personalities were thus as important as regimes, and not all countries were attractive to lenders. By 1975 Peru was no longer considered creditworthy by most banks, and in any case, only a limited number had been attracted to the country in the first place. Argentina failed to attract lenders until the fall of President Isabel Perón in 1976 and the advent of economic czar José Martínez de Hoz, a steel executive well known in U.S. and European financial circles.

The availability of funds and a relatively limited market where they could be invested profitably and, in the eyes of creditors, safely, sparked strong competition. Not only was it a high priority for the major banks to appear at the top of the league tables of syndicated loan managers— as in the securities industry today—but considerable financial income was involved. Lead managers could make as much as 1 percent of the loan in management fees, paid up front at the time of signature. During the mid- to late-1970s, these lead management fees, not counting those paid to participants in the syndicates, probably exceeded $100 million annually in the case of Latin American borrowers alone. Fierce competition for a share of this pie resulted, serv- ing to intensify the market forces that were driving the lending anyway.

The depreciation of the U.S. dollar during much of the 1970s, together with real dollar interest rates that were close to zero when adjusted for U.S. inflation and mostly negative against the rise in the commodity export prices affecting the borrowers, fueled the appetite of the borrowers. Loans from the World Bank and its regional development bank cousins had a heavy component of strong currencies, whose risk was (and still is) passed on to the borrowers, because these institutions are usually encouraged to borrow in the markets of surplus countries. Thus, even though loans carried apparently moderate nominal interest rates, they were very expensive in dollar terms. In 1975 a typical World Bank loan carrying a nominal interest rate of 8 percent in fact cost the typical Latin American borrower (whose export prices are denominated in dollars) about 18 percent in U.S. dollars versus a syndicated bank loan of 1 percent over the London Interbank Offered Rate (LIBOR), or 8.5 percent. Add to that the lack of conditionality on commercial bank loans, which could usually be drawn down in a lump sum, and the case for borrowing from commercial banks was clear.

The case was in fact apparently so compelling that only the most skeptical—skeptical about floating interest rates, commodity price

prospects, and developing country governments' external borrowing—
resisted it.

Warning Signals

Since the growth of bank lending was so obviously rapid, it is
perhaps surprising that more concerns were not publicly expressed
about the trend. No one looking at the statistics on the growth of debt
could fail to be impressed by the rapid build-up of external debt, even
only up to 1979. The deterioration of such ratios as debt to exports or
interest burden to export earnings was also apparent, albeit with some
delay.

It was of course the international recession and high interest rates
of 1980–82 which brought the debt build-up to a crisis. Interest payments ballooned, and for a time they were paid for by even more
borrowing, while export earnings fell drastically. So the conclusion is
inescapable that the international economic crisis of 1980–82 precipi-
tated the demise of the Latin American economies, but it is also true
that the borrowers and lenders set themselves up for this risk by
excessively aggressive external borrowing and lending in the 1970s.
The Asian countries, which were also hit hard by the 1980–82 crisis,
rode out the storm much better because they owed much less and at
better terms.

Of course, after each of the two major oil price increases, there was
a good deal of discussion about the financial needs of the oil-importing
developing countries. In 1974 the IMF quickly created a Special Oil
Facility to accommodate some temporary needs of the oil importers,
although in fact the largest users of this special credit window turned
out to be Britain and Italy. The World Bank in the 1970s accelerated
the large expansion of lending begun in 1969–70, after Robert Mc-
Namara became president of the bank, and, of course, commercial
bank loans rose sharply. There was discussion about the idea of a
"safety net," which would help cushion the shock for the oil-importing
developing countries of further possible rises in the price of oil. By the
time the Iranian revolution and renewed world inflation made possible
the second round of oil price increases, nothing had been done on the
question of a safety net. "Early warning systems" were also discussed;
somewhat more was done on that score, as I discuss later, but with
limited practical results.

The events that began with the tripling of oil prices in 1979 were
certainly not entirely the result of that price increase. But the combination of a huge increase in import bills with plummeting export prices

and extremely high interest rates proved disastrous to the most highly indebted countries, mainly the large debtors in Latin America. This combination helped to trigger the crisis that manifested itself in 1982. Although the crisis could hardly have been foreseen, it is proper to ask whether the lenders made themselves sufficiently aware of relevant economic information, especially on short-term external debt. Another legitimate question is whether the available information was not by itself enough to make both lenders and borrowers more cautious and more aware that they were becoming increasingly vulnerable.

The main source of statistics about the public medium- and long-term (but not short-term) debts of developing country governments has historically been the World Bank.[10] Although membership in the Bank requires countries to submit data promptly on debt and other economic information, there are inevitably long delays in receiving and process-ing it. The increasing number of member countries and the growing complexity of debt information in the late 1970s made it more difficult to obtain and process up-to-date information.

Just before the Mexican crisis broke, the World Bank issued its annual report for the year ending June 1982. It reported the external medium- and long-term debt outstanding for Latin America and the Caribbean at $125 billion for the end of 1980. That was accurate enough, as far as it went. However, the short-term bank debt and the debts of the private sector not guaranteed by states or their agencies—both measures clearly excluded from the World Bank numbers—would have added approximately another $100 billion to that number. More-over, the growth of total debt from the end of 1980 to mid-1982 added another $85 billion or so to the published figure of $125 billion. Anyone looking at that figure in August 1982, therefore, should have realized that it omitted, by definition, the major portion of the actual debts.

In other words, the generally available information from the most respected source was incomplete. With some effort, lenders could have obtained the necessary statistics elsewhere. The Federal Reserve Board, as well as the Bank for International Settlements (BIS) in Basel, Switzerland, have for many years published statistics that approximate international lending. By mid-1977 the availability and clarity of this information improved substantially as the Federal Reserve, the Comp-troller of the Currency, and the Federal Deposit Insurance Corporation (FDIC), jointly concerned by the growth of international lending by U.S. banks, began a "Country Exposure Lending Survey," summa-rized every three months in a press release.

Another problem with the availability of statistical information was that much of the growth of debt, especially in the case of Mexico in 1980–81, was in the form of short-term debt to banks. Since short-term financing is normally part of a trade transaction—for example, an advance against a future export or a credit that is repaid when an import is sold—it is often watched with less care than longer-term debt. Short-term debt, however, is a good indicator of financial stress, since it is much easier to arrange quickly than is more permanent financing. As table 2-5 shows, even by 1979 the growth of short-term debt was already much faster than trade requirements, reflecting the use of short-term financing by governments and some state enterprises to cover increasing budget deficits.

How did the leading international financial institutions react to the debt numbers? Again, the reaction was mixed. Official institutions are naturally cautious in their public pronouncements, and the multilateral ones—such as the IMF, the World Bank, and the Inter-American Development Bank—especially so, since they want to avoid public debates with their shareholding governments. For example, it would have taken a very discerning reader to detect signs of debt trouble ahead in the texts of the two most widely read World Bank documents, the *Annual Report* and *World Development Report.* The 1982 issues, for example, which came out in mid-1982, a few weeks before the Mexican crisis, referred only briefly to the subject of external debt. On the other hand, a rather careful reading of the individual country economic reports published with increasing frequency by the World Bank from the early 1970s on would have given a somewhat more balanced picture. The IMF's reports, which are not public, were undoubtedly critical, while its annual published reports were generally quite cautious.[11]

Another problem faced by most international financial agencies was their proclivity, which still continues today, for classifying countries according to their levels of income and industrialization, and whether they are oil-importing or oil-exporting, both categories that hid the mounting debt problem. Categories such as "middle-income oil importers" are broad enough to include Argentina and Chile, on the one hand—large borrowers and relatively modest exporters of manufactured products—and, on the other hand, some East Asian countries that are export-oriented, high-savings economies with relatively modest external debts. No standard of classification can do justice to each particular country, but a case could be made for dividing countries according to their relative level of savings and external borrowing. Countries that survived the oil shocks well had relatively high and growing domestic savings and held back external borrowing. Most sub-Saharan countries of Africa had very low savings, as a result of poverty-level incomes, and were knocked out by the first oil shock; the East Asians survived without borrowing too much; the Latin Americans, whether oil importers or exporters, borrowed in order to offset relatively stagnant savings and to finance high consumption and investment, and in the end, they were knocked out, too. To characterize countries as "middle-income" or "industrializing" simply obscures the basic question faced by some of the Asian and Latin American countries: to save and export or to spend and borrow?

In the 1970s major international commercial banks geared up to analyze the economies of the countries to which they were increasing their lending. The effectiveness of this economic work is questionable, however. First, the economic departments of banks were sometimes, some would say often, overruled by lending officers who had to demonstrate that their bank was willing to take the lead in major loans, even though economists (and even the loan officers themselves) may have had doubts about the borrowing country or enterprise. Most of the major international banks, at least in the United States, set country lending targets—as opposed to limits—which loan officers were anxious to meet, especially if they wanted a good year-end bonus. Second, some of the economic work was flawed by the obsession with the pseudo-science of "country risk analysis." Certainly, the practical results of country risk analysis show that much of it was a failure. Country risk analysis assumed that risk could be measured in probability statistics, such as those used by insurance companies, which rely on historical information about thousands if not millions of cases, while in fact the important countries to be evaluated were only a few.

As the lending side of banks was worrying in varying degrees about risky lending to developing countries, the deposit-receiving side was competing hard to provide banking services to wealthy depositors, many from Latin America. The growth of "private banking," which is now a hot new service offered by large commercial banks in North America, in fact dates from the 1970s and early 1980s. A quick reading of the statistics would have told many of the banks that the money they were lending on the asset side to governments was coming right back to them on the liability side as deposits from individuals in those countries, not a good recommendation for the economic policies pursued by the borrowing governments being appraised in the country risk exercises.

The country risk analysis episode is a sad one for bank economists, although not all were guilty. Among the reasons beyond those mentioned was the natural inability of most evaluators, in a period of world inflation, to visualize a worst-case scenario. When the price of sugar was twenty-one cents per pound in 1976, it was obviously hard to visualize a situation in 1984 in which it would be four cents. Furthermore, country risk cannot generally be measured by a composite sum, since usually one key variable causes the accident in each case. Iran went the way it did, not because of a composite rating, but because of the inability of the shah to deal with Islamic fundamentalism; Mexico ran into financial trouble because of excessive government expectations after 1979; Argentina and Chile because of the impact of simplistic theories about reducing inflation through real appreciation of the exchange rate; the Philippines because of accumulated borrowing and the cost of economic favoritism and Pharaonic public investment; and so on. Other factors were obviously influential, but in the end the key to accurate credit projections depends on distinguishing a few, perhaps only one or two, crucial variables. Often large international banks, especially in North America and Japan, failed in that process. Although also large lenders, the continental Europeans tended to reach somewhat more clear-cut and cautious credit judgments.

Capital Flight

One cannot show convincingly that either external or internal factors were more important in the build-up of debt, since they tended to interact. It is clear, nevertheless, that the ease with which external credit could be obtained by most of the governments of the more advanced Latin American economies and some of the companies in them tended to postpone difficult economic decisions.

As in the case of debt, easy-come-easy-go is also the story of capital flight. As shown in table 2-6, budget deficits tended to expand rapidly as tough decisions to increase the prices charged by public enterprises were delayed and balance-of-payments deficits on current account rose sharply in a number of countries as exchange rate decisions were postponed or altogether disregarded.

The overvaluation of exchange rates was especially dramatic in Argentina and Mexico before they were forced into huge devaluations in 1982, while Brazil kept a realistic rate and then devalued aggressively in 1983, promoting the export gain of 1983–85. In the period of the external borrowing bonanza, investment projects that should have been carefully screened in an era of austerity were happily started. However, the very beneficiaries of this largesse often realized that it could not go on forever and therefore tended to shelter their extra savings in foreign currencies, whether on a small scale by buying dollar notes for safekeeping at home or in a domestic bank or, on a larger scale, actually moving substantial sums abroad to place them in real estate or financial investments.

"Capital flight" is, of course, a term fraught with value judgments.

Table 2-6   Argentina, Brazil, and Mexico: Deficits and Exchange Rates, 1980–1986 (Percentages of GDP)

| | | Public Sector | | Balance of Payments Current Account Deficit (GDP) | Index of Real Exchange Rate[c] (1982 = 100) |
		Savings[a] (GDP)	Deficit[b] (GDP)		
Argentina	1980	0.9	−7.6	−3.2	33
	1981	−6.3	−15.9	−3.7	42
	1982	−8.9	−16.7	−3.7	100
	1983	−7.2	−15.6	−2.9	95
	1984	−4.1	−12.5	−3.5	87
	1985	2.0	−4.0	−1.6	104
	1986	n.a.	n.a.	−3.4	87
Brazil	1980	−0.4	−9.1	−5.3	102
	1981	−1.6	−7.1	−4.3	97
	1982	−0.3	−6.2	−5.8	100
	1983	n.a.	−3.0	−3.3	137
	1984	n.a.	1.6	0.0	154
	1985	n.a.	−3.2	−0.1	163
	1986	n.a.	n.a.	−0.9	150
Mexico	1980	−2.5	−7.0	−3.6	71
	1981	0.6	−14.7	−5.2	65
	1982	−4.2	−17.6	−1.6	100
	1983	0.2	−8.9	3.7	109
	1984	−0.1	−8.7	2.5	96
	1985	−0.6	−9.9	0.3	96
	1986	n.a.	n.a.	−1.1	126

Sources: Inter-American Development Bank, *Economic and Social Progress in Latin America* (1985, 1986); International Monetary Fund, *International Financial Statistics* (for exchange rate calculation); also Angus Maddison, *Two Crises: Latin America and Asia, 1929–38 and 1973–83* (OECD, 1985).

[a]For the central government and autonomous bodies, current revenue less current expenditures, including interest; for state enterprises, operating income less interest; financial entities such as banks are excluded. Negative savings means that the public sector is borrowing its entire contribution to public investment plus the portion shown of current expenditure.

[b]Does not include indexation of government internal debt as part of the deficit in the case of Brazil; the data thus exaggerate the real public sector deficits of Argentina and Mexico, where the inflation component of interest is not deflated in the data shown.

[c]Actual exchange rate average for year shown divided by domestic price index multiplied by U.S. consumer price index. If 1982 is taken as a rough equilibrium point, numbers below 100 represent overvaluation of the exchange rate; above 100, undervaluation.

When the Japanese export their savings into U.S. Treasury paper and the international capital market, that is generally considered a "capital movement." When individuals in Latin America or Africa and even some European countries do the same, it is considered "capital flight." The implicit value judgment in the latter case is that money should be kept home, even though "home" may be politically unstable and saddled with overvalued exchange rates and low relative interest rates.

There is, of course, nothing new about capital flight out of turbulent places. Latin America has had a long tradition of both turbulence and capital flight, as have some European countries. Historically, the ebb and flow of capital resulted from a mixture of political and economic reasons, but the movement of funds out of three countries in particular—Argentina, Mexico, and Venezuela—during the period from 1979 to 1982 resulted from an increasingly overvalued exchange rate. When this rate was combined with excessively expansionary policies, mostly public expenditure in Mexico and Venezuela and monetary stimulus in the midst of a too rapid banking liberalization in Argentina, a large-scale export of funds resulted.

For several of the major borrowers from 1979 on, there was a rapid deterioration in public finances and in the balance of payments, as shown in table 2-6. This was true despite the fact that Mexico and Venezuela had a rapid growth in their merchandise exports, because of oil prices, in the two years starting in 1979. The point was that most governments passed on the prosperity resulting from large-scale external borrowing or oil-induced export increases in the form of large public expenditures and domestic credit expansion. The only exception among the heavily indebted countries was Brazil, which slammed on the brakes in an austerity program announced at the end of 1980. The austerity was the result of the delayed effect of the oil price rise and of a substantial tightening in the terms of lending by the international commercial banks. Brazil was also the only major country that did not have a significant real appreciation of its currency. The others made the dollar and other foreign currencies increasingly cheap and attractive to their residents. That fact, combined with a domestic credit expansion far larger than that of domestic financial savings, set the stage for capital flight. As international reserves began to fall in 1981, massive outflows resulted, especially in Argentina, Mexico, and Venezuela.

It has been argued that the existence of exchange controls in Brazil and Colombia played the major role in preventing the capital flight that took place elsewhere.[12] The arguments tend to be both long and inconclusive. Were the well-managed exchange rate policies the reason for the containment of capital flight, or was it the existence of controls, regardless of exchange rates? Experience in other cases strongly suggests that controls at the wrong price are ineffective. At the same time, it is equally clear that total freedom at the wrong price can be very costly indeed.

There have also been arguments about the amount of capital flight, quite aside from questions of definition. For example, if a Latin American company makes a deposit in a New York bank for the purpose of guaranteeing a loan to that company, is the deposit capital flight? Statistics are hard to come by. Taking one's money abroad is considered unpatriotic, and no one likes to advertise it. As a result, "capital flight" estimates are usually taken to be the unexplained remainder in balance-of-payments statistics. This often is taken to be the "errors and omissions" item, which simply reconciles the movement of international reserves (a known item) with all the other (estimated) items. If errors and omissions are positive, this means more foreign exchange inflow is coming in than can be explained (for example, from drug exports); if they are negative, it could be capital flight, but it could also be smuggling into countries that restrict luxury imports.

Capital flight could also be, and often is, hidden in trade, either by underreporting exports (earnings that legally have to be brought back home) or, more often, by overinvoicing imports (thus enabling more foreign exchange to be purchased at favorable official rates applicable for most imports). Such maneuvers show up in reported trade and current account deficits that are larger than in reality. It is, therefore, simplistic to take the reported current account deficit and subtract known financing and uses of financing, such as the accumulation of reserves, and label the difference "capital flight," as some have done.[13]

Table 2-7 gives a rough idea of the trend of capital flight, which accelerated sharply from 1981 on. Measured either from the balance-of-payments statistics, which are often rough estimates, or from what is known about Latin American deposits in banks outside, the trend is the same: a sharp rise in capital flight in the period from 1981 to 1983. The coincidence in the two trends is as striking as the fact that the deposits of private Latin Americans in banks outside were rising sharply in 1982–83 (item 2c in table 2-7) while their governments and central banks were losing their foreign reserves (item 1f). Much of this occurred in the last stages of the large-scale build-up of external debt, which ended in 1982. The actual amounts of capital flight were no doubt much larger, perhaps as much as double the range shown in the table, because of physical investments, such as real estate, financed out of inflated trade invoicing or hidden exports and because some of the external borrowing was stimulated by the desire for capital flight— as in the Philippines, for example—so that actual capital flight became almost impossible to measure. Whether capital flight was as much as

Table 2-7 Capital Flight: Two Approximations (Data for the Eight Largest Latin American Economies, in Billions of Current U.S. Dollars)

	1977	1978	1979	1980	1981	1982	1983	Total 1977–1983
1. Flows: balance-of-payments measure								
"Net" capital flight (a + b − f)	0.4	0.7	7.0	1.0	−8.5	−10.6	−8.8	−18.8
Gross capital flight (c + e)	−0.2	−0.1	5.9	−0.2	−9.0	−21.3	−17.7	−42.6
a. Current account deficit	−10.4	−15.7	−16.6	−23.7	−35.7	−36.7	−5.1	−143.9
b. Long-term capital	14.8	22.8	19.6	25.1	42.1	28.2	10.0	162.6
c. Short-term capital	−2.1	−1.8	3.3	5.1	1.5	−11.2	−10.5	−15.7
d. Other exceptional financing*	0.5	0.9	1.1	1.3	0.9	10.1	9.0	−23.2
e. Errors and omissions	1.9	1.7	2.6	−5.3	−10.5	−10.1	−7.2	−26.9
f. Net changes in official reserves	4.8	7.8	10.0	2.4	−2.1	−19.1	−3.9	−0.1
2. Stocks: banking deposit measure								
a. Lat. Am. deposits in BIS reporting banks	29.5	38.2	47.8	49.2	54.9	46.2	53.0	—
b. Less: central bank net reserves (other than IMF and gold)	21.0	28.8	38.8	41.2	39.0	19.9	16.0	—
c. Deposits of private Latin Americans in BIS reporting banks† (a − b)	8.5	9.4	9.0	8.0	15.9	26.3	37.0	—

Sources: International Monetary Fund, *International Financial Statistics,* and Bank for International Settlements (BIS) Annual Reports.

Notes: minus signs indicate outflows.

Argentina, Brazil, Chile, Colombia, Ecuador, Mexico, Peru, and Venezuela are the eight economies for which information is presented here.

*Mostly short-term loans to governments from official sources.

*This is an approximation. Not all banks are included in the BIS reporting system; several adjustments have to be made to central bank reserves, and some state agency deposits are included under private deposits.

†This is an approximation. Not all banks are included in the BIS reporting system, several adjustments have to be made to central bank reserves, and some state agency deposits are included under private deposits.

$100 billion from the mid-1970s to 1983 is hard to prove. Such a number would amount to a third or so of disposable savings for a long period, an unlikely although not impossible proportion; but the number is certainly not the whole savings wealth of Latin America, as some claimed in early 1986, when the balance-of-payments problems of Mexico led a number of U.S. bankers and other observers to ascribe the problems of Latin America largely to capital flight.[14] In any case, it is clear that large-scale capital flight was primarily an affair of the early 1980s and had by and large diminished by 1984–85, after the large devaluations by the major debtors.

For the three countries in which capital flight was a major factor— Argentina, Mexico, and Venezuela—the drain was in the range of $30 to $40 billion in 1982 and 1983 alone, or 3 percent of GNP and as much as 25 to 30 percent of disposable savings. Capital flight was already a factor in the slowdown of growth which started at the end of the 1970s in Argentina and Venezuela; in Mexico, the balloon created by high oil income and massive external financing kept growth going at full speed until 1981, while in Brazil, the necessary adjustment to higher oil prices halted further economic expansion in 1979.

Conclusion

During the 1970s, the majority of Latin American economies sharply increased their dependence on foreign borrowing from commercial banks. Even though the statistics were not easily available, the signs of this increasing reliance were clear by 1979, three years before the crisis broke. Among these warning signs were the rising ratios of debt to exports and to foreign exchange reserves, which meant that debt was rising significantly faster than the ability to service it; the rising proportion of short-term debt at a rate quicker than the growth of trade would have justified; and the increasing burden of interest payments as a proportion of exports and savings. These signs, however, did not necessarily spell a crisis. As the Turkish debt crisis had shown earlier in the 1970s, the underlying illness usually erupted only when lenders lost confidence and stopped lending. But by 1981 the doubts that had troubled the lenders in 1979–80 were largely dissipated by the heady tonic of world inflation, and the merry-go-round spun around one last time, sharply increasing the level and burden of debt for another year or so.

There is thus little doubt that most Latin American countries and their external commercial lenders had got themselves into a vulnerable position by 1979. That should have been the point for more caution, and indeed it was for some borrowers—especially Brazil from the end of 1980 on—and for some lenders, who cut back. But the leaders in lending went on, fortified by rosy global statistics and driven by the tonic of world inflation. Most of all, these lenders did not look closely enough at what the borrowing governments were doing with the money.

Two statements in 1981 by prominent men of finance reflect the differing views about the large debt of a number of developing countries. The men were Henry Wallich, for many years a student of developing countries as a professor of economics at Yale and then a governor of the Federal Reserve from 1974 to 1986, and Walter Wriston, widely regarded as the leading international banker and innovator in financial services of his time. Both were perceptive in different ways—Wallich, in anticipating trouble ahead, and Wriston, in believing that this trouble would not bring down the international financial system.

> It is sometimes thought that the usual rules of lending do not apply to sovereign borrowers. It has been said that lending to countries is less risky than lending to businesses or individuals because a country, unlike a business or an individual, will always be around. Country lending, it is said, is free of final bankruptcy and definitive loss. All that is needed is occasional rescheduling that gives the borrower a breathing space and does not significantly affect the earnings or capital of the lending banks. In my judgment, this is too complacent an attitude. . . . The past few years' experience suggests that our ability to anticipate future problems in this sphere is modest. (Henry Wallich, at the International Conference of Banking Supervisors, 1981)

> It is no secret that over the years a lot of intellectual capital has been invested in the proposition that massive defaults in the Third World will cause a world financial crisis. Those who have taken this view since 1973–74 have been proved wrong, and those of us who believed the market would work proved correct. (Walter Wriston, International Monetary Conference, 1981)

(3)

Core Problem: The Role of the State and State Enterprise

A central factor that gave impetus to the rapid growth of external debt in the 1970s, and hence to the severity of the economic and social crisis of the 1980s, was the pervasive and rapidly expanding role of the state in most of Latin America. The easy availability of foreign loans to governments and their agencies was exemplified by the fact that the external debt of the public sector grew almost ten times from 1973 to 1983, while that of the private sector quadrupled. With the notable exceptions of Chile, Colombia, and some of the Central American economies, governments, some with a leaning toward so-called strategic projects and industries (a leaning not unusual in military governments), were eager takers of foreign credits. External borrowing financed growing public sector deficits. However, even in the case of Chile, where the rapid growth of external debt in the late 1970s was concentrated in the private sector, government exchange rate policies and official assurances that they would not change provided the key incentive for excessive external borrowing.

During this same time, official and private foreign lenders expressed their understandable tendency to avoid risk by lending mainly to governments and especially to their enterprises. By 1982 over 80 percent of the total external public debt of the region was owed by the public sector, and the proportion has subsequently risen as some

---

A modified version of this chapter appears as chapter 4 of the book by Bela Balassa, Gerardo M. Bueno, Mario Henrique Simonsen, and myself, *Toward Renewed Economic Growth in Latin America* (Washington, D.C.: Institute for International Economics, 1986), sponsored by the Council of the Americas, the Getulio Vargas Foundation, and the Institute for International Economics of Washington, D.C.

governments have taken over the foreign obligations of bankrupt private sector companies.

The economic crisis that has engulfed most of the countries of the region since 1982 has provoked a lively debate about whether state intervention has gone too far. As some countries have moved from military to elected civilian governments, particularly Argentina and Brazil, the consensus seems to be for more private initiative and less state control. However, as of 1986, effective progress in reducing the role of the state in most of the larger economies has been slow.

Historical Setting

The rapid expansion of the role of the state in most of Latin America is part of a worldwide phenomenon of the last twenty years which was accelerated by the inflation and energy crises of the 1970s. Latin America has not been unique; moreover, there have been significant differences among countries of the region. The most rapid growth in public expenditures, especially through state enterprise, took place in Mexico, Peru, and Venezuela, largely because of the expansion of state oil companies. Much earlier, in the 1940s, there had been a considerable expansion of the state role in Argentina under Perón. There was a more moderate longer-term trend toward a larger state role in Brazil and Colombia. Overall, growth was roughly similar in public consumption, much of it for subsidies, and in public investment. Everywhere, however, the state today plays a significant role as investor and, except for Chile, as regulator.

Despite the shortcomings of official statistics, which generally include capital formation by state enterprises as part of private investment (thus greatly underestimating the role of the government in the economy), the rough data available suggest that, in several of the largest Latin American economies, the government and its enterprises at the end of the 1970s accounted for a far larger proportion of gross capital formation than in some of the advanced industrial countries, such as France, Sweden, and the United Kingdom, where the public sector has traditionally played a major role in investment. Much of the growth of the public sector was in fact concentrated in state enterprises (table 3-1).

The inclination to rely on state intervention and enterprise for a wide variety of activities is partly the result of historical tendencies, especially in Spanish America. In these countries, the Spanish colonial tradition of special concessions and monopolies for particular enterprises has lasted in various forms for over four centuries, and the resulting tendency on the part of large areas of business is to look to

Table 3-1   Growth of the Public Sector, 1970–1982

Country	Public Sector Outlays as Percentage of GDP		Of Which State Enterprises		Estimated Share of State Enterprises in Gross Domestic Investment	Public Sector Deficit as Percentage of GDP	
	1970	1982	1970	1982	(1978–1980)	1970	1982
Argentina	33	35[a]	11	12	20	1	14
Brazil	28	32[a]	6	11	39	2	17
Chile	41	36	5	10	13	5	2
Colombia	26	30	6	10	9	4	2
Mexico	21	48	10	26	24	2	17
Peru	25	57	4	32	15	1	9
Venezuela	32	66	17	45	45	3	4
Weighted average	28	42	9	19	29	2	9
Malaysia	36	53	4	34	33	12	19
South Korea	20	28	7	4	23	4	3
France	38	48	6	7	13	1	3
Japan	23	27	8	8	11	2	6
Sweden	52	66	4	6	11	2	10
United Kingdom	43	49	10	11	17	3	6
United States	22	21	10	9	4	1	2

Sources: Inter-American Development Bank, *External Debt and Economic Development in Latin America,* Appendix on Public Finances (1984); International Monetary Fund, *World Economic Outlook* (1985); Peter R. Short, *The Role of Public Enterprises: An International Statistical Comparison* (1984); William R. Cline, "Debt, Macro Policy, and State Intervention: The Next Phase for Latin America," *Journal of Interamerican Studies and World Affairs* 27, no. 4 (1985–86): 155–72; national statistics for Asian and European countries.

[a]The peak figures for Argentina were 42 percent and for Brazil 35 percent; both pertain to 1981.

the state for protection. Personal relationships with the government are often essential to business success. Thus, some large private businesses often end up as the keepers of a privilege granted by the state, rather than as Schumpeterian entrepreneurs fighting it out in the marketplace.

In addition to these historical reasons, the small size of most domestic markets helps to explain why the bracing winds of competition and privatization of enterprise are not universally accepted in Latin America. The GNP of the whole of Latin America and the Caribbean is about equivalent to that of West Germany, while the average Central

American economy has a national market comparable to Albuquerque, New Mexico, or Newark, New Jersey.

During the 1970s only Chile successfully opened up its economy in a major way and sharply reduced the role of the state in production and distribution. The centralized nature of its regime, however, has limited the usefulness of its example for other countries, and the credibility of the Chilean experiment has been reduced by the costly results of its economic policy in the period 1978–81. At that time the government actively encouraged large-scale external borrowing by several of the largest private groups in the economy, and it assured these groups that the policy of maintaining a fixed exchange rate would be continued in the face of increasing overvaluation. Even in this case, therefore, the government played an active role in stimulating external borrowing.

Historical reasons plus the relatively small size of domestic economies thus favored those who advocated that the state have a major role in industrialization. The views of the United Nations Economic Commission for Latin America (ECLA), referred to in Chapter 2, fell on receptive ears. Not only did the articulate and forceful personality of its 1950s chief and guiding spirit, Raúl Prebisch, contribute to the influence of the proponents of a larger state role, but the decline of primary commodity prices in real terms in the twenty years after the Korean War and their especially sharp fall up to the mid-1960s gave special force to the argument. It was not, however, until international bank lending started to soar in the 1970s that governments obtained the resources to dramatically expand state enterprise. By then, of course, the rationale for moving out of commodity exports and industrializing at almost any cost had been diluted by the recovery of commodity prices stimulated by the Vietnam War. However, partly as a result of the typical lag with which economic decisions are often made, based on the perceptions of phenomena which may in fact already be superseded, governments in several countries forged ahead with state industry, buoyed by easy financing from abroad.

The rapid increase in the role of state enterprise in the 1970s was thus the combined result of history and economic circumstances. It was accompanied by rising nationalism and a growing tendency to regulate investment flows and prices. The same set of circumstances favored the larger established private enterprises as well. At the same time, foreign investment was in effect discouraged through restrictions on ownership and profit remittance as well as by red tape. In particular, smaller enterprises cannot afford to go through endless *trámites* (bureaucratic red tape). This, perhaps even more than taxes and regulations, is responsible for the existence of a large "informal sector," or black market.[1]

Despite these obstacles, by the late 1970s there emerged a trend in some countries, such as Brazil and Colombia, to open up and deregulate economies. This effort was spearheaded by a group of industrialists engaged in exports. At the same time, the evident costs of past excessive external borrowing by the public sector led to widespread condemnations of the large-scale role of governments as economic regulators. Increased freedom of the press and public discussion that accompanied the replacement of military regimes by elected civilian governments, especially in Argentina and Brazil, heightened the reaction against the past.

Regulation

Even today the larger Latin American countries are among the most regulated market economies in the world, at least on paper. Price controls, restrictions on foreign investment inflows and on profit remittance outflows, import barriers, credit allocation, and high corporate income tax rates combined with discretionary reduction mechanisms, as well as limits on the firing of employees, are among the most important economic regulatory mechanisms (table 3-2). In a number of Latin American countries, the web of regulation is maintained by undertrained and underpaid administrators. The potential for corruption is great.

Taxation is generally considered by many economists as a subject to be treated separately from regulation. However, in most Latin American countries, there is a strong regulatory component to the tax systems, partly because in those countries tax rates for nominal profits are high and are therefore offset through investment tax credits and other concessions for particular activities. The state thus acts to motivate or inhibit certain types of investment, further weakening the forces of the market.

Despite the bureaucratic importance of the regulatory apparatus, there is in fact widespread avoidance of regulations. There are many reasons for this. One is the natural tendency for controls to give rise to their own antidotes: price controls generate cartelization and the practice of obtaining a high ceiling with each price adjustment; interest rate controls create a parallel and sometimes usurious nonbank market; foreign exchange restrictions and excessive protection often lead to smuggling and to overinvoicing of imports and undervaluation of exports; under credit allocation systems that, for example, generally consider agriculture to be "good" and services to be "bad," one finds that

Table 3-2 State Economic Regulations

Regulation (1985)	Argentina	Brazil	Chile	Colombia	Mexico	Peru	Venezuela
Price controls, nine basic staples[a] (number)	9	9	0	9	5	9	9
Price controls, five basic manufactures[b] (number)	5	5	0	5	5	5	3
Mandatory ceilings on bank interest rates (yes or no)	yes	yes	yes	yes	yes	yes	yes
Foreign direct investment limitation in:							
Industrial companies (yes or no)	no	no	no	yes	yes	yes	yes
Banks (yes or no)	yes	yes	no	yes	yes	yes	yes
Maximum domestic corporate profits tax rate (percentage)	33	35	30[c]	40	42	50	50
Withholding on after-tax profits remitted abroad[d] (percentage)	17.5	25	40	40	55	40	20
Workers' mandatory profitsharing in industrial companies (yes or no)	yes	yes	no	no	yes	yes	yes
Fringe benefits as percentage of average industrial wage	80	80	65	65	60	50	60
Limitations on reductions on employment (significant or insignificant)	S	I	I	S	S	S	S

Sources: Business International Corporation, Investing, Licensing, Trading Conditions Abroad, data for Argentina February 1985, for Brazil January 1985, for Chile October 1985, and for Peru March 1985; Price Waterhouse, Doing Business in Chile (October 1985); Price Waterhouse, Doing Business in Mexico (June 1984); Price Waterhouse, Doing Business in Venezuela (August 1985).

[a]Wheat, bread, meat, poultry, sugar, vegetable oil, milk, soft drinks, basic pharmaceuticals.
[b]Cement, steel, cars and trucks, fertilizer, and tires.
[c]First-category tax of 10 percent levied on income, 30 percent levied on taxable income net of first-category tax.
[d]In addition to profits tax.

agricultural credit is rising rapidly even though real farm output is not; limits on labor dismissals are circumvented by temporary employment; and so on. In general, in order to avoid excess exposure to controls, most business groups in Latin America keep their operations divided into many separate companies, thus avoiding visibility. Kidnappings of corporate chieftains in a number of countries have only served to reinforce the tendency toward corporate anonymity.

Another important factor in the case of taxation is that the benefits of avoidance are so great, because of unrealistically high rates, that there is simple evasion. Hence, the underground economy. The unregulated economic sector, which has been estimated, perhaps with some exaggeration, to provide between 45 and 70 percent of urban employment in Peru, is largely the result of exaggerated tax rates and unbelievably complex tax and business (especially labor) regulations. Only the most skilled and specialized lawyers can understand the complexities involved. The informal sector in Peru includes some sizable industrial operations, concealed by a multitude of smaller establishments. Large, well-known companies cannot evade taxes outright, so they naturally stretch the law as much as regulations allow.

Nonetheless, there is a cost to excessive regulation. Investment decisions responsive to unbiased market signals are discouraged, and money is channeled instead to activities that are artificially stimulated by tariffs, tax concessions, and special credit allocations. The automobile assembly plants that popped up in most of the medium-sized economies of Latin America in the 1960s and early 1970s are a prime example of this type of uneconomic investment.[2] They created little employment at the cost of large fiscal subsidies and were naturally encouraged by high duties on finished cars plus fiscal incentives for local assembly. The wide use of such industrial policies tends to have an unfavorable effect on the growth of remunerative employment. From 1960 to 1970, employment in the manufacturing industry—the most highly paid on average—in the two highly export-oriented economies of South Korea and Taiwan rose by an average of 9 percent a year in comparison with 17 percent annual growth in industrial value. In Mexico and Colombia, on the other hand, which were among the best performers in Latin America but were much less export-oriented than the East Asian economies, the comparable percentages were 4 and 8.

It is tempting to compare the East Asian countries to the Latin American ones, although the different nature of their economies and political systems makes such comparisons somewhat unfair. Nonetheless, the differences between the two types of regulation are instructive.

- Instead of prohibitions and restrictions, the regulation of East Asian economies is more in the form of state support, through special credit, tax, and import arrangements, for activities that are considered important.
- Corporate tax rates are lower in the East Asian countries.
- While strong protectionism exists in some East Asian countries, it tends to be for a limited range of consumer goods which have little effect on production costs in the economy at large.
- Most important, in the East Asian countries, explicit state encouragement of certain activities takes place in a context of broadly realistic prices, especially the exchange rate, and of limited price distortions because inflation is, in general, moderate.

Proper prices, however, may not be enough to spur sustained growth unless the tax system also promotes growth. Despite the mitigating effect of evasion and legitimate avoidance, corporate tax rates in most of Latin America tend to be high, as noted in table 3-2. They are offset by tax credits for various types of investments, but their dubious effects on employment and growth have been the subject of much analysis.[3] Tax credits combined with subsidized state loans and low import tariffs for investment in machinery tend to create excess capacity, slow employment growth, heavy corporate debt to equity ratios, and, hence, weak corporate cash flows. Another feature of tax regimes is their complexity. Despite years of apparent tax incentives favoring decentralization of economic activity through small enterprises and agro-industry, most Latin American economies except Brazil and Colombia tend to remain concentrated around the capital city and to have only limited rural industrialization.

The difficulties of administering overly complex income tax systems with underpaid and undertrained personnel mean that direct taxation provides limited revenue despite high nominal tax rates. Inflation further complicates the task. In 1982, for example, only 6 percent of central government current revenues of Argentina came from income and profit taxes; the comparable figures were a low 13 percent in Brazil and 15 percent in Peru,[4] with the bulk of the latter generated by a few oil and mining companies. As a result, there is a tendency in several countries to place heavy taxes on domestic trade and in some cases also on foreign trade, both of which are relatively easy to collect. High import tariffs are thus not always simply the product of protectionism but also of the need to collect revenues for the government, creating two conflicting objectives—if protectionism works, then imports are sharply cut and the revenue-collecting objective cannot be met. Foreign trade is sometimes restricted by the implicitly undervalued exchange rate, which affects imports because of high import duties, and the overvalued rate created on the other side by taxes on traditional exports. This type of policy stands in sharp contrast to what has happened in the fast-growing economies of East Asia.

It is obviously a vast generalization to describe the regulatory and tax systems of Latin American economies in these terms. Some countries, such as Chile, Colombia, and Mexico, have relatively strong income tax systems; the Central American economies have traditionally been moderate on trade and investment regulations and have maintained fairly low protection from imports in comparison with the other economies of the region. On average, however, it is probably not unfair to characterize the economic situation of the 1970s and early 1980s in Latin America as one of increasing regulation and taxation, most of it indirect and biased against foreign trade.

State "Enterprise"

There is a general view that state-controlled companies are inefficient. There are also inefficient private sector enterprises, but it is nonetheless true that waste and inefficiency are far greater problems for state-owned companies. If such an enterprise fails, it is the taxpayers or the population at large, through inflation, who pay for the losses; in the case of private enterprises, however, it is usually the shareholders and their creditors who pay.

As far as state enterprises are concerned, on the one hand, there are a number of well-run public utilities and a few successful commercial and industrial enterprises, such as CVRD (mining and metals processing in Brazil) and CODELCO (copper mining, smelting, and refining in Chile), while, on the other hand, there is a vast array of inefficient, money-losing state-run companies in commercial ventures ranging from airlines to steel mills. Admittedly, some of these do not operate at a loss, particularly the state oil companies, but their tax contributions to the national treasury are no doubt less than they would be if the companies were run as private sector enterprises. Some state enterprises, such as the state-owned mining companies in Chile and Peru or the nationalized banks in Mexico, are the result of state takeovers. And finally, a wide variety of companies have been rescued from bankruptcy by the state because of political pressures to maintain employment. The same pattern can be found in the Philippines, where the government is responsible for more than five hundred state enterprises, many of them formed originally as private ventures by friends of former president Ferdinand Marcos who were able to achieve large personal gains by defaulting on state-guaranteed financing. In general, Latin American state enterprises have been large contributors to public sector deficits.

The reasons already reviewed for the rising role of state enterprise, especially in Mexico, Peru, and Venezuela, are clear, even though complex: a combination of historic and economic forces, fueled in the 1970s by the availability of foreign credit. Even in Brazil and Colombia, where state enterprise plays a smaller role, its participation in the economy nearly doubled in the 1970s (see table 3-1). Among the more advanced developing countries, only Malaysia, a commodity exporter and relatively large international borrower, showed a growth in state enterprise which exceeded that in Latin America. Meanwhile, in Western Europe, where a number of countries are considered the natural habitat of state enterprise, its role in their economies did not increase in the decade of the 1970s. The Latin American experience was thus a unique one in that period.

Despite the fact that there are successful and productive industrial state enterprises—the cases of CODELCO in Chile and CVRD in Brazil have been noted—two facts stand out: (1) the headlong growth of external borrowing by state enterprises in major Latin American economies in the 1970s and early 1980s in order to finance a growing proportion of public investment; and (2) the growing contribution to public sector deficits of state enterprises (table 3-3). Consistent data are hard to find, but in rough numbers the deficit of state enterprises in the seven largest Latin American economies accounted for one-quarter of the public sector deficit in the mid-1970s but rose to about one-half in the years 1980–82, while the overall public sector deficit doubled from about 4 to 8 percent of GNP. State enterprises thus accounted for three-quarters of the deterioration in public sector finances.

Deficits and borrowing are, of course, two sides of the same coin. The availability of external credit stimulated public investment in the second half of the 1970s, especially through state enterprises that were considered attractive by lenders. For international suppliers, most of whom can finance their equipment export sales with credit guaranteed by their own governments—especially in the case of Europe, Japan, and Canada—state enterprises in large, semi-industrialized developing countries have traditionally been a happy hunting ground. Despite convoluted bidding procedures, complexity is sometimes a cover for directing the business to a particular supplier. Often the availability of financing tied to the equipment sale is enough to tip the decision in one direction.

For commercial bank lenders, state enterprise borrowers provided

Table 3-3 State Enterprise and Public Investment

	Argentina		Brazil[a]		Mexico	
Number of state enterprises (1985)	297[b]		471[c]		677[d]	
	Average *1980–81*	*1983*	*Average* *1980–81*	*1984*[e]	*Average* *1980–81*	*1984*
Public sector investment (percentage of GNP)	12.7	11.9	6.7	6.1	11.6	7.6
Of which state enterprise[f]	4.9	5.0	4.3	3.8	7.6	4.2
Private sector investment	7.7	4.2	15.6	10.2	14.1	10.6
Public sector deficit (percentage of GDP)	5.7	15.7	8.1	10.5	11.2	6.9

	Argentina			Brazil[a]			Mexico		
	1980	*1982*	*1984*	*1980*	*1982*	*1984*	*1980*	*1982*	*1984*
Outstanding external public debt of state enterprise (billions of dollars)	14.5	28.6	37.6	32.0	46.7	53.3	15.4	32.3	50.6

Sources: Inter-American Development Bank, *Economic and Social Progress in Latin America* (1984, 1985); national statistics.

[a]Public investment for Brazil is only for 10 largest state companies. Deficit data for Brazil do not include the cost of indexing public debt.

[b]Argentina's largest state enterprises: YPF, Gas del Estado, Segba, ENTEL, Aerolineas Argentinas, Agua y Energia, Ferrocarriles Argentinos, Elma.

[c]Brazil's largest state enterprises: Petrobras, Siderbras, Electrobras, Telbras, CVRD, RFFSA.

[d]Mexico's largest state enterprises: PEMEX, CFE (Comision Federal de Electricidad), CONASUPO, FERTIMEX, SIDALMEX, Empresas Ferroviarias.

[e]Estimated.

[f]Excluding social security system.

the security of a government-guaranteed loan combined with the likelihood of cash flow and related business opportunities that generally come with lending to companies. Given the energy crisis and the high commodity prices of the 1970s, natural resource state companies were especially attractive to commercial banks, oil companies in particular. Petroleos Mexicanos (PEMEX), the Mexican state oil monopoly, was considered the best credit in Mexico after the federal government itself and was often used by the government as a channel for its own external borrowing; it thus became difficult to disentangle what the borrowing was for, even though a major portion was used to finance the development program of PEMEX. It did not matter much if the oil company was an exporter or an importer of oil. PEMEX was a favorite long before it became a major oil exporter in 1976, as was the Brazilian state oil company, Petrobras, which was an oil importer as well as a major producer. As of 1982, almost 40 percent of the medium-term debt of the Mexican public sector was in the PEMEX name. Bankers were also eager to lend to Petroleos de Venezuela, the state oil monopoly, which emerged after the foreign company nationalizations of 1974, but the Venezuelan government refrained and Petroleos remains debt-free.

Naturally enough, public investment tended to emphasize energy and mining. That is also what lenders found attractive, given high energy and mineral prices. Substitution of oil imports was an obvious priority, while rapid economic growth generated an even faster growth of demand for electricity. With Latin American economies growing at about 6 percent on average, planners estimated that electricity demand would increase 50 percent faster, or by 9 percent per year, doubling every eight years. The bulk of the expansion of generating capacity came in the form of hydropower, for which Latin America has a huge potential. It obviously made sense in order to save expensive oil; however, it also has an investment cost about three times higher than conventional oil-burning thermal plants. As a result, public investment in energy, which is almost entirely in the hands of the state, ballooned. From close to 3 percent of GNP in 1973, public investment in energy almost doubled to about 5 percent in 1980–81.

The decision for this massive investment assumed that growth would continue without major interruptions. The counterparts to nuclear plants and oil shale projects in the United States were dams and transmission systems in Latin America. However, when the world recession began to be felt in 1981 and was then followed by a gradual but profound weakening of the international oil market, energy investment projects were hit hard. In North America, uneconomic private sector projects have subsequently been reorganized or mothballed at very substantial cost to bank creditors and bondholders, while the state-sponsored investments of Latin America still carry the full value of the debt. This puts a major burden on government budgets and taxpayers.

The past energy investment has obviously left in place good facilities and a strong base for future growth. But the economic costs have been high. While it would be incorrect to say that public investment in natural resources, energy, and related fields has been costly and inefficient, there are major investments that have turned out badly because of poor planning or that are not needed today because of the unexpected downturn in demand for energy.

Since energy has absorbed such a large proportion of public investment, it has naturally attracted the most attention. It is also true that some of the showpiece industrial projects have turned out badly. The following is a sample of some state investments that have not turned out well:

- The Las Truchas steel complex in western Mexico: built with the help of loans from suppliers and from the World Bank, which argued internally about the merits of the investment. Its accumulated losses since 1976 are probably close to the original investment of $800 million. Production costs at the plant are reportedly twice those of South Korean steel mills.
- The Majes irrigation project in Peru, on which about $700 million has been spent since 1970 on a water diversion scheme: so far only about six thousand hectares are irrigated, and no money is left to begin the hydroelectric plant intended along with the irrigation. When and if completed, the scheme will likely have the highest capital cost per acre of irrigated land in the world.
- The Brazilian nuclear power program, on which about $4.2 billion has been spent since the plan was announced in 1975: of the plants proposed, not one was operating by 1986, and at least another $3 billion was needed, not counting interest, in order to commission the first two units of 1,200 mw each in the first half of the next decade.
- The Açominas two-million-ton steel plant in Minas Gerais, Brazil, was built in the late 1970s at a cost of more than $2.5 billion, almost entirely with external borrowing, some of which was apparently diverted to financing the central government deficit. While its operating efficiency is no worse than that of most of the rest of the state steel sector, because of its high investment cost, Acominas is likely to incur heavy losses after its start-up in 1986, five years behind schedule.

- In addition, several large transport projects, especially subways, have had huge cost overruns. The capital investment on subway projects, such as that of Mexico City, works out to about $2,500 per inch of route.[5] In that regard, Latin America is no different from the rest of the world, but it is in no position to afford the costs.
- A different type of problem was faced by the expansion in the late 1970s of the state-owned Cobriza copper mine in the Central Andes of Peru, a project undertaken with the help of multilateral development banks. After start-up in 1981, the ore reserves were found to be inadequate to sustain economic production for the size of the facilities built with the loans.

Many problems of state enterprises are not of their own making. Politicians have an ambivalent attitude: on one hand, they like to talk about the need for efficiency in the state, but on the other, they often do not hesitate to cut back salaries of the management of state enterprises, to support price controls on output, and to impose all kinds of operating restrictions. The simplest purchase and travel permit may well require ministerial approval. Unrealistically low salaries for high-level professionals encourage a brain drain to the private sector and in many instances to international agencies.

Every government believes that its state enterprises are different. In general, however, well-run state enterprises fall along industry lines rather than geographical ones. Electric utilities have, by and large, avoided the excesses of other state enterprises, as have some of the oil and mining companies that were originally run privately, mostly by foreign companies. In the case of the electric utilities, the role of the World Bank since the early 1950s in maintaining discipline through the requirements attached to its loans has paid off; the Inter-American Development Bank further supported these efforts from the 1960s onward. In the case of manufacturing, international financial agencies have been much less successful: lending has been smaller, objective standards are more difficult to set, and the state tends to be a notoriously bad marketer of products that have to compete in commercial markets. Some state industries, such as steel in Brazil, have in general operated well at the plant level but have nevertheless faced heavy losses because of excessive reliance on debt financing.

The longstanding impression among the public in many Latin American countries that state enterprise is inefficient and sometimes corrupt has been heightened in recent years. This is a salutary by-product of the debt crisis and of the freer public discussion that has accompanied the return to democracy in several countries. But despite the fact that

Table 3-4   Social Welfare Indicators

	Argentina		Brazil		Chile	
	1960	1980	1960	1980	1960	1980
Average life expectancy at birth (years)	65	70	55	63	57	67
Infant mortality (per 1,000 live births)	61	45	118	77	114	43
Population per doctor	740	530	2,670	1,700	1,780	1,920
Population per medical assistant	750	430	2,810	820	640	450
Percentage of minimum daily calorie requirements supplied	n.a.	125	n.a.	109	n.a.	114
Enrollment in school (as percentage of age group)						
Primary	98	116	95	93	109	117
Secondary	23	56	11	32	24	55
Adult literacy rate	91	93	61	76	84	93
Percentage of population with access to piped water	51	58	32	56	63	78
Electricity consumption per capita (kw/hour)	513	1,406	325	1,149	598	1,058
Energy consumption per capita (kg coal equiv. per year)	1,057	2,161	375	1,102	797	1,137

Sources: World Bank, *World Development Report* (1982, 1983, 1985);
Inter-American Development Bank, *Social and Economic Progress in Latin America,*
various annual issues.

state enterprises in Latin America have received about $80–100 billion in foreign loans in the decade form 1973 to 1982, there is remarkably little public information over a period of years showing elementary numbers for sales, value added, profits, subsidies, expenditures on investment, and so on. The exceptions have been mentioned. Much can be done to create an awareness of the problem through better information.

Basic Public Services

Most Latin American countries have made significant progress in providing basic public services in the last twenty years. While there are still large deficiencies in the quality and equitable distribution of services, especially education and health, overall progress has been

	Colombia		Mexico		Peru		Venezuela		Average All Upper Middle Income Countries	
	1960	1980	1960	1980	1960	1980	1960	1980	1960	1980
	53	63	58	65	47	58	57	67	57	64
	93	56	91	56	163	88	85	42	103	62
	2,640	1,920	1,830	1,260	1,910	1,390	1,510	950	2,606	1,689
	4,220	1,220	3,650	1,420	2,210	690	2,840	370	2,678	1,010
	n.a.	108	n.a.	121	n.a.	99	n.a.	112	n.a.	115
	77	128	80	120	83	112	100	104	88	104
	12	46	11	37	15	56	21	39	20	48
	63	81	65	83	61	80	63	82	61	76
	54	56	38	50	45	51	50	80	n.a.	50
	244	890	313	972	265	567	601	2,298	150	1,137
	494	970	713	1,684	417	807	3,014	3,039	462	987

comparable to the average of the middle and upper group of developing countries. Beginning in 1981, however, the extremely high proportion of government expenditure on debt service has undercut the provision of basic public services. For the seven largest countries of Latin America, the share of interest on domestic and external debt in central government outlays has grown from 8 percent in 1975 to about 20 percent in 1984.[6] This increase—especially in recent years, when economies have been depressed and tax revenues have stagnated in real terms—does not augur well for the future provision of basic government services. In order to keep up the growth of services provided by the government, there is likely to be a move, at least in some countries, for the private sector to substitute for the government in providing some services.

The remarkable progress achieved in the last two decades can be seen in increased longevity statistics, sharp reductions in infant mortality, improvements in diet and the availability of medical care, higher rates of literacy and enrollment in primary and secondary school, and substantially better availability of basic services such as electricity, water, and sewage, as well as road transport (table 3-4). Except for Peru, which has had the slowest rate of economic expansion of any of the major Latin American economies since 1965, these countries have done better than the average of the upper middle-income countries or the upper tier of developing countries.

The distribution and the quality of these services are controversial, but the lack of statistics makes judgments difficult. There are obvious regional disparities, such as the rich South versus the poor Northeast in Brazil, or the similar disparity between the coast and the Sierra in Peru, as well as urban versus rural areas in general. Clearly, basic services are much less available in rural areas, which account for only about 30 percent of the total population in the larger countries. (In some of the highly industrialized East Asian countries, such as South Korea or Taiwan, the rural population is still almost 40 percent of the total.) The lack of public services in the rural areas of Latin America contributed in the period up to 1981–82 to high immigration into major cities and to the increasing centralization of economic activity. Conversely, following the debt crisis the return of individuals and families to the countryside[7] in order to escape urban unemployment is likely to put future pressure on governments to increase public services outside the main cities. On the political plane, this shift back to the countryside may well mean a change in the character of rural voters, away from the traditionally conservative agrarian parties.

There is little doubt that public services, such as education and health, are, on average, of poor quality in much of Latin America. The reason is simple: no money. For example, with a public school enrollment of 19.2 million and a total annual education budget of $3.3 billion in 1985, Mexico could afford to spend only $174 per public school student; Brazil could afford only about $100. This compares, for example, with $840 per public school student in the case of a recently industrialized country such as Spain. Repeater rates in public schools are high, while retention in rural areas is low because of the lack of teachers and facilities combined with the pressure to find early employment on the part of the students.

The public sector controls the bulk of energy supply in most Latin American countries: production of electricity for public use is almost entirely in the hands of the state, and government oil companies are either monopolists or major factors in oil production and distribution. On the whole in Latin America, during the 1960s and 1970s the state did a creditable job in stimulating and providing energy and related services. The shortages that existed in electricity in several countries fifteen or twenty years ago are gone, although part of the comfortable surplus comes from the depression of most economies after 1982. In oil the rise of prices after 1973 has spurred a major effort on the part of oil-importing countries: Colombia became a net exporter in 1986 because of a policy of deliberate stimulus to private producers combined with more realistic domestic oil prices; Argentina, because of successful exploration by private producers and the state oil company, is now self-sufficient; and Brazil has cut its oil import needs from 70 percent of total oil consumption in 1973 to about 45 percent today, the result of successful offshore exploration by Petrobras combined with the equally successful although costly government-sponsored alcohol fuel program.

Relatively abundant energy plus low product prices in the oil-exporting countries have given Latin America a relatively high use of energy in relation to its GNP; compared to the East Asian developing countries, energy consumption per person in Latin America in 1981 was more than twice as high on average. Much of that has gone into private transport. Latin Americans have on average one car for every five families, compared to one for every sixteen in East Asia.[8] These averages, of course, conceal heavy concentration among higher income groups. Even so, the type of development that has taken place in most Latin American countries is illustrated by what has happened in energy: a stimulus to consumer demand through low or subsidized prices, emphasis on consumption rather than savings, and an important although not exclusive role for the government in providing basic services, as well as a major role for it in regulating the economy. It is difficult to quantify the extent to which governments have deliberately stimulated this development, or whether they have simply responded to historic and social forces favoring this pattern.

Conclusion

Easy borrowing by governments led to a sharp expansion of the public sector in the majority of Latin American economies in the 1970s. While some of this expansion was the natural result of development and income growth, much of it was diverted to subsidies for urban populations and to investment in dubious state-sponsored projects. How much was efficient investment is difficult to know. Moreover, some countries did not participate in the statist trend to the same extent as others. While state enterprise and excessive regulations were on balance a net drain on economies, shutting out private enterprise while raising the cost of basic industrial and agricultural inputs and subsidizing staples for the urban populations, the record of government in providing basic services was laudable. On average, Latin American countries did better in providing basic education and health, as well as public electricity and water, than most of the countries in other developing areas. Yet only limited amounts were borrowed abroad for these purposes, which create far more employment per unit of expenditure than big state enterprise investments. The lesson for the future is clear—especially today, at a time of high unemployment and, with a few exceptions, of low economic growth: redirect limited public resources toward essential investment and basic social services that will quickly provide employment and in the longer run benefit populations. Given the level of public sector management in most countries and in Latin America in particular, high-cost state capitalism has been shown by the borrowing binge of the 1970s to be a costly and mostly inefficient path toward self-sustaining growth.

(4)

The Crisis Erupts: Mexico, Latin America, and the International Economy, 1980–1982

The easy borrowing by major Latin American governments during the 1970s was based on the unstated assumption that the world economy would continue more or less on the same path: moderate growth with low real interest rates. As long as export growth was enough to cover the interest cost of the debt, it was argued, there would be no problem.[1] The possibility of a deep recession combined with high interest rates was considered unthinkable, even though the world economy had come close to that in 1974–75.

Beginning in 1980 there was a dramatic break with the past in the United States. A major economic downturn, far larger than expected and the deepest of the postwar period, was accompanied by record-high interest rates (table 4-1).[2] This pattern spread to most of the other major industrial countries, except Japan, and by the end of 1981 had become virtually worldwide. There followed a drastic fall in the price of internationally traded raw materials, and by 1982 the volume of international trade also fell.

Not only was a deep recession combined with high interest rates unthinkable, but its eventual sequel, the suspension of new lending, was equally so. Borrowers had assumed that they would go on borrowing.[3] But the chain of events brought the bad news piecemeal, and the real message was hard to hear. First came the rise of international interest rates in 1980 and 1981; second, the decline in export earnings in 1982; and finally, from mid-1982 onward, the suspension of new commercial bank lending to Latin American borrowers and a sharp curtailment in East Asia. It was this sequence that in August 1982 ended the ability of Mexico to pay its scheduled debt obligations.

Table 4-1 The International Recession, 1980–1982

| | Year and Quarter | | | | | | | | | | | |
| | 1980 | | | | 1981 | | | | 1982 | | | |
	1	2	3	4	1	2	3	4	1	2	3	4
Real GNP percentage change												
U.S.A.												
a. Quarter-to-quarter	4.1	−9.1	0.3	5.2	8.0	−1.3	1.8	−5.5	−5.9	1.2	−3.2	0.6
b. Year-to-year	1.6	−0.7	−1.5	−0.1	0.9	3.0	3.3	0.6	−2.8	−2.2	−3.4	−1.9
West Germany (year-to-year)	4.7	1.0	0.8	−0.6	−1.3	−0.1	0.6	0.8	−1.0	−0.1	−1.4	−1.3
Japan (year-to-year)	5.3	3.9	4.0	3.9	3.8	4.2	3.9	3.0	2.5	3.2	3.1	3.7
Unemployment (average percentage rate for quarter)[a]												
U.S.A.	6.7	7.1	7.4	7.0	7.8	7.2	7.2	7.8	9.3	9.2	9.5	10.1
West Germany	3.6	3.0	3.1	3.4	4.6	4.2	4.5	5.3	6.8	6.2	6.4	7.2
Inflation (CPI percentage change over previous year)												
U.S.A.	16.7	14.2	7.6	11.8	11.3	8.7	11.6	6.7	3.8	5.5	7.3	1.4
West Germany	5.6	5.8	5.1	5.2	5.6	5.8	6.7	7.1	5.2	4.7	5.0	3.5
Japan	7.4	8.3	8.3	7.9	6.6	4.9	4.2	4.0	3.1	2.5	2.7	2.3
International non-oil commodity prices (index 1980 = 100)	102	99	99	99	92	85	82	80	79	75	72	72
Interest rates (last month of quarter)												
U.S. prime rate	19.5	11.5	13.0	21.5	17.0	20.0	19.5	15.8	16.5	16.5	13.0	11.5
London interbank offered rate (LIBOR), 6-month dollars	19.6	9.9	13.9	16.4	14.8	17.3	18.1	14.8	15.4	16.0	11.9	9.5

Sources: U.S. Dept. of Commerce, *Survey of Current Business*, and OECD International Data Bank.
[a] Japan omitted because its unemployment rate stayed stable at about 2 percent.

Unlike the previous problems of individual debtors such as Indonesia and Brazil in the 1960s, Turkey in 1977, and Poland in 1981, the crisis in Mexico spread throughout the Latin American region as well as the Philippines. This was the result of Mexico's unusual standing as an international borrower; it was not only a top-rated borrower but the largest as well. Mexico's financial demise thus shocked international banks. The crisis was complicated by an already jaundiced view of Latin American governments by many banks because of Argentina's invasion of the Malvinas, or Falkland Islands, earlier that year. Argentina did receive the tacit if unenthusiastic support of several Latin American governments; in fact, however, there was little material support and much behind-the-scenes manipulation to get Argentina to stop the war.[4]

It was especially the rise in interest rates that hit the larger Latin American borrowers hard. The fact that their external debt had in 1981 reached the equivalent of three times one year's export earnings, and that almost 70 percent of it was at floating interest rates, meant that countries were caught between the two blades of a financial scissors: declining export incomes and rapidly rising obligations for interest payments abroad. The squeeze was all the tighter because now there was no ability to finance this large difference. The East Asian countries were hit almost as hard by the loss of markets due to the recession and by the decline in the markets for their manufactured exports; however, their relative external debts were much lower, as was the proportion of loans at floating interest rates. Except for those of the Philippines, the problems in East Asia were far more manageable.[5] Major Latin American borrowing countries, on the other hand, found that the burden of interest payments as a proportion of exports doubled from 1979 to 1981. When exports fell off in 1982 and bank lenders lost confidence, the music stopped.[6]

There is thus no great mystery about the origins of the debt crisis in Latin America: first, and most important, an extremely high level of external debt, most of it at floating interest rates; second, the impact of a very large rise in international interest rates, mostly denominated in dollars at a time of a rising U.S. dollar, upon the service of this debt; third, an eventual, but not immediate, decline in export earnings due to a deep international recession; and finally, as in most debt crises, a loss of confidence on the part of lenders, who initially started to lend at shorter terms and eventually stopped altogether, precipitating the suspension of debt service.

The high level of external debt and consequent vulnerability to rises in international interest rates are the critical factors. This can be made clear by contrasting the case of Colombia with those of large debtors such as Brazil, Mexico, or the Philippines. With an external debt two-and-a-half times its annual merchandise export earnings in 1982, and with 60 percent of the debt at long-term maturities with fixed interest rates, Colombia was able to avoid a major refinancing of its commercial bank debt because interest service stayed within reason. Although economic growth slowed sharply, to a large extent because of the effects of recessions in neighboring countries upon Colombian exports, Colombia still had the best growth performance of any of the major Latin American economies in the period 1981–85.[7] In contrast, by 1982, large debtors—whether oil importers, such as Brazil or the Philippines, or oil exporters, such as Mexico—had external debt-to-exports ratios of three or four to one; most of the debt was at floating rates, so that an enormous inflow of capital was needed to maintain economic growth and at the same time service the debt.

The case of Mexico is the most telling. Between 1979 and 1981, the years of peak export growth because of high oil prices, its external debt to banks nearly doubled. With an external debt by 1981 equivalent to three times exports, an interest rate of 10 percent would have required 30 percent of exports just to pay the interest on the debt. But for 1981 the average interest on the debt had risen to about 17 percent, so that 51 percent of export earnings were required to cover interest. The stage for the crisis was then set because the debtor—other things being equal—would need to raise its borrowing abroad by two-thirds in the short space of a year or so in order to pay interest without disrupting its economy. When that became impossible, the crisis arrived.

The United States and the International Crisis, 1980–1982

The United States has been at the center of the international economy since World War II. Yet, even today, after the record growth of imports of the 1980s, the U.S. economy is still far more self-contained than those of other industrial countries. Nonetheless, because of its sheer size, the United States has a considerable impact on others. In 1984, U.S. imports accounted for 19 percent of world trade, up from 13 percent in 1980. The U.S. capital market is by far the largest and most varied; as an example, the U.S. stock market accounts for almost half of the market capitalization of companies listed on the stock exchanges of the world.[8] The U.S. dollar is by far the most widely used currency in international trade and capital movements; for example, it accounts for 79 percent of the currencies of deposit in the Euromarket.[9]

As a result of its international economic importance, the United States is somewhat like a friendly giant on a playground: he is amiable, but any move he makes immediately affects everyone else there. This type of relationship has given rise to the saying that when the United States sneezes, the rest of the world catches pneumonia. No other economy can make a similar claim. Even Japan and West Germany, each with about 8.5 percent of world trade, do not by themselves come close.

The international economic downturn of 1980–82 was not only a U.S. affair but U.S. policy played the key role. It started with the trebling of oil prices, which OPEC put through in the wake of the Iranian revolution. World inflation exacerbated the demand for commodities, especially oil, and in turn the upsurge of oil prices fed the inflation. Investment then started to sag, intensifying the stagnation-with-inflation, or "stagflation," which most industrial countries had suffered in varying degrees since the first round of major international oil price increases in 1973–74. By the first quarter of 1980, U.S. inflation was running at an unbelievably high annual rate of 16.7 percent, while dollar interest rates had gradually been going up since mid-1978, to almost 20 percent in the three-month Eurodollar deposit rate in March 1980.[10] The burden of the inevitable adjustment needed to cut down inflation fell upon the Federal Reserve, which severely tightened credit in order to offset the fairly easy fiscal policy being followed in an election year. A large drop in output ensued in the second quarter of 1980, with a resulting short-lived drop of interest rates to the 9 to 10 percent level. As the November 1980 election approached, credit policy was loosened again, and the economy rebounded at the end of 1980 and beginning of 1981, but at the cost of renewed inflation and sky-high interest rates, which hovered around 16 to 19 percent for most of the twelve months starting in October 1980.

The elimination of inflation was the paramount domestic priority of the incoming Reagan administration in January 1981. With the continuation of a loose fiscal policy, the burden of fighting inflation had to be assumed again by the Federal Reserve. The resulting tight monetary policy coincided with accelerating deregulation of interest rates in the U.S. banking system; this culminated with the creation of interest-paying checking deposits (NOW, or notification-on-withdrawal accounts) at the beginning of 1981. A prolonged period of high interest rates ensued (see table 4-1). It was only broken in August 1982, when the Federal Reserve, afraid of the possible consequences of the Mexican debt crisis upon major U.S. banks, relaxed.

The depth of the 1980–82 recession was combined with wrenching downward wage adjustments in major industries, exemplified by President Reagan's strong stand against the federal air controllers in 1981.

Inflation came down sharply and since 1983 has stayed at the 3 to 4 percent level. The successful fight against inflation was helped by the effect of relatively high interest rates on the international value of the dollar. The large differential between high U.S. interest rates and interest rates elsewhere, as well as strong growth in the United States in 1983–84, attracted a growing inflow of foreign capital to the United States, strengthening the dollar and thus making imports more attractive to American buyers. Hence the sharp rise in U.S. imports, with its favorable impact on the cost of living in the United States.

Overall, the cost of these policies upon large debtors everywhere, but especially the commodity-producing economies in Latin America, was considerable. The need for an attack on inflation is not in question. The point is simply that the difficulty of the task was so great that there was bound to be a worldwide cost. The 1980–82 recession was a turning point, not just because of its extent and special nature, but because it in effect completed the enormous job of readjusting the world economy after the inflationary period that had begun as far back as the Vietnam War.

While it was not generally realized in 1982, the elimination of inflation brought into the open a trend that had started after 1973, namely the replacement of expensive energy-intensive raw materials with lighter weight, less energy-intensive materials. The long-term consequences for most commodities have been devastating. After 1982, contrary to expectations, the raw materials exported by developing countries did not rebound in price, as in past economic recoveries, but instead continued to decline steadily from year to year, making recovery more difficult. The 1980–82 international recession was thus not just another cyclical economic event; it was a watershed in the economic history of the postwar period.

The Explosion of Short-term Debt

The explosion of international borrowing at short maturities by several Latin American governments from 1979 on represented a major change in attitudes toward external debt. Until then borrowers had paid much attention to getting the finest terms possible, especially long maturities on new loans. Banks used maturities as a rationing device, limiting longer maturities to the very best borrowers. In the high liquidity period after the first oil price run-up in 1973–74, maturities to twelve years were in some cases possible, but for most of the decade eight years was the normal limit, with some loans of up to ten years. Brazil was traditionally concerned with keeping maturities as long as possible. Mexico, on the other hand, was far more concerned about the rate of interest itself, as measured by the margin, or "spread," over the traditional benchmark for Eurolending, the London Interbank Offered Rate (LIBOR).[11] Because Mexico was an oil exporter starting in 1976, and also because of its proximity to the United States, it was considered by bankers to be a better credit risk than Brazil and traditionally obtained the lowest spreads among Latin American borrowers (table 4-2).

Beginning around 1979, however, a number of major banks began to worry about the creditworthiness of their developing country customers in general and about the oil importers in particular. Spreads became higher, large syndicated loans became harder to organize, and final maturities shortened. Brazil, the debtor most affected by the near trebling of international oil prices during the course of 1979, suffered the most. On the other hand, however, international banks continued to seek the profitability of lending to the more developed and resource-rich among developing countries. In order to reconcile their doubts with their desire to lend, which was driven in part by the huge increase in liquidity created by high world inflation and increased inflow of the petrodollars, lending at short maturities became attractive. The main objective was to have a higher proportion of loans for self-liquidating trade-related purposes, such as financing imports or exports. In this way, it was felt, lending would be more secure.

Not all countries were enthusiastic about the new short-term lending. Brazil continued to be cautious and to emphasize longer maturities. However, the need to finance the doubling of oil import costs in 1979–

Table 4-2   Maturities and Spreads on Gross New Publicized Syndicated Loans to Brazil and Mexico, 1973–1981

	1973	*1974*	*1975*	*1976*	*1977*	*1978*	*1979*	*1980*	*1981*
Brazil									
Average final maturity (years)	14.3	10.4	5.0	6.2	6.1	10.6	10.8	6.8	8.2
Average spread over LIBOR (percentage)	0.8	1.0	1.8	2.0	2.0	1.5	0.9	1.4	2.1
Mexico									
Average final maturity (years)	11.7	7.8	5.0	5.5	6.8	8.0	7.8	7.3	7.5
Average spread over LIBOR (percentage)	0.5	0.8	1.5	1.6	1.6	1.1	0.8	0.7	0.7

Source: Financial Statistics, Organization for Economic Cooperation and Development, Paris. I am grateful to the OECD Financial Markets Division for having specially prepared the data shown here.

80 forced it to draw upon previously unused short-term lines of credit and to resort to other short-term, although renewable, loans. The trend-setter had been an oil import "acceptance facility," organized in 1974 by Wells Fargo Bank. Oil imports into Brazil were secured by accep-tances, supposedly trade-related, short-term paper, which were paid off by the loan as the oil was imported into the country. Then the facility would revolve until its maturity, being renewed as each acceptance came due. Through devices such as these, banks were able to appear as if they were providing short-term, business-related lending when in fact it was simply a form of permanent financing of the balance of payments. In 1980, Brazil, which had used short-term borrowing less than the other major debtors, nonetheless had to obtain about 80 per-cent of its net borrowing from banks in short-term form, at original maturities of less than a year (table 4-3).

In the case of Venezuela, the short-term borrowing had a different and more specific cause, namely the legal requirement that foreign borrowing had to be approved by Congress. A loophole, however, exempted loans with an original maturity of less than two years—the

Table 4-3   The Growth of Short-term Bank Debt, 1978–1982 (in Billions of U.S. Dollars, Outstanding at End of Year)

	1978	1979	1980	1981	1982
Argentina, total	7.0	13.4	19.9	24.8	25.7
Of which short-term	3.5	6.9	10.4	11.6	13.9
Brazil, total	32.9	38.6	45.7	52.5	60.5
Of which short-term	9.3	11.3	16.2	18.2	21.1
Mexico, total	23.2	30.9	42.5	57.1	62.9
Of which short-term	7.4	10.7	18.8	27.8	29.9
Venezuela, total	14.0	20.8	24.3	26.2	27.5
Of which short-term	7.6	12.7	14.3	16.1	15.8
Latin America, total	97.1	129.0	162.9	196.6	214.2
Of which short-term	38.3	54.4	75.2	91.4	98.6
1. Rate of growth of total, %	30.3	32.9	26.3	20.7	9.0
2. Net disbursements by banks	22.6	31.9	34.0	33.7	17.6
3. Interest paid to banks (est.)[a]	9.0	15.3	22.3	32.2	30.4
4. Net transfer from banks (2 less 3)	13.6	16.6	11.7	1.5	−12.8

Source: Basic data from Bank for International Settlements. These exclude offshore banking centers such as the Bahamas, Grand Cayman, and Panama. This omission probably leads to an underestimate of 10 to 25 percent in outstandings and flows. Author's estimates of interest paid are based on LIBOR plus an average margin of 1.25 percent.

Note: The data encompass short-term debt with an original maturity of up to and including one year.

[a]Interest received from banks on reserves deposited abroad has not been netted out.

original reason for this having been that such borrowing was necessary for the day-to-day working of state enterprises. Instead, the loophole was widely used for what was in effect long-term borrowing, circumventing Congress. The system was understood and accepted by banks and the government, both of which knew that long-term investments were being financed with renewable shorter-term loans. As a result, Venezuela had a fairly steady proportion of about 50 percent of its external borrowing from banks undertaken at renewable short-term maturities (see table 4-3).

Once again the most telling case is Mexico. Between the end of 1979 and the end of 1981, Mexico almost doubled its external debt to banks; moreover, $17 billion of the $26 billion increase in two years was at short term. This enormous increase in short-term debt took place at the very time that the average price of Mexico's oil exports went from about $13 per barrel to $36, fueling the largest increase in export earnings in Mexico's modern history. Meanwhile, however, public expenditure rose just as quickly, helped by the combined effect of the increase in external debt and the higher tax revenues from oil. The frantic pace of public expenditure—both in current expenditure, including large-scale subsidies to food staples and fuel, and in a massive public investment program—raised public sector outlays from Mex. $1.3 trillion in 1979 to Mex. $2.8 trillion two years later, or from the equivalent of 41 to 47 percent of the GDP.[12] Foreign bank borrowing financed about 20 percent of the increase.

Thus, for the two-year period after 1979, short-term borrowing by a number of Latin American countries became the main way to get around the resistance of some major bank lenders to continued large-scale lending. At the same time, short-term lending helped the banks to convince themselves that they were keeping their borrowers on a shorter financial leash.

The government officials in charge of external borrowing were regularly praised in the international financial press for their prowess in assembling "jumbo" loans at the finest possible "spreads," and they were in most cases willing to go along with short-term borrowing. Often they had no choice, since it was the only way to get the large amounts that their governments wanted to borrow. An equally important driving force, however, was "spread fixation"; market standing, especially in the press, was often equated with the spread over LIBOR that the borrower paid. A one-year loan at three-eighths of 1 percent over LIBOR, the sort of interest then paid by a top-rated international borrower such as France or Sweden for medium-term loans, looked like a much better deal for Mexico, for example, than a smaller eight-year loan at three times the spread. The fact that the spread would be of almost no importance when base interest rates rose to 20 or 21 percent in mid-1981 was not considered back in 1979.

Short-term borrowing is not by itself bad, as long as it is used for genuine short-term purposes. The trouble arises when the purpose is really long-term, so that the nonrenewability of the short-term loan puts the borrower in a cash squeeze. As the proportion of short-term debt rises, the risk of a squeeze increases. For Latin America as a whole, short-term debt rose from about 15 percent of total external debt at the end of 1973, or about 25 percent of the exports of that year, to 16 percent of total debt in 1979, but about 43 percent of exports. By 1981 these ratios were up to 43 and almost 70 percent, respectively.[13]

The growth of short-term debt led to two problems: first, the risk that lenders might not renew the loans increased sharply; and second, the lack of information among lenders about one another's lending also increased. As bank lenders found out in the second half of 1982 that others had lent more than was imagined, the realization speeded the nonrenewal of short-term loans, and the crisis spread from Mexico to the other major Latin American debtors.

In a perfect market, we are taught, there is perfect information. In the case of short-term lending, however, the information flow that the Euromarket has for longer-term lending does not exist. The fact that short-term lending is considered self-liquidating induces bank lenders to ask for less information from the debtor than they would for a longer-term commitment. This is normal, except that the new short-term loans to Latin American countries were not self-liquidating but simply balance-of-payments loans disguised as commercial transactions. In addition, since short-term loans were supposed to be less risky, banks were less inclined to "syndicate" the loans, or spread the risk among many banks. As a result, little public information was available about short-term lending, except with great delay, after 1977. Borrowing countries were eager to disguise short-term borrowing, which is usually a good indicator of money problems. Short-term loans were thus often channeled through various state banks and agencies, making it hard to obtain reliable numbers on short-term debt. Since most countries did not have stabilization programs with the IMF in the late 1970s, the IMF was not able to get good up-to-date information on the explosion of short-term debt until it was too late.

Short-term borrowing, however, did not cause the debt crisis. It simply enabled borrowing to continue at a time of hesitation by major commercial bank lenders. The short-term borrowing led to two or three additional years of still very high growth of foreign debt, greatly increasing the potential vulnerability of major borrowers to a future international economic crisis. For Brazil there was at first little choice as it faced a 60 to 70 percent increase in the average price of its imports (because of oil) in the period 1979–81; in fact, however, Brazil started to cut back new external borrowing at the end of 1979. For Mexico, an oil exporter, the reverse was true: export earnings more than doubled between 1979 and 1981, but it nevertheless borrowed abroad with even more vigor than in the past. It did so in order to finance the breakneck growth of public expenditures and, indirectly, to finance a growing volume of capital flight stimulated by the combination of buoyant private savings facing unrealistically low interest rates at home and an increasingly overvalued exchange rate for the peso in relation to the U.S. dollar. In the case of Argentina, the financial crisis started in 1981 as public expenditure went out of control and capital fled the country, again because of a grossly overvalued exchange rate. The South Atlantic conflict in April and May 1982 immediately led to a suspension of new lending by banks and to a de facto default by Argentina. More than anything else, the crisis in Argentina in the spring of 1982 paved the way for the really big crisis later that year—the Mexican default. Once the banks put the brakes on new lending, some sort of crisis became inevitable.

A careful reading of the statistics of the Bank for International Settlements (BIS), the important Basel-based international institution that was created in the 1920s to administer the Dawes plan for German reparations, could by mid- to late 1981 have revealed that something was amiss. As international interest rates were racing up and new net lending began to slow down, the new lending barely covered the interest flowing back to the lenders. In the case of Latin America, this "net transfer" from the banks to the borrowers fell from $17 billion in 1979 to $12 billion in 1980 and to almost nil in 1981 (see table 4-3). As if they were on a treadmill, both lenders and borrowers were exhausting themselves just to stay in the same place. Clearly, something was wrong.

How much did countries borrow simply to pay interest? Such calculations are, of course, highly subjective, since they depend on choosing a "normal" base period. The amounts of interest paid above that base are then considered to have been the additional amount that countries were obliged to borrow in order to meet interest payments. If we take 10 percent as the base rate paid to banks, which was in fact the average rate in 1978 before the run-up international interest rates, and then take the actual rates paid above that in subsequent years and compound the difference at the going interest rate of each subsequent year, we get something on the order of $40 to $50 billion as the amount of external debt which was added by the high interest rates of 1980–82. However, significant as this number appears, it has to be interpreted with great care. High interest rates did indeed lead to external borrowing, but on the other hand, if borrowing countries had taken effective austerity measures earlier—as Brazil tried to do in 1980, but with only limited success—they could have avoided a substantial increase in their external debt (table 4-4).

Mexico Defaults

The Latin American debt crisis seemed to burst upon the world as a complete surprise in August 1982. Only a few top people in the Mexican Finance Ministry and a few not-so-top people in the U.S. Treasury had been warning for several months that a Mexican default was likely.

On Thursday, August 12, Mexican Finance Minister Jesus Silva Herzog, who had been in office only since March of that year, telephoned U.S. Treasury Secretary Donald Regan, Federal Reserve Chairman Paul Volcker, and the Managing Director of the International Monetary Fund, Jacques de Larosière. He told them that Mexico had almost run out of foreign exchange reserves and could no longer make payments on its external debt.[14] The following day Silva Herzog and his director of public credit, the youthful Angel Gurría, as well as Banco de Mexico Director General (i.e., governor) Miguel Mancera and

Table 4-4   Interest Rates and External Borrowing from Banks, 1978–1982 (Amounts in Billions of U.S. Dollars)

	1978	1979	1980	1981	1982	Cumulative Total
1. Actual interest payment to banks	9	15	22	32	30	108
2. Actual average rate paid to banks (percentage)	10.0	13.4	15.4	18.0	14.8	
3. Amount which would have been paid at 10%	9	12	15	18	21	75
4. Difference between 1 and 3 plus compounding at current interest rate = borrowing due to interest above 10%	—	4	9	17	14	44

Source: Calculated by author from data of Bank for International Settlements. As noted in table 4-3, these data underestimate total debt to banks by about 10 to 25 percent.

his deputy, Alfredo Philipps, began a round of negotiations in Washington, D.C.

The Washington discussions, held over the "Mexican weekend," from Friday, August 13, to Sunday, August 15, made two points clear: first, there would be a moratorium on amortization payments of debt to commercial banks; second, in the meantime there would be an international package of emergency loans from various official sources. An implicit but extremely important additional point was that interest payments would continue as scheduled.

The subsequent unfolding of the Mexican debt crisis took much longer than was originally thought. Already, during this first weekend of discussions, there were strong disagreements between the United States and the Mexicans—whose numbers now included Mexican Energy Secretary José Andrés Oteyza—on the terms of an advance U.S. oil purchase, which Secretary Regan wanted at a substantial discount over then-prevailing international oil prices. But the main reason for the delay was the turn of political events in Mexico on September 1. That day, in his last annual message to Congress and the nation, outgoing President José López Portillo announced the state takeover of all Mexican commercial banks as well as the imposition of exchange controls. On August 5, the president had allowed a sweeping devaluation to a two-tier exchange system with partial controls, but the measure could not stem the tide of capital flight; by the end of the month, López Portillo had to take dramatic political measures. Not only were the banks nationalized—the bombshell measure—and blamed for having encouraged capital flight, but exchange control was reimposed for the first time since it was abandoned in 1954. Dollar-denominated deposits of about $12 billion in the Mexican banking system were forcibly converted into pesos, causing large losses to small U.S. investors and others who had been attracted by high dollar interest rates in Mexico.

The September 1 measures were clearly political. In the previous month or so, López Portillo had become convinced that a crisis such as the one he was facing could not go unblamed. Two close advisers, Carlos Tello and José Andrés Oteyza, were instrumental in convincing him to take political action. Tello, the son of one of Mexico's illustrious foreign ministers, Manuel Tello, was a distinguished career civil servant, economist, and academic, who at a young age had been named planning and budget minister at the beginning of the López Portillo administration in December 1976. He had been an advocate of a stronger public sector and more aggressive public spending, a position that quickly put him at odds with Finance Minister Julio Moctezuma

Cid. After a year of infighting, President López Portillo dismissed them both. The experience radicalized Tello, who then moved to the decorously remote Colegio de Mexico, Mexico's top economic research institution. From there he criticized the government's economic policies and headlong external borrowing, renewed his links with a group of Cambridge University economists who had been fellow students of the noted economist Joan Robinson, and sought their ideas on Mexico. Led by Dr. Ajit Singh, a group from Cambridge moved to Mexico by mid-1982 to give advice to Tello.

Oteyza was less academically inclined than Tello. Despite his youth, he had also been named a minister in 1976, secretary of national patrimony, in effect controlling mining, energy, and industry as well as the price control system. From this powerful post Oteyza steadily gained influence within the administration, especially in the final months of crisis. It was Oteyza, with the support of the economic arguments of Tello, who convinced López Portillo that the commercial banks had to take the blame for the crisis. After all, they were highly concentrated in ownership and in turn owned or controlled a large proportion of Mexican industry and services. Exchange control would work, despite the eighteen hundred-mile-long border with the United States, Tello and Oteyza argued, but first the root cause of evil, the enormous economic power of the banks, had to be attacked by putting them in the hands of the state.

Needless to say, this advice was anathema to Finance Minister Silva Herzog and President-elect Miguel de la Madrid. Both men were consulted in a perfunctory fashion just before the September 1 measures were announced. Miguel Mancera, the Banco de Mexico governor, had only a few months before written a well-publicized and articulate pamphlet, *On the Inconvenience of Exchange Control.* As a result of the September 1 measures, he had no choice but to leave and was replaced by Tello himself. Tello, partly because of his Cambridge economic advisers but mostly because of his own convictions, then set out to put into place a program to enforce exchange controls, lower interest rates, and stimulate government spending as an antidote to the inevitable austerity provoked by the interruption of new bank lending to Mexico. In the end Tello wanted to use the threat of default to get the banks and the IMF to agree to such a program. It was not to be.

The reaction of Mexican business groups to the bank nationalization, and to a lesser extent to the imposition of exchange controls, was one of stunned silence. They knew that the power of the Mexican state could not be questioned, especially on a popular issue such as bank nationalization, but they also hoped that the new president might change or at least palliate the measure when he was inaugurated three months later. That did indeed happen, although the nationalization itself was irreversible. Abroad, Mexico's creditors said little, an act of prudence on the part of holders of a shaky and volatile debt. Secretly, however, many international bankers were not displeased that the debts of the Mexican banks, which had made many doubtful loans to businesses in trouble, were now the debts of the Mexican state.

Toronto

In early September 1982, about five thousand bankers, government financial officials, and reporters gathered in Toronto for the ritual of the joint annual meeting of the governors of the International Monetary Fund and of the World Bank. Each year the 150 or so governors of each institution, 300 in all, meet to decide the policies of both institutions. Over the years the gathering has become the biggest financial gathering in the world, with bankers and deal-makers hustling their wares to government officials.

While the meeting had an official agenda, in fact the minds of the delegates were firmly fixed on Mexico. Somehow, at the time, many believed that Mexico was an isolated case,[15] although a most important one. After all, the debt reported by the international institutions did not appear that large, although, as we have seen, the statistics were out of date and did not include the critical factor of short-term debt. The mood wavered between nervously upbeat and deathly worried. Some help would be needed to tide Mexico over, the U.S. delegation conceded, but the chief adviser to U.S. Treasury Secretary Regan in Toronto, Under-Secretary for Monetary Affairs Beryl Sprinkel, a conservative monetary economist who was formerly chief economist of the Harris Bank in Chicago, had been adamantly opposed to and was still unenthusiastic about an increase in IMF quotas, the chief item on the agenda in Toronto. Although IMF resources had been cut in half in the previous decade in relation to world trade, the U.S. Treasury position was that nothing new was needed at that point. Over the next few weeks, the Treasury position changed dramatically as commercial bank lending ground to a halt, and, one by one, the major debtors found that they could pay neither the interest nor the principal without new loans and refinancings. Debt begets debt; if the U.S. Treasury were suddenly unable to borrow, there would surely also be a huge crisis facing the U.S. government.

The real turning point was Brazil. At first Brazilian financial authorities, led by the longstanding economic czar and planning minister, Antonio Delfim Netto, put on a good front and said everything was fine.[16] A few new loans, mostly to finance European equipment exports, were announced. But it was clear that the virtual cut-off of new net lending from banks, plus the commodity export slump combined with still very high oil prices, was leading to a rapid decline of Brazil's foreign exchange reserves. Finally, by late November the Brazilian government had to swallow its pride and admit defeat; just like Mexico three months earlier, it had to seek a moratorium on the repayment of principal to commercial banks. But even then the Brazilian authorities maintained that a general rescheduling was not necessary and that only a one-year refinancing would be needed.[17]

After Brazil it was only a matter of time before other countries in the region followed suit: Venezuela in February 1983, followed by Chile, Peru, Ecuador, and Uruguay. Only Colombia avoided a formal rescheduling, given its relatively moderate debt, with the predominant portion from official institutions at long maturities, while Panama, a relatively small but highly indebted economy, more or less hung on. Other countries, such as Costa Rica and Jamaica, had been in and out of debt reschedulings almost continuously for several years, while the Dominican Republic, caught between high oil prices and dramatically low sugar export prices, plus the usual budget deficit, had been postponing foreign payments since before Mexico.

The Pattern of Rescue

The rescue efforts made on behalf of Mexico had one simple objective, to avoid a major disruption in the international financial system. The strategy was based on a basic but at least debatable premise, namely that the major debtors faced a temporary "liquidity crisis" (a cash squeeze) rather than a problem of "solvency" (a basic inability to pay).

Although the premise was debatable, the objective of avoiding an international financial panic was indeed achieved. While there was much press comment about the questionable solidity of major—especially U.S.—banks,[18] and their already depressed stock prices fell even more, no major bank failed because of its Latin American loans.

To some degree, the conflict between liquidity and insolvency is a matter of words and definitions. In fact, since the basic objective at the time was to avoid an immediate international financial crisis, there was little point in debating the issue of whether the problem was temporary or permanent. There were thus, in retrospect, few practical alternatives to what was done. But the question was to become important later, once the initial international financial containment operation for Mexico had been successfully launched. At that point, from about 1984 onward, there indeed arose a legitimate question—was the debt strategy viable for the long term? To a substantial degree, the debate between liquidity shortage and insolvency is a red herring. The fact was that no major debtor could service interest without additional financing and major austerity measures that required a sharp curtailment of economic growth. How long this condition continues determines whether the problem is one of solvency or of liquidity. But the answer is largely a matter of definition with little practical application. If a country can resume debt service and economic growth in, say, five years, does the resulting present value today of its debt, at about 50 cents on the dollar, mean that the country is illiquid or insolvent?

Mexico set the pattern of rescue for the other major Latin American debtors as well as for the Philippines. Because Mexico's external debt to the international banking system was so large, it was not possible to delay interest payments and drag out discussions on the principles of refinancing, as had happened in Poland after March 1981. It was essential for the safety of the major international banks, especially in the United States and Britain, that the regular inflow of interest payments be kept up without delay. Otherwise, under general accounting and banking regulatory rules, any significant interruption would have required large charges against the income of those banks. While there was more leeway from regulators in the banking centers of other countries, the basic danger was in fact the same.

The first step was to find cash to beef up Mexico's foreign exchange reserves so that essential payments, especially interest, could continue. This was done through a package of emergency financing from official sources: $1 billion in advance purchases by the United States from Mexico of oil for its strategic petroleum reserve; $1 billion in U.S. Department of Agriculture's Commodity Credit Corporation credits for purchases by Mexico of U.S. staples (wheat, rice, and so on); and a package of $1.85 billion from the central banks of major European countries, Japan, and the Federal Reserve. The Federal Reserve provided half the original total of $1.5 billion and was the driving force behind the large emergency loan. The other half was channeled through the BIS. The Mexican request for a bridge loan of $750 million was originally viewed skeptically by several of the European central banks, which are the core members of the BIS, but the U.S. view carried the day. To this sum Spain, due to its special solidarity with Latin America, added $175 million, which the United States matched, making a total of $1.85 billion.

Once Mexico had the prospect of cash to keep going, the second step was to organize the discussion with the commercial bank lenders. In the case of Mexico, these numbered between 800 and 1,000—no one knew exactly at the time, since Mexican government paper had been spread out among small, local U.S. banks, especially in Texas and California. The Federal Reserve was again instrumental in solving this problem by inviting the known bank lenders to a meeting at the New York Federal Reserve on August 20. The Federal Reserve supported the idea of creating a committee of banks which would coordinate the effort of rescheduling, since the banks ranged from sophisticated banks in the major financial centers of the world to relatively small, local institutions in the hinterlands of the United States and elsewhere. The committee of creditor banks was supposed to "advise" Mexico, but its real function was to coordinate the position of the lending banks. The Federal Reserve tapped Citibank and the Bank of America, the largest bank lenders to Mexico, to chair the committee of fourteen major banks from around the world, along with a third cochairman from the European banks, whose representatives initially balked at being visibly associated with the Mexican problem.

By the end of August, Mexico and its bank lenders had two key elements in place: (1) emergency public funds to keep Mexico's foreign payments going, and (2) a mechanism to discuss in a more or less orderly way how to refinance the amortization owed to almost a thousand different bank lenders. This was no mean achievement, especially in the record time of two weeks. There is little doubt that the U.S. authorities, especially Chairman Volcker and the Federal Reserve, and also the Treasury, particularly Deputy Secretary McNamar, were decisive in making these things happen. At the same time, the fact that the Mexican financial authorities, led by Finance Minister Jesus Silva Herzog, prided themselves on their sense of international financial responsibility and on their easy access to economic policymakers in Washington, D.C., greatly eased matters. It is quite possible that if the initial debt crisis had occurred in a different large Latin American debtor, the pattern of rescue might well have been different, without an initial cash infusion and with far more confrontation between lenders and borrower—the kind of problems that had existed in Poland a year earlier.

President López Portillo's nationalization of Mexican banks and of foreign currency deposits on September 1, 1982, threw the carefully crafted crisis prevention plan into disarray. The new central bank head, Carlos Tello, was not at all in favor of the type of IMF-led austerity that most major lenders expected. Finance Minister Silva Herzog, normally open and accessible, virtually disappeared for a couple of weeks, evidently in the midst of a personal crisis about what to do: continue to represent a government with which he disagreed, or resign and leave matters to an unknown successor who was likely to leave a mess for his great friend and longstanding colleague from the Banco de Mexico, incoming President Miguel de la Madrid, due to be inaugurated in only three months. In the end, Silva Herzog rolled with the punches and struggled to put together an austerity program despite Tello's opposing point of view. The encouragement of incoming President Miguel de la Madrid, who had to sit publicly powerless on the sidelines, was clearly a factor in the decision.

During a visit to Washington at the end of October, Silva Herzog cleverly used the IMF to soften Tello's resistance. By November 10, a stabilization program had been agreed upon with the IMF. The centerpiece was a cut in the estimated public sector deficit from the very high level of about 17 percent of the GNP in 1981 to about 8.5 percent in 1983, a drastic reduction. The program thus endorsed a shock treatment for the Mexican economy, as opposed to the views of those, such as Tello in Mexico and many others elsewhere, who advocated gradualism. Clearly, economic growth was going to grind to a halt; inflation was supposed to come down from the 100 percent plus levels it reached in the second half of 1982 after the second sizable devaluation of more than 400 percent. Indeed, inflation did decrease, but not until a year later, because in the meantime increases in the prices of goods and public services—such as flour, electricity, and fuel—which were essential to cut the budget deficit, inevitably stoked the fire of inflation.

The IMF agreement, reached in principle before the inauguration of President de la Madrid on December 1, 1982, was the cornerstone for the next and final step, a "new money" loan from all the banks that had outstanding loans to Mexico. The amount estimated to be needed by Mexico for the first year of the IMF program, after huge public sector cuts, was $5 billion, compared to about $15 billion of net new borrowing from banks in the halcyon days of 1981. Of all aspects of the Mexican program, this was the only really innovative one. The IMF managing director, Jacques de Larosière, a sprightly Frenchman who had until 1978 held the job of directeur du trésor, perhaps the most prestigious career post in the French government, considered the new loan an essential ingredient in order to make the Mexican sacrifices tolerable.

On November 16, again at the Federal Reserve Bank of New York, the main bank lenders to Mexico were called together to hear de Larosière. There, in the words of Joseph Kraft,[19] "he sprung a trap upon the bankers." After explaining the austerity program agreed upon with Mexico, he told the bankers that $5 billion of new loans from them would be needed for Mexico in 1983. "Before the Mexican program could be presented to the IMF board for approval," he said, "there would have to be concrete undertakings from the bankers that the $5 billion would be forthcoming." De Larosière gave a deadline of

December 15 for commitments, only four weeks ahead. Most of the bankers were stunned by the ultimatum. If there was no loan, he said, there would be no IMF standby credit and stabilization program.

The IMF, with the help of the Federal Reserve, thus gave rise to "involuntary," or "nonmarket," lending, in essence a mechanism to force Mexico's lenders to stick with it in sickness as they had in health. The $5 billion amounted to about 7 percent of the approximately $70 billion in loans which banks had outstanding to the public and private sectors of Mexico, including short-term loans.

After difficult discussions within the committee of banks, its members decided that every bank lender would have to put up new money equivalent to 7 percent of its exposure. Clearly, large banks realized that the money would be extremely difficult to raise from the smaller, less exposed banks unless the terms were attractive to them. That required, despite opposition from Angel Gurría of Mexico, substantial up-front fees and relatively short maturities for refinancing the approximately $20 billion in principal falling due from August 1982 to the end of 1984. In the end an agreement was quickly reached between Gurría and the committee of banks and announced on December 8, only three weeks after the meeting with de Larosière. The agreement called for front-end fees to the banks of about $260 million,[20] a large sum indeed in the light of Mexico's feeble reserves and balance of payments.

The rush to get the Mexican default out of the way thus came at a price. In the short term there was a significant financial cost; but more important, in the long term there was at least the possibility that the containment strategy might not be viable. Was there a practical alternative? At the time, the facts of the situation probably precluded a slower and more deliberate approach. Mexico alone accounted for perhaps 10 percent of all Euromarket placement of funds and for a higher proportion of medium-term lending. These loans had been placed among a far larger number of banks than for any other borrower; five large U.S. banks had close to the whole of their capital tied up in loans to Mexico. The potential for a major international financial crisis, especially coming at the end of a deep international recession and after record-high interest rates, was certainly there.

The role of personalities was critical for the success of the Mexican rescue. Paul Volcker and his colleagues at the Federal Reserve, especially Anthony Solomon, president of the Federal Reserve Bank of New York, had the vision to understand the world importance of a possible Mexican default. The New York Fed got into high gear to help the committee of lead banks to persuade reluctant banks in the United States to go along with the rescue of Mexico, and similar roles were played by central banks in Germany, Britain, Japan, France and elsewhere.

De Larosière, a diplomatic but forthright person, showed that a public international organization, despite some inevitable bureaucratic foot-dragging, could rise to the occasion. This was in contrast to the World Bank, where a new president since 1981, A. W. (Tom) Clausen, former head of the Bank of America, faced two problems: (1) the fact that the bank was organized to finance long-term development projects, such as dams, highways, schools, and irrigation systems, and was not equipped to handle economic emergencies; and (2) an increasingly unsympathetic attitude on the part of the U.S. Treasury and Congress toward a larger World Bank role.

Two other key participants were R. T. (Tim) McNamar, the deputy secretary of the Treasury, and William Rhodes, the Citibank executive who became the leading banker on reschedulings. McNamar, an athletic Californian with a warm personality, was given most of the Treasury duties on the debt crisis by Secretary Donald Regan. He was instrumental in getting the various U.S. agencies to come up with the initial emergency loan package and in helping to develop the whole pattern of the rescue. Rhodes was the key player in the steering committee of banks; after more than twenty-five years at Citibank, he had long experience in Latin America and was a forthright "can-do" type, with the talent to bridge the gap between his strong-willed chairman, Walter Wriston, and the official agencies. Wriston, undoubtedly the leading international banker of the time and the man who many others claimed was the intellectual author of overlending to developing countries, was not liked by government agencies. The Federal Reserve, in particular, mistrusted him because of the aggressive posture of his bank as a strong advocate of deregulation and liberalization of the financial system.

The Mexican Precedent

Mexico created the precedent for other major debtor countries in Latin America as well as for the Philippines. Instead of the foot-dragging that had occurred in Poland a year-and-a-half earlier, within ten weeks the crisis of one of the two largest debtors in the world had been neatly defused. The personalities involved in the process were all positive action-oriented men; they were not contemplators. An immediate problem had to be resolved and they did it. Within less than a year, Mexico had reduced its public sector deficit to the level negotiated with the IMF and had built up, because of massive real wage cuts and the ensuing drastic fall in imports, a large trade surplus, far beyond anything imagined a year earlier. The Mexican case seemed to show that a financial shock treatment did indeed work. By September 1983,

Finance Minister Silva Herzog had been elevated from the representative of pariah debtor to the "Finance Minister of the Year" by *Euromoney,* the noted international money magazine that, like much of the rest of the financial press, specializes in personalities and hero worship.

Thus, Mexico had shown that a turnaround was possible. Despite its huge debt (nearly four times the annual value of its foreign exchange earnings), it had been able to pay interest, rebuild its reserves, and help its commercial bank lenders avoid an enormous crisis. The financial press saw it as a triumph of the ability of the international financial system to weather a crisis. Clearly, the model was worth emulating.

In fact, as the $5 billion loan for Mexico was being arranged in late November, Brazil was on its way to default. The Brazilian crisis was inevitable after lending by commercial banks stopped in mid-1982. While it appeared that a few new loans were still being announced in the fall,[21] these represented decisions made earlier. By November, international reserves were running low. The crucial moment for Brazil came in mid-December 1982, when the international branches of the state-owned Banco do Brasil, the country's largest bank, were unable to honor maturing deposits from other international banks. Brazil had been using the interbank market, through overseas branches of major Brazilian banks, increasingly since 1979 as a revolving source of financing to cover the balance-of-payments deficit. Normally the interbank market is the logical place where banks put excess funds to work for short periods, from overnight to a few months. It is an unstated assumption that funds can automatically be withdrawn at maturity, but Brazil and Mexico, which had large commercial bank subsidiaries of their own in London and New York and had access to interbank funds, had used the interbank market as a permanent source of financing. This was especially so in the case of Brazil, and in mid-December 1982, a major rescue operation had to be mounted to keep the interbank funds within the Banco do Brasil. It was clear then that the music had stopped for Brazil, too.

As in Mexico, the initial rescue package for Brazil was put together quickly and was in place by the end of February 1983. The immediate crisis was palliated by a short-term loan through the BIS for $1.2 billion. Subsequently, Brazil twice postponed repaying this loan, provoking unusually stern public rebukes from the president of the BIS, Fritz Leutwiler, who was also president of the Swiss National Bank. The centerpiece of the rescue package, however, was a $6 billion credit from the IMF, the largest package it had assembled to date. As in Mexico, de Larosière used the IMF credit as a bargaining chip to get the banks to agree to a $4.4 billion "involuntary" loan. It was even harder to raise such money for Brazil than for Mexico; after all, Brazil was already in its third year of austerity and nevertheless still faced major financial problems. Many banks were leery of having to make yet another large nonmarket loan. Finally, the Brazilian military government, by then in its eighteenth year, was showing signs of fatigue and did not appear to have the determination of the new de la Madrid administration in Mexico.

On the other hand, the private sector of Brazil owed less abroad than did Mexico and was far more able to withstand the impact of the gradual devaluation of the cruzeiro. Since 1964, the cruzeiro had never been overvalued for long, so that the local currency value of the foreign debt of the Brazilian private sector rose gradually. In contrast, the Mexican private sector faced a sudden fourfold nominal increase in the peso value of its external debt of about $17 billion from the middle to the end of 1982.[22]

There were also differences between Mexico and Brazil in the success of the initial rescue effort.[23] In the case of Brazil, a different bank was put in charge of each part of the package (new money, rescheduling, and the maintenance of trade lines and interbank deposits), an impractical arrangement that led to disputes among the lead banks. By the end of February 1985, a single bank committee was in charge, once again under the direction of William Rhodes of Citibank. Brazil had no sooner reached an agreement with the IMF than it was unable to meet the financial program targets, triggering the deferral of the loans from the banks and of the IMF standby credit itself. Brazil was, from the standpoint of the banks, clearly not a success.

Despite the differences, however, the rescue packages for Mexico and Brazil were basically similar: an eight-year rescheduling of the principal due to commercial banks (covering two-and-a-half years of amortization in Mexico, and about one year in Brazil), the maintenance of a somewhat reduced level of trade lines and interbank deposits, and large involuntary loans. Of course, the new loans were much smaller— by about two-thirds to three-quarters—than those of the previous year. This obvious and unavoidable fact, combined with declining prices for most raw materials, meant that overborrowed debtors would have to undergo major belt-tightening (or "adjustment," in the language of economists), with or without the IMF.

(5)

Buying Time: Lenders and Debtors, 1982–1985

The Crisis Containment Strategy

The crisis containment operations mounted on behalf of Mexico and Brazil succeeded in their main objectives. An international financial crisis was avoided as a result of emergency financing packages and of a fairly drastic cut in the standard of living of the debtors, who were thus able to cut back imports and thereby generate the large trade and foreign exchange surpluses needed to pay interest on their debts. Lenders helped by refinancing the principal, but interest was by and large left untouched. From 1984, most debtors other than Peru went along with the refinancing rules set by the creditors, hoping that in this way they could maintain some access to credit, especially revolving credit to finance trade.

Despite the initial success of the containment strategy, by 1985 involuntary lending by commercial banks had fallen off sharply. At the same time, the export earnings of most countries other than Brazil were stagnant or falling as a result of weak commodity prices. Except for Brazil in 1985–86, economic growth did not revive, so that real per capita income for Latin America in the mid-1980s stayed roughly where it had been a decade earlier. By 1985 only the austerity component of the containment strategy seemed to be firmly in place; new financing and export growth appeared on their way to failure.

Economic frustration led to a period of "adjustment fatigue" among some of the main debtors. After the stagflation of 1985, Mexico was shocked by the drop of oil prices in 1986, and a very difficult economic and political period set in. In Brazil, on the other hand, the fall in oil import prices gradually brought with it increasing economic benefits;

this, combined with the impending return to an elected civilian government, ushered in a period of relative optimism and rapid economic growth. In 1983, the Brazilian authorities had resolved to make their export drive a success by keeping their exchange rate competitive and in 1986 began an unorthodox experiment to beat inflation. For Mexico the oil price drop of 1986 had an effect equivalent to a capital outflow of about $7 billion a year, quite the opposite of what was happening in Brazil. The world economic environment thus proved critical to the pattern of recovery in both countries. In general, however, there was frustration with the more traditional IMF solutions involved in the initial containment strategy.

The new management at the U.S. Treasury under the second Reagan administration sensed that something was changing in 1985 and that a more involved, growth-oriented public position would be required by the United States. The result was an initiative by Treasury Secretary James A. Baker III at the annual meeting of the IMF and the World Bank in Seoul in October 1985. Baker called for a renewal of some commercial bank lending to troubled debtors and a major expansion in World Bank lending to help reorient their economies toward private sector investment and growth. For the fifteen or so most indebted developing countries, Baker suggested that commercial banks provide an additional $20 billion in total net new lending over three years, somewhat below the $11 billion provided in emergency financing in 1983 but well above the numbers of 1984 and 1985, while the multilateral development banks, especially the World Bank, were to increase their net lending over the same three years by about $3 billion annually to about $6 to $7 billion. The approximately fifteen debtor countries—mostly in Latin America—were to respond by intensifying their pace of economic reform.

Although the Baker Initiative was of necessity somewhat vague, it put the U.S. government on record as concerned and in effect passed the ball from the IMF to the World Bank. It also implicitly recognized that commercial bank lending to troubled debtors was at that point nearly dead. The Baker Initiative is thus an important watershed in the debt problems of Latin America.

The original containment strategy was a quick response to the immediate problem in Mexico. Lenders stressed the case-by-case approach, but in fact there was a generalized response to the problems of all major developing country debtors. Procedures and prescriptions were the same in all cases. The first step was always austerity. This "adjustment" was to be accompanied by the recovery of the world economy. Recovery would in turn lead to the growth of exports from the debtors; thus, as a result of austerity and a major cutback of imports, the burden of debt would decline in relative terms. Within four to five years, it was hoped, the burden of debt as a proportion of exports would have dropped to the point where commercial banks would once again resume lending of their own free will.[1]

As with most strategies and projections, however, the outcome of the original containment strategy was a mixture of success and failure. Major debtors were successfully weaned from the massive external borrowing of the past. Considerable social pain and political difficulty, particularly in Argentina, accompanied this change, but there were no revolutions. Where the containment strategy was a disappointment, however, was in the failure of economic growth to resume in most of Latin America.

By 1984–85 the average per capita income of the region had fallen to the level of ten years before. Thus, simply to achieve by 1990 the real per capita income levels of 1980 would require an unlikely economic expansion in the second half of the decade. With the exception of Brazil, the value of Latin American exports stagnated after 1982, in conjunction with the worldwide depression of commodity prices. The projected involuntary lending from commercial banks did indeed take place, but the actual money that could be drawn was much less than the projected figures; repeatedly, countries were unable to follow the IMF programs that were the precondition for the loans. In 1983–84 Brazil had no less than seven different programs with the IMF.

The Debtors' Austerity

Of all the elements in the containment strategy, austerity was the most effective and the most immediately felt. The reason was simple market economics: when the money runs out, the belt has to be tightened, with or without the IMF. Mexico was the most conspicuously successful case of adjustment. President de la Madrid, a former career officer with the Banco de Mexico, and Finance Minister Silva Herzog were convinced that drastic action was needed[2] and that there was a large amount of fat in public expenditures that could be cut with only moderate pain. Moreover, because of the political support of the trade unions (referred to below) the highly centralized Mexican government was able to ensure that austerity would not be breached because of wage demands. Largely through government control and cooperative unions, therefore, real wages fell about 30 percent between 1982 and 1984.

In 1984, however, the Mexican economy continued to suffer from high inflation and no growth. The inflation was the result of long-delayed increases in the prices of controlled products, which took place beginning in 1982: first the exchange rate, then fuel, public transport, electricity, and basic foods. Past subsidies for these items had been a major cause of the public sector deficit. Because these items make up the bulk of the consumer price index, by definition any increase in their price is translated into an increase in the official price index, intensifying inflationary expectations. In order to achieve growth with less inflation, the rate of devaluation was slowed down in mid-1984, bringing down the relative prices of dollar-related items, such as fuel and imported staples, while the economy was stimulated by Keynesian public spending. The tactic worked for a while but at the cost of stagnation in exports, which became increasingly uncompetitive in the booming U.S. import market. Non-oil exports to the United States did rise by 24 percent in 1984, but exports elsewhere stagnated because the peso was substantially overvalued in relation to rapidly depreciating European currencies, while in the same year Brazil increased its manufactured exports to the United States by 53 percent. The 1984 pump-priming episode in Mexico showed that growth without a strong base of exports was not self-sustaining. And the economic policy pursued in late 1984 and early 1985 unwittingly led to greater dependence on oil exports, which were already declining in price, and made Mexico even more vulnerable to the big drop in world oil prices in early 1986.

The case of Brazil stood in sharp contrast to Mexico in 1985–86 (table 5-1). Initially, in 1983, inflation was roaring along at about 160 percent, compared to 100 percent in 1982, and Brazil was unable to comply with successive IMF programs. Interest arrears mounted, and Brazil was unable to repay the $1.45 billion in short-term credits that had been coordinated by the BIS at the end of 1982. However, Brazil was already beginning to benefit from lower oil import prices, augmented by the effects of conservation and the substitution of domestically produced alcohol for petroleum. Planning Minister and economic czar Antonio Delfim Netto, aided by the youthful Central Bank head, Carlos Langoni (succeeded by another economist, Affonso Pastore), as well as by the experienced finance minister, Ernane Galveas, was determined to avoid the mistake of 1979, when he had primed the pump through fiscal expenditure and allowed the exchange rate to appreciate in real terms. A major devaluation of the cruzeiro was accomplished in February 1983, and from that point on the currency was devalued at a rate faster than that of domestic inflation. Brazil thereby gained exchange rate competitiveness against the U.S. dollar and was able to remain more or less competitive against the European currencies and the yen. In contrast to Mexico, Brazil was poised to take full advantage

Table 5-1   Brazil and Mexico, 1981–1986

	1981		1982	
	B	M	B	M
Real GDP percentage change	−3.4	8.0	0.9	−0.5
Inflation, CPI (Dec. to Dec.),				
percentage	93	29	103	99
Real exchange rate (1980–82 = 100)	103	114	113	83
Terms of trade (1980 = 100)	84	99	81	82
Annual impact (billions of dollars)[a]	−4.4	−0.2	−4.7	−4.6
Merchandise exports, f.o.b. (billions				
of dollars)	23.3	19.4	20.2	21.2
Value of Brazil oil imports, c.i.f.				
(billions of dollars)	11.0		10.1	
Value of Mexico oil exports, f.o.b.				
(billions of dollars)		15.0		16.5
Interest on external debt, incl.				
short-term (billions of dollars)	9.2	8.2	11.3	12.2

Sources: International Monetary Fund, *International Financial Statistics;* Morgan Guaranty Trust, *World Financial Markets* (May 1987); and author's estimates based on national statistics.

of the big U.S. import boom in manufactures in 1984. The Brazilian industrial sector, which was operating with about 40 percent of its capacity unused, was able to exploit its competitive edge. The performance of Brazilian exports in 1984, led by industrial products, made up most of the 5.7 percent expansion in GNP that year.[3]

The lesson to be drawn from these contrasting cases is that economic recovery depends upon the combination of a favorable world environment and the economic measures taken by individual governments; neither side of the equation can work by itself. The sharp devaluation taken by Brazil in 1983 was a courageous, difficult, and, in the short run, inflationary measure, but the fact that it showed results within about a year, partly because of the U.S. import boom, made the tough medicine far easier to take. But in Mexico the reverse happened: the gradual decline of the oil market in 1984 coincided with the highly inflationary consequences of long-delayed increases in controlled prices and the run-up of international interest rates that year. To some degree this setting contributed to the government's lack of resolve in persevering with the difficult measures started in 1982. The economic experiment to end stagflation failed, and Mexico found itself in an even more vulnerable position when international oil prices unexpectedly collapsed in early 1986.

The point is not to minimize the importance of successful or unsuc-

1983		1984		1985		1986	
B	M	B	M	B	M	B	M
−2.5	−5.3	5.7	3.7	8.3	2.7	8.2	−3.8
164	81	215	59	242	64	75	106
86	79	86	92	85	91	74	65
82	79	88	78	88	77	108	60
−4.8	−5.9	−3.7	−6.8	−3.5	−6.5	+1.8	−9.4
21.9	22.3	27.1	24.2	25.6	21.9	24.5	14.1
8.2		6.9		5.7		3.0	
	16.0		16.6		14.8		6.3
9.6	10.1	10.2	11.7	9.7	10.2	9.0	8.3

Note: B = Brazil; M = Mexico.

[a]Estimates the trade gain or loss for the year shown if terms of trade had stayed at 1980 levels.

cessful policy decisions by governments but to place them in the relevant international context. The circumstances of each country in Latin America were, of course, different in degree.[4] Two of the extremes, as we have seen, were Brazil and Mexico. But the country that suffered the worst deterioration of its terms of trade was Chile. In the early 1980s, Chile relied on copper for about half of its export earnings; from 1980 to 1985, however, the world price of copper fell by about 35 percent. To some extent, this decline was the result of expanded output by the Chilean Corporacion del Cobre (CODELCO). Admittedly the lowest-cost world producer overall, CODELCO expanded its output by 27 percent during the same period in a virtually flat world copper market. Chile's autocratic government was able to hold back wages and government outlays, maintain a reasonably competitive exchange rate, and make ends meet despite the fact that interest expense on the external debt averaged about half of export earnings. And Chile was the only country to which commercial banks provided a steady flow of new money. The price for this flow was government financial support of the private sector debt and, of course, austerity and its inevitable corollaries, extremely slow economic growth and a sharp decline in per capita income, at least initially.

Peru, with a lower overall external debt, could not make ends meet despite a sharp cut in real wages. Government expenditures, both until mid-1985 in the Belaúnde administration and under Alan García afterward, could not be held back because of military outlays and public enterprise investment. The restoration of export taxes in 1984, as a revenue measure, helped to dim the prospects for any export-led recovery.[5] Somewhat in contrast, Venezuela, with a relatively moderate external debt, was able to ride out the post-1982 storm with a combination of exchange and fiscal measures discussed in the next chapter, but at the cost of a sharp decline in income.

The most complex case was probably that of Argentina. The economic drag resulting from a high external debt, much of which had financed arms purchases and capital flight, and a long history of economic decline and sharp ideological conflicts were only two elements in the complicated political and economic equation. Beginning in December 1983, the first eighteen months of the Alfonsín administration, the first civilian government since the military coup against the widow of President Juan Perón in 1976, were not auspicious as government indecision and spiraling hyperinflation fed on each other. By March 1984, the Argentine government was falling very much behind in its payments of interest to the banks, threatening to cause losses to the large U.S. banks. At the annual meeting of the Inter-American Development Bank in Punta del Este, Uruguay, that month Finance Minister Jesus Silva Herzog of Mexico rounded up his colleagues from Brazil, Colombia, and Venezuela and, with U.S. Treasury support, organized a $300 million loan to help Argentina reduce its arrears and, most importantly, to help the banks.

In June 1985, under a new economic team headed by Economy Minister Sourrouille, in a sharp departure from traditional remedies against high inflation, the Alfonsín government launched the Plan Austral, reminiscent of the Plan Pinay launched in France in 1952. Wages were frozen along with prices, exports were stimulated by a large devaluation, and the windfall to exporters was taxed to help reduce the budget deficit. New hope was infused into the economy. By mid-1986 the inevitable question of how to end the freeze without restarting inflation was the most urgent economic question in Argentina.

There is little doubt about the extent of the austerity in Latin America as a whole. As finance from outside dried up, incomes dropped, and imports fell far more than most observers had expected.[6] Already in 1982, total imports had declined by about one-fifth (table 5-2), and a trade surplus was rapidly building up. Import prohibitions and increased import tariffs sprang up in most countries, but these basically affected consumer and luxury imports, a minor portion of the total. The drop in imports, which totaled 40 percent from the high of 1981 to the low of 1983, was largely the result of a decline in domestic

Table 5-2   The External Readjustment of Latin America and the
Caribbean, 1981–1986 (Amounts in Billions of Dollars)

	1981	*1982*	*1983*	*1984*	*1985*	*1986*
Exports, f.o.b.	95.9	87.4	87.5	97.7	91.0	78.3
Brazil	23.3	20.2	21.9	27.0	25.6	24.5
Others	72.6	67.2	65.6	70.7	66.4	53.8
Imports, f.o.b.	97.6	78.3	56.0	58.3	58.5	59.9
From U.S.	41.9	33.6	25.1	29.0	30.1	30.4
Trade balance	−1.7	9.1	31.5	39.4	33.5	18.5
Current account balance	−39.9	−40.6	−8.9	−0.2	−4.0	−14.2
Terms of trade index (1980 = 100)	91	90	86	88	87	80

Sources: United Nations Economic Commission for Latin America and the
Caribbean, annual *Preliminary Overview of the Latin American Economy;* and U.S.
Department of Commerce, *Latin America Trade Review* (1985, 1986).
   Note: The above data are slightly different from those shown elsewhere in the
text.

production and demand, itself the result of cuts in credit to the private
sector and a sharp drop in incomes and purchasing power. By 1984
Latin America and the Caribbean as a whole had a negligible deficit in
the current account of the balance of payments, which meant that the
region did not import capital for its economic functioning. However,
the financial improvement also reflected a deep economic recession,
the sharpest since the 1930s.

The trade surplus that built up after 1982 averaged about $35 billion
annually, or about 4 percent of the GDP, twice the relative level of
Japan's trade surplus in the early 1980s. The size of the surplus and
the fact that it was, in the aggregate, exclusively the result of import
cuts give an idea of the size of the economic sacrifice made by most of
Latin America after 1982. The cost was also considerable for exporters
to Latin America. Trade within the region fell about the same as total
imports, which collapsed from a peak of almost $100 billion in 1981 to
$56 billion in 1983 (see table 5-2). In the case of the United States, the
loss of exports was felt especially in the machinery and equipment
industry, which was already weakened by the rising dollar. Machinery
and equipment exports to Latin America fell from $19 billion in 1981
to less than half that two years later. No precise estimate exists of the
employment cost of Latin American austerity upon its trading partners,
but it would probably not be an exaggeration to put the loss of employment for the United States in the range of about half a million jobs lost
directly.[7]

The Cost of Austerity

Despite the healthy aspects of belt-tightening, it is nevertheless clear that when the austerity crunch came after 1982, governments squeezed the private sector first and themselves second. Admittedly, with a growing burden of interest cost as a proportion of government expenditure—in the range of 15 to 20 percent in 1983–84—it was not easy to cut government expenditures. Mexico was the exception, achieving big cuts in 1983 and 1984,[8] especially in current outlays. While central governments were trying hard to cut back deficits, state enterprises continued to spend, so that overall internal banking system credit to the public sector fell only marginally. In most countries, domestic credit cuts, guided by the IMF and designed to reduce import demand and conserve foreign exchange, fell heavily upon the private sector (table 5-3). Adding to this effect was the natural reluctance of banks inside each country to lend to domestic companies hard hit by recession and inflation. The private sector, especially larger industrial companies, was devastated in most countries, leading to sharp declines in investment and employment plus the de facto bankruptcy of major corporations. This in turn was accompanied by the very large real wage cuts that took place in 1983 and 1984.

Although a generalization to which there are evident exceptions, it is not an exaggeration to say that the private sector and its workers have paid for the major part of the belt-tightening in much of Latin America since 1982. Because the private sector is by far a larger employer than the state, despite the large economic role of governments in some Latin American economies, its share of austerity and economic depression has been larger. The danger for the future is that when economic expansion begins anew, the public sector might relax and start spending again.

The per capita GDP of the region fell almost 10 percent between 1981 and 1985 (see table 5-3), and there was an even larger drop in actual per capita income. Not a single country in the region avoided a major drop in income during those four years.[9] With the exception of Argentina and Colombia, the average real wage of salaried workers also fell sharply, especially in 1983. In that year in Mexico, real wages fell by 21 percent, a testimony to the willingness of Fidel Velázquez, head of the Confederación de Trabajadores Mexicanos, the labor arm of the official government party, to use his considerable power to support the austerity efforts of the government.

Needless to say, the drop in income was accompanied by an increase in unemployment. With the exceptions of Chile and Colombia, official unemployment statistics, as shown in table 5-4, generally underesti-

Table 5-3   The Domestic Impact of Adjustment

GDP per capita, cumulative change 1981–85 and change 1986 (percentage)

	1981–85	1986
Latin America[a]	−9.5	1.2
Argentina	−17.7	3.9
Brazil	−3.0	5.7
Colombia	−0.5	3.0
Chile	−9.1	3.2
Mexico	−3.6	−6.3
Peru	−14.6	5.9
Uruguay	−19.1	4.2
Venezuela	−20.8	−1.0

Gross fixed investment (as percentage of GDP)

		1980–81	1983–84	1985
Argentina	public sector	12.7	11.1	13.3
	private sector	7.7	4.4	
Brazil	public sector[b]	6.7	6.8	5.1
	private sector	15.6	11.3	12.1
Mexico	public sector	8.0	9.5	9.5
	private sector	11.1	8.8	10.4

Domestic banking system credit (as percentage of GDP)[c]

		1981	1983–84	1985
Argentina	public sector	5.3	9.3	10.0
	private sector	26.0	13.2	22.7
Brazil	public sector[b]	2.2	5.5	1.2
	private sector	14.5	10.8	20.3
Mexico	public sector	13.9	18.1	22.1
	private sector	13.7	9.4	12.3

Sources: United Nations Economic Commission for Latin America and the Caribbean, *Preliminary Overview of the Latin American Economy* (1985, 1986); Inter-American Development Bank, *Economic and Social Progress in Latin America, 1985;* additional (1985) data from IADB.

[a]Author's estimate, after adjusting official data for Cuba downward in 1981–85 period. 1986 excludes Cuba.

[b]Central government, decentralized agencies, and 10 largest state enterprises.

[c]Outstanding credit divided into GDP.

mate the extent of unemployment. In general terms, it is probably true that there was no net employment growth at all in Latin America as a whole after 1981, with the possible exception of Brazil after 1984. During the period 1982–85, the labor force of about 200 million was growing by close to 3 percent, or about 6 million per year, the result of rapid population growth, which lasted until the early 1970s. Therefore, unemployment grew by at least 25 million, and most of that was among the young.

Table 5-4   Income and Employment Adjustment, 1981–1986

Total Latin America	*1986*
Population (millions), midyear	406
Gross Domestic Product (in billions of current dollars)	730 (est.)

	Cumulative Change, 1981–86
Population	+11.8 %
Gross National Income per capita	−14.0% (est.)
Gross Domestic Product	+5.9%

Employment in manufacturing (1980 = 100)

	Argentina	*Brazil*	*Colombia*	*Chile*	*Mexico*	*Peru*
1985	89	88	82	96	95	83

Official rates of urban unemployment (percentage) (1980 = 100)

	1980	*1981*	*1982*	*1983*	*1984*	*1985*	*1986*
Brazil	6.3	7.9	6.3	6.7	7.1	5.3	3.8
Colombia	9.7	8.2	9.3	11.8	13.5	14.1	14.2
Mexico	4.5	4.2	4.1	6.7	6.0	4.8	n.a.
Venezuela	6.6	6.8	7.8	10.5	14.3	14.3	11.8
Peru	10.9	10.4	10.6	9.2	10.9	11.8	10.6
Chile	11.8	9.0	20.0	18.9	18.5	17.2	13.4

Average real wage rate index (1980 = 100)

Argentina		89	80	100	127	108	109
Brazil		99	99.5	89	83	85	88
Chile	100	109	108	97	97	93	95
Mexico		103	93	77	72	71	68
Peru		99	100	84	71	60	64

Education and health as percentage of public expenditure

	1979	*1983*
Argentina	10	9
Brazil	14	11
Mexico	23	12

Source: United Nations Economic Commission for Latin America and the Caribbean, *Preliminary Overview of the Latin American Economy* (1985, 1986).

Unemployment was combined with increasing inflation. Excluding Bolivia, where inflation rates exceeded 2,000 percent in 1984 and 11,000 percent 1985, the average inflation rate in the region rose from 55 percent in the period 1979–81 to well over 100 percent in 1983 and remained at about 150 percent in 1984 and 1985. With real wages declining in most countries, major contributors to inflation were the long-delayed devaluations, especially in Argentina and Mexico, and the equally necessary increases in regulated prices, especially electricity, fuel, and basic staples such as flour and cooking oil. Finance ministers thus faced a Hobson's choice: delay the price increases even more and intensify inflation because of increasing public sector deficits, or carry out the increases and cause inflation anyway. Only major wage and income reductions, such as those in Mexico in 1983, allowed public sector deficits to be reduced at the same time that inflation was also cut back, albeit with great difficulty.

Why was there no social upheaval? Up to 1986, at least, there had not been a revolution anywhere, although long-repressed frustration could well lead to future explosions. There were, of course, disturbances such as the riots and looting in São Paulo and elsewhere in Brazil in April 1983, and the more serious riots in Santo Domingo in April 1984, which left some fifty persons dead. There were general strikes almost everywhere. But the lack of an explosion is still surprising, given the depth of the income and welfare decline after 1982. Part of the tension was probably eased by a population movement back to the countryside, where farm incomes tended to improve as a result of the large devaluations carried out by most countries. At the new, more depreciated exchange rates, domestic farm products did better against imported foodstuffs, and farm output and incomes improved in most countries after the debt crisis.

The brunt of the income and employment drop was no doubt borne by the lower and lower-middle income groups, although there is little conclusive evidence on the subject. Of course, "lower" and "lower-middle" comprise the vast majority of the urban population, with the upper income group a minute part of the population. The sociological view of "middle class" is very different from its economic position, which in Latin America is at the top of the income spectrum. The "lower-middle" income groups are also not far from the top and typically include salaried factory workers as well as civil servants and teachers. The fairly rigid antidismissal labor laws in most Latin American countries, which are a factor against hiring workers during economic upturns, probably helped to preserve jobs during the downturn that began in 1982. For the lowest income groups, the general income drop has probably led to increased malnutrition, higher rates of infant mortality, and deterioration in already dramatically bad housing conditions. Sketchy data for Brazil show an increase in nationwide infant mortality in 1983 and 1984; surveys of poor areas in Mexico City show a deterioration in the quality of nutrition.[10]

Finally, it is possible that the boom that ended around 1980–82 left enough good memories to provide a psychological cushion against despair. The return to elected government in Argentina in 1983 and in Brazil in 1985, as well as the popular attention that elections enjoyed in Colombia and Mexico in 1982, Venezuela in 1983, Peru in 1985, and in several Central American countries, may also have given populations hope. Indeed, in most of these elections, voter turnout was unusually high. If and when electorates realize that political hope is a mere illusion, however, a severe social backlash becomes a possibility.

Despite its considerable costs, the crisis containment strategy of 1982 did succeed in its major objective, preventing a major international banking crisis. The key was austerity, and the result was the build-up of a large trade surplus to service interest on a bloated external debt. The other two elements of the debt strategy—a favorable world economic environment and continued capital inflow—had less clear results. The world economic environment helped some countries, basically oil importers with a large manufacturing base capable of exports (e.g., Brazil), and hindered others, the oil exporters; most countries fell somewhere in between. As far as a continued inflow of capital was concerned, this was mainly a task for the commercial banks, at least until 1984–85.

The Commercial Banks

The international commercial banks that had been active in lending to Latin America were shell-shocked by the debt crisis. Not only were there wholesale staff eliminations and redeployments in the international groups of large and middle-sized banks, but, more important, the debt crisis led to the stagnation and then the rapid shrinking of the international syndicated loan market, a mainstay of the increasing profitability of the major international banks during the 1970s. The debt crisis coincided with the increasing deregulation of banking in major financial markets. The realization that about one-third of Euromarket loans were outstanding to troubled debtors, mostly in Latin America, speeded the so-called flight to quality: international lenders and investors strengthened their preference for highly liquid securities issued by first-class borrowers, such as bond issues by major corporations of European governments. The resulting trend toward "securitization" was, in any case, under way, but the debt crisis undoubtedly speeded the process.

Another less important by-product of the debt crisis was the virtual demise of consortium banking, which had flourished in the early and mid-1970s but was already seriously wounded before the debt crisis began. At the start of the syndicated loan boom in the late 1960s and early 1970s, a number of large international banks felt that they could have a strong network for international loans by creating independent, specialized banks with a major shareholder from each financial market, including, in a number of cases, OPEC countries. Thus, for example, Orion Bank, one of the larger and more successful consortium banks in London, has as its shareholders Chase Manhattan, Royal Bank of Canada, National Westminster, Westdeutsche Landesbank, Credito Italiano, and the Mitsubishi Bank. Smaller banks were also attracted to the concept as a way of having an international presence and, in theory at least, pooling the costs. By the late 1970s, there were about thirty major consortium banks, most of them in London. But as the syndicated loan boom gathered momentum in the late 1970s, the parent banks increasingly found that they were competing with their own consortia offspring; gradually they withdrew their support, leaving the consortia in stagnation or selling them off to one shareholder—as occurred with Orion, which was sold in 1981 to the Royal Bank of Canada. The withdrawal of support was speeded by the debt crisis and by the fact that most consortium banks, as one-product institutions, were not able to adapt to the changes in international capital markets which had already begun in the late 1970s as a result of deregulation.

The debt crisis in Latin America hit the largest U.S. banks especially hard, even though they held directly only about 35 percent of the debt of Latin American borrowers. Another 30 percent or so was in the hands of European banks, about 15 to 20 percent in Japanese banks, and the balance in banks around the world, including Arab banks and the foreign branches and consortia participants of Latin American banks. The large U.S. banks attracted the most attention for a number of reasons. First, they had been the leaders in lending to Latin America; they had the clout to put together large syndicates, and their relationships in Latin America went back many years. Second, strict U.S. accounting and regulatory reporting requirements, including the need to report quarterly results, brought substantial and immediate public attention to the Latin American loans. Third, the bulk of the international debt rescue effort took place in New York and Washington, tending to give it a U.S. flavor in press reports. And finally, the U.S. money center banks (located in New York, Chicago, and San Francisco), as well as the remainder of the top dozen U.S. banks, held about three-quarters of the U.S. bank exposure to Latin America as well as to all other developing countries.

The Regulatory Impact

The treatment of reserves against doubtful and bad loans in the United States undoubtedly played a major role in determining the attitude of large U.S. banks to the debt crisis. In some continental European countries, banks are able to create loan loss reserves in anticipation of the real need to do so, thus mitigating the impact on their income statement when bad loans do arise. In the United States, however, the need to report quarterly results and the vigilance of the tax authorities make it difficult and unattractive for banks to reserve large amounts against a rainy day without at the same time drastically cutting their profits and depressing the prices of their shares. The share prices of large U.S. banks were already depressed in the years before the Mexican crisis in August 1982. Domestic loans, troubled because of the recession, as well as the doubts of securities analysts about international loans, had already driven down their share prices well before the crisis (table 5-5). No large money center U.S. bank was able to raise capital in the U.S. equity market after 1978 until 1986, when Citibank issued a large number of shares. After the Mexican crisis, stock prices of large banks stabilized at low levels, roughly half those of the rest of the market in terms of earnings. This made it even harder to build up capital, and a number of banks had to resort to financial stratagems, such as selling off their office buildings and leasing them back, thus creating a large cash infusion, albeit at the cost of future office occupancy expenses. The most notable case was the sale of the Bank of America headquarters to investors for $600 million in 1985.

The financial troubles of large banks, which press and public opinion laid to their rash international loan expansionism, provoked legislative and regulatory pressure to disclose loans to developing countries and, in general, made new lending of this type more difficult. This merely reinforced the natural tendency of the banks to cut off lending. In Europe and Japan, central banks and bank regulators tightened requirements for the creation of reserves against possible losses on loans to Latin American and other troubled debtors. The worst credits would have to be totally written off within four or five years.[11]

In the United States, during the fall of 1983, there was a legislative struggle to approve the U.S. share of the increase in the quotas for government contributions to the IMF. A political storm broke out both on the right and the left against "bailing out" the banks. Both left and right drew from the long U.S. populist tradition against banks, particularly strong in the Midwest since the depression. The Reagan administration had to compromise in order to maneuver the bill through the House of Representatives, with help from the Democrats, at the end of November 1983. The result was a bill that mandated tighter requirements for bank loans to developing countries, including the creation of special reserves, the amortization of one-time refinancing fees over the life of the restructured loan (in order to avoid the income incentive to banks of large up-front fees, such as in the first Mexico refinancing),

Table 5-5 Impact of Latin American and Philippine Loans upon U.S. Banks

Exposure of Largest U.S. Banks to Large Developing Country Debtors, End 1982

	Top 9 Banks[a]		Next 15		Next 185	
	Billions of Dollars	*Percentage of Capital[b]*	*Billions of Dollars*	*Percentage of Capital[b]*	*Billions of Dollars*	*Percentage of Capital[b]*
Mexico	12.9	45	5.1	38	6.4	23
Brazil	13.3	46	3.9	29	3.2	11
Others[c]	20.1	69	6.4	47	5.1	18
Total	46.3	160	15.4	114	14.7	52

Largest banks[a]	1981	1982	1983	1984	1985	1986
Exposure to all Latin America and Caribbean as percentage of capital (end year)	est. 169	172	163	148	125	109
Stock price to annual earnings ratio (banks)	5.6	6.4	6.2	7.8	7.9	8.1
New York Stock Exchange mean stock price to annual earnings ratio (all listed stocks)[d]	11.4	12.2	13.9	10.7	12.0	16.2

Sources: Federal Financial Institutions Examination Council, "Country Exposure Lending Survey of U.S. Banks," April 24, 1987, press release; New York Stock Exchange, *Fact Book 1987.*
[a]Top nine "money center" banks: Six from New York, plus Bank of America, Continental Illinois, and First Chicago.
[b]Shareholders' equity, including reserves for loan losses and subordinated debentures.
[c]Argentina, Chile, Philippines, and Venezuela.
[d]Including negative ratios.

and additional disclosure and capital requirements. While the legislation gave wide discretion to regulatory agencies,[12] the message to
banks was nevertheless clear: reduce your loan exposures in risky
developing countries.

The impact of shaky international loans and of the ensuing disclosure requirements is much higher for the top nine U.S. money center
banks, which have about 70 percent of the total U.S. bank loans to
Latin American borrowers, than it is for the rest of the banks (see table
5-5), with the exception of a few other large banks. Under the burden-
sharing principle first adopted in the Mexican case in 1982, all banks
had to participate in refinancings and new involuntary loans in proportion to their exposure. Refinancing agreements of government debt
prevented banks from selling out their loans, but there was more flexibility in the case of the private sector, where in fact a growing volume
of loans was sold or traded by the smaller lenders. For the large banks,
selling off their large loans would have been impossible except at very
large discounts that would have endangered their capital and their
independent existence. The way out for them was to increase their
capital as much as possible while lending as little as possible to troubled
debtors, mostly in Latin America. By the end of 1986, the results of
this general policy had borne fruit. The exposure of the nine largest
U.S. money center banks to Latin America had fallen to 109 percent of
their capital, compared to 172 percent only four years earlier (see table
5-5).

The gradualist approach of leading U.S. banks to reducing their
exposures has been the subject of criticism in the United States and in
Europe from a number of press, academic, and Wall Street analysts.[13]
Investors in bank stocks had already discounted the bad loans, the
argument goes, so why not reflect reality once and for all in balance
sheets? While there is indeed merit in "marking to market" a portfolio
of investments, this is difficult to do when these investments are not
tradable or liquid. Moreover, some observers greatly underestimate
the cost of a drastic write-off policy, even if more generous tax and
regulatory incentives existed. Anatole Kaletsky, in his 1985 book, *The
Costs of Default,* estimates that for the nine largest U.S. banks in 1983,
the creation of loan loss reserves of 6 percent per year of their loans to
Argentina, Brazil, Chile, Mexico, the Philippines, and Venezuela would
have reduced their earnings per share—that is, net after-tax income—
by 54 percent; at 9 percent, the earnings reduction would have averaged 81 percent, and so on.[14] The impact diminishes each year but is
nevertheless huge. By 1986, the impact would have been much less,
but still large. For example, loss reserves of 20 to 25 percent—the
proportion of reserves taken by Citibank and other major banks in the

spring of 1987, or somewhat over half the average market discount on the small volume of Latin American loans traded—would have created a large accounting loss for at least one year, as it did for 1987, even though the Latin American loans of the banks involved were only about 6 to 7 percent of their total assets—with the reserves equivalent to only 1.5 percent of assets.

The reason for this asymmetry between a modest proportion of troubled loans in total assets and a high potential impact of such loans on profits is leverage. Banks use a relatively modest amount of capital to generate loans and other assets fifteen to twenty times the value of their capital. Profitability for large banks is usually in the range of 0.5 to 1 percent of total assets, or a return of about 8 to 16 percent on invested capital. A small change in the valuation of assets, as a result of the creation of a loss reserve or of a write-off, for example, can thus have a large impact on profitability. Banks with a strong capitalization combined with relatively high profitability—Morgan Guaranty is the best-known example—are obviously in a better position to absorb the impact of loss reserves.

Most money center banks were not in a strong financial position in the period beginning with the U.S. recession in 1981 and followed by the Latin American debt crisis in 1982–83. Only major changes in tax policies, allowing the use of part of the pretax profits to create nontaxable reserves, as well as the easing of accounting and regulatory rules, could have achieved that objective. In fact, the trend was the other way: a tightening of U.S. corporate tax rules and of regulations affecting the international portfolios of banks. During the period of a well-publicized crisis for U.S. farmers, as well as debate over the Gramm-Rudman-Hollings mandatory deficit-cutting legislation, it would have been surprising had it been otherwise.

The trend of bank regulation, plus the unavoidable facts of the economics of commercial banking in the first half of the 1980s, meant that a major part of the debt strategy was very difficult to achieve. Instead of a steady but modest stream of some bank lending to troubled countries in the 1982–85 period, as official strategists had envisaged, there was significant lending in the aftermath of the initial scare and then rapid retrenchment (table 5-6). Large involuntary loans made in 1983 and 1984 were in some cases partially or not at all disbursed, and short-term trade lines were cut in a number of countries, such as Argentina, Peru, Mexico, Venezuela, and, to a lesser degree, Brazil. Net lending in effect declined to only about $2 billion in 1984.

Combined with the decline of private investment from abroad and the slow growth of development loans from international agencies, the practical effect was a drastic slowdown of external capital inflows into

Table 5-6   Trends in Commercial Bank Lending to Latin America,
1981–1986 (in Billions of Dollars)

	1981	1982	1983	1984	1985	1986
Publicized new loan commitments	33.8	29.2	15.6	17.5	8.1	3.2
Argentina	2.7	1.6	1.8	4.2	3.7	0.0
Brazil	5.8	5.8	4.5	6.6	—	0.2
Mexico	10.5	9.9	5.1	3.9	0.1	0.3
Others	14.7	12.0	4.2	2.7	4.3	2.7
Actual change in outstanding						
loans	33.7	17.6	11.0	2.0	9.3[a]	3.3
Argentina	4.9	0.8	1.1	−1.5	4.1	1.7
Brazil	6.9	7.9	0.5	4.5	1.2	2.7
Mexico	14.6	5.8	6.4	1.6	0.8	−0.8
Others	7.3	3.0	3.0	−2.5	3.1	−0.2

Sources: Morgan Guaranty Trust, *World Financial Markets,* various issues; Bank
for International Settlements, *The Maturity Distribution of International Bank
Lending,* semiannual issues, 1980–87.
   [a]Data for 1985 and 1986 are not strictly comparable with those for earlier years
owing to an expansion in statistical coverage and to the decline in the relative value of
the U.S. dollar.

Latin America. The task of economic recovery thus became even more
difficult. The growth of external debt was cut back drastically; in
principle a good thing, but coinciding with stagnant prices for most of
the main commodity exports of the debtors, this threatened to jeopard-
ize the original containment strategy. By May 1985 Chairman Volcker
of the Federal Reserve was voicing his concern about the lack of
commercial bank financing,[15] and on June 19, 1985, while Volcker was
on a visit to Japan, Vice-Chairman Preston Martin cast doubt on the
whole strategy, calling for interest rate concessions to the debtors.
Later, the depth of the controversy was exposed when Volcker publicly
rebuked Martin. Nevertheless, the argument reflected a real problem.

The Rescheduling Ballet

Much of the attention to the debt question in the international
financial press after 1982, as well as in the major debtor countries
themselves, was devoted to the rescheduling of existing debt. The
large-scale reschedulings of principal were presented as heroic feats on
the part of bank syndicates and finance ministers.

The reschedulings, summarized in table 5-7, took place first during
1982–83, in the initial heat of the crisis. Immediate maturities were
stretched for the relatively short periods of seven to ten years. Then,

in a second major round of reschedulings during 1984–85, "multi-year rescheduling agreements" (MYRAs) covered the principal repayment of several years, up to 1990 in the case of Mexico, and stretched them typically for fairly long periods, fourteen years for Mexico and twelve to thirteen years in most other cases. The MYRAs represented a major improvement, not only in coverage and maturities, but also in reducing cost. Except for small countries, the fees and commissions charged Mexico and other countries in 1982 and 1983 were gone, and the margins, or "spreads," over the LIBOR base rate were cut back substantially, from an average of 2.25 percent in the first reschedulings to about 1.25 percent to 1.50 percent in the second round, and even farther in the third round of 1986–87.

Despite these great efforts, the rescheduling of amortization was not economically meaningful to the debtors. In the aftermath of the Mexican crisis, statements were often made to the effect that the Latin American debt would never be paid back, as if it were indeed supposed to be paid back. Even before the debt crisis, it was true that most Latin American countries would not be net repayers of debt until the early part of the next century at the earliest. In other words, they would continue to be net importers of capital, a normal state of affairs for a developing country.[16] Questions about whether or not the debt would be paid back are therefore off the mark. For example, very few people expect the U.S. national debt to be repaid. It is simply a permanent financing mechanism: the U.S. Treasury borrows as maturities fall due and thus continuously renews the debt. The only important issues about such financing are whether the debt grows too rapidly—which it certainly did in the case of most large Latin American borrowers—and whether the interest gets paid. The crucial issue is interest, not principal: a dollar of interest paid today is worth twelve times more than a dollar of principal paid thirty years from now.[17]

Rescheduling of principal was a recognition by the lenders that normal market lending had ended. Rescheduling simply maintains the lending already made. The debt then becomes frozen in nominal terms and goes down in real inflation-adjusted terms so that debtors in real terms are in effect "paying back" the debt gradually, at the same rate as world inflation. Hence the economic justification for some nonmarket or involuntary lending, such as was begun with the loan of $5 billion to Mexico in 1982–83, equivalent to 7 percent of lending banks' exposure, or more or less the rate of world inflation at that time.

Rescheduling nevertheless creates a serious problem for individual lenders. In a normal market, some lenders would indeed expect to be paid back, while others would make new loans. Rescheduling freezes the positions of the lenders at the time of the stretch-out; because bank

Table 5-7.   Latin America: Rescheduling of Medium-term External Debt with Private Banks, 1982/83 to 1986/87 (in Millions of U.S. Dollars)

| | First Round, 1982/1983 | | | Intermediate Round, 1983/1984 | | |
| | Maturities | | New Credits | Maturities | | New Credits |
Country	Amount	Years	Amount	Amount	Years	Amount
Argentina	13,000	Sept. 82–83	1,500	—	—	—
Brazil	4,800	83	4,400	5,400	84	6,500
Costa Rica	650	82–84	225	—	—	—
Cuba	130	Sept. 82–83	—	103	84	—
Chile	3,424	83–84	1,300	—	—	780
Ecuador	1,970	Nov. 82–83	431	900	84	—
Honduras	121	82–84	—	—	—	—
Mexico	23,700	Aug. 82–84	5,000	12,000c	Aug. 82–84	3,800
Panama	180	83	100	—	—	—
Peru	400	83	450	662	Jul. 84–85	—
Dominican Republic	—	—	—	—	—	—
Uruguay	630	83–84	240	—	—	—
Venezuela	—	—	—	—	—	—

Source: United Nations Economic Commission for Latin America and the Caribbean, *Preliminary Overview of the Latin American Economy* (1985, 1986).

Note: For each round, the first column refers to the total amortization commitments rescheduled and the second to the years covered by the maturities rescheduled.

loans cannot easily be sold, unlike securities, the lenders can be stuck with an unwanted customer. However, if the customer pays the interest regularly, the rescheduling is simply as if the lender were covering each payment of principal with a new loan of the same amount. The total amount of the debt does not change in nominal terms.

The economic aspects of rescheduling were not always understood by the debtors. Partly for that reason, and partly for domestic political reasons—in order to show something good coming out of the debt problem—after 1982 finance ministers of some Latin American debtors spent a great deal of their time and prestige on the rescheduling of existing debt. Constant visits were made to New York, London, and Tokyo; large delegations were tied up for weeks in discussions with the lawyers for the banks; lavish ceremonial signings of debt reschedulings trumpeted the progress of debt negotiations. To say that much of this wheeling and dealing was a waste of time would be an overly harsh judgment, but certainly much of it was unnecessary. By spending

Second Round, 1984/1985		New Credits	Third Round, 1984/1985		New Credits	Fourth Round, 1986/1987		New Credits
Maturities			Maturities			Maturities		
Amount	Years	Amount	Amount	Years	Amount	Amount	Years	Amount
13,500	82–85	4,200	13,500	82–85	4,200	—	86–	—
—	—	—	15,500	85–86	—	—	87–	—
280	85–86	75	280	85–86	75	—	86–	—
82	85	—	82	85	—	—	86–87	—
5,932	85–87	1,085[b]	5,700	85–87	714[d]	—	88–	—
4,630	85–89	200	4,800	85–89	—	—	—	—
220	85–86	—	220	85–86	—	—	85–	—
48,700	85–90	—	48,700	85–90	—	43,700	85–90	6,000[3]
603	85–86	60	603	85–86	60	—	—	—
—	—	—	—	—	—	—	—	—
790	82–85	—	790	82–85	—	—	—	—
1,600	85–89	—	2,130	85–89	45	—	—	—
21,200	83–88	—	21,200	83–88	—	—	86–	—

[a]In some cases, these include maturities already rescheduled in 1982/1983.
[b]Also includes 1986 and US$150 million underwritten by the World Bank.
[c]Private sector commitments.
[d]Includes US$150 million underwritten by the World Bank.
[e]Includes US$750 million underwritten by the World Bank. In addition, there is a US$1,700 million contingent credit by private creditors.

so much time with their erstwhile lenders, now turned into bill collectors, some debtors actually began to believe that real economic progress was being made, when in fact a purely mechanical rearrangement of obligations was being put into place.

In the meantime, however, after the first involuntary loans, new bank lending fell off rapidly, increasing the net transfer of funds from debtors to banks. The multiyear rescheduling arrangements in fact indirectly helped to speed up the net decline in bank lending; because reschedulings had at the beginning been accompanied by some involuntary loans, the fact that several years of maturities were now being folded into a single package made it difficult to have more than one involuntary loan. The new loan would come at the time of the rescheduling, instead of each succeeding year. Thus, the progress of the MYRAs in lengthening amortization periods and reducing effective interest spreads was offset by the decline in net new lending which accompanied their introduction.

One interesting consequence of the debt crisis is that Latin America has by and large been bypassed by the financial innovation in world capital markets in the 1980s. The mushrooming growth of borrowing through securities and the introduction of new hedging mechanisms, such as interest rate and currency swaps, used to convert fixed interest rates into floating rate obligations or vice versa, or obligations from one currency into another, have not been evident in Latin America. Because of the realities of rescheduling, the dialogue of Latin American borrowers has been not with the innovators in the financial markets, as it had been in the 1970s, but with the erstwhile lenders turned into bill collectors. The "bill collectors" have been assigned to the "work-out," or troubled loan, part of the commercial banks, while their colleagues in the capital markets and treasury areas of the same banks have been handling the new and exciting transactions. In the meantime, countries as diverse in income as Malaysia, South Korea, Indonesia, and India have been moving ahead rapidly to tap securities markets and to reduce their use of bank loans as vehicles for commercial borrowing.

An important area of rescheduling concerns private sector debt. For Chile this was the largest part of its external debt, and it was especially important in Argentina, Mexico, Venezuela, and Colombia. Each case was somewhat different, but the funds involved were about $75 million for the region as a whole, or one-quarter of the total regional debt to banks. The problems of servicing the private debt were more complex than those of the public sector. This was so because not only was foreign exchange unavailable from the central bank, but the indebted companies were also unable to come up with enough local currency to buy foreign exchange, even if it had been available. Private funds were especially limited after sizable devaluations took place and a sharp recession cut into sales and cash flow.

The countries that had large devaluations of the exchange rate after long periods of overvaluation faced the most complex problem and needed to establish exchange subsidy schemes for the private sector. The model was FICORCA in Mexico,[18] under which private sector debtors were in effect able to fix the rate several years ahead at a fraction of its likely future price. Without FICORCA, a wholesale default by the Mexican private sector would have been unavoidable. Although such schemes undoubtedly had a cost—namely, creating central bank credit at a time of already rapid inflation—they were instrumental in helping creditors who had made loans for which, in most cases, they bore the full commercial and exchange rate risk. Latin American governments thus bent over backward to accommodate lenders. In the case of Chile, where a few large groups owed about half the external debt,[19] the lenders put special pressure on the government, especially in 1983–84, to assume the debt. This was never formally done, but the government in effect supported a plan to bail out the two largest commercial banks in the country, which in turn controlled the largest industrial groups. In the case of three similar but much smaller bank failures in Brazil in late 1985, the government refused to accept the pressure of external lenders to guarantee their external liabilities.

The idea that lenders might take equity in their erstwhile borrowers in order to clean up their debts has been a last resort. United States banks, which were the predominant lenders to the private sector, were not allowed to take equity except in minority positions (until a change in 1987), and they obviously avoided as much as possible the write-offs or write-downs of debt which would have resulted from its conversion into equity. Overall, a total of perhaps $3 billion of the debt to banks of the Latin American private sector was converted to equity or quasi-equity up to 1986. The transactions were usually made possible because of an exchange subsidy to the debtor or because the debtor was prevailed upon to give fairly generous conversion features to the lenders.[20]

A different set of problems arose in the case of private and public sector debts to suppliers. Those that were guaranteed by the governments of the exporting countries, primarily Japan and European countries, were dealt with through the longstanding mechanism known as the Paris Club[21] an informal gathering of government representatives and official export credit agencies usually chaired by the French Treasury. Paris Club refinancings among government creditors have over the years established a fairly set pattern: no refinancing without an IMF program, one year of refinancing at a time, but, on the other hand, fairly generous conditions on interest rates combined with a short leash on repayment periods for the refinancings. The major difference from commercial bank refinancing has been the willingness of export credit agencies to capitalize interest, at least partially, since government organizations, unlike banks, do not have to write down the value of a loan if the interest on it is postponed. Some $8 billion of Latin American debts to suppliers, including some interest, were refinanced through the Paris Club in the years 1983–85. The most complex negotiations were in the case of the Mexican private sector debt to Paris Club members, where the latter unsuccessfully pressured the Mexican government to assume the debts instead of simply making the foreign exchange available for the service.

As in all debt problems, there were inevitable disagreements between lenders and debtors regarding the legitimacy of certain debts. Perhaps the thorniest case was that of about $7 billion of debts owed by the Venezuelan private sector to various suppliers and banks. Many of these loans had never been registered with the central bank, as exchange regulations required, and the authorities suspected that some if not many of these debts were in fact phony claims of the debtors upon themselves in order to obtain foreign exchange at the special concessionary exchange rate applicable to debt repayment. The registration process was thus very slow, leading to write-offs by legitimate creditors.

In conclusion, the greatest contribution to the debt strategy devised in 1982 came from a somewhat unexpected quarter, namely, the debtors themselves. The balance-of-payments impact of the inevitable belt-tightening was quicker and larger than had generally been expected. Other remedies, such as the growth of Latin American exports and a continuation of some capital inflows, were not fully successful. Total exports stagnated—although they did reasonably well in the case of Brazilian and Mexican manufactured products—largely because of falling commodity prices. Capital inflows, despite major efforts by banks and international agencies, were of minor importance. By early 1986 a larger than expected fall in international oil prices had changed the debt outlook completely for the two largest debtors: buoyancy and growth seemed to await Brazil; another crisis, likely to be more serious than that of 1982, seemed likely to befall Mexico. By 1987, in yet another turn of events, it was Brazil that was in crisis: the excessively long price and exchange rate freeze imposed in March 1986 led to the collapse of foreign exchange reserves at the end of the year. In February 1987, Brazil, the world's largest debtor to the commercial banks, suspended interest payments to them, as it had done briefly in 1983.

(6)

Financial Policemen: The Role of the IMF and the Multilateral Agencies

The Strategy of the Fund and the Commercial Banks

A key role in applying the debt containment strategy beginning in 1982 was played by the International Monetary Fund. The Federal Reserve, especially Chairman Paul Volcker, was instrumental in designing the strategy and helping the IMF to apply it. It is therefore important to understand the role of the IMF and, beginning to look to the future, to analyze the long-term merits of the debt strategy. Can the approach established in 1982 work for the future? If not, what elements need to be modified or replaced?

For more than thirty years, the IMF had played the role of financial policeman in Latin America, and in 1982 it was able to move quickly into action. The decisive personality of its chief, Managing Director Jacques de Larosière, speeded the process and added a dimension that had not existed in previous rescue packages: "involuntary," or "non-market," lending. These factors gave the IMF strong credibility with debtor countries during the initial stages of the debt crisis. Domestic financial officials knew that unpopular austerity measures had to be taken; the IMF thus helped governments swallow the medicine, which politicians would have preferred to postpone.

Acceptance of the IMF as a key intermediary by the banks and the borrowers came only after the Mexican crisis in August 1982. Before that, debtor countries had feared that an IMF presence would call their creditworthiness into question, and lenders appeared to encourage such

An earlier version of this chapter appeared in Kuczynski, "The IMF and the Debt Crisis," in *The Political Morality of the International Monetary Fund,* ed. Robert J. Myers (New York: Carnegie Council on Ethics and International Affairs, 1987).

an attitude.[1] In retrospect, if both borrowers and lenders had been convinced of the extent of their troubles, valuable time and money could have been saved by earlier intervention.

The IMF undoubtedly played a necessary and constructive role in the early stages of the debt crisis. As an organization designed to deal with temporary problems, the IMF tended to believe that the debtors' predicament was short-term; in practical terms, this view led to measures encouraging more external borrowing rather than interest relief and to an emphasis on internal austerity rather than on action that could in time rekindle economic growth.

Hence, the IMF by and large endorsed the view of the largest bank lenders that most of the troubled debtors faced a short-term problem. Within a few years, it was argued, financial discipline would overcome the debt problem, and countries would be able to return to normal borrowing from banks. The huge size of the external debt, averaging in 1982 about four times the annual exports of the larger debtors, was not considered unmanageable and, it was thought, would gradually be diluted as export earnings picked up. While few observers in 1982–83 would have considered continued erosion of commodity prices likely, that possibility was simply not taken into account in the projections of the IMF and the bank lenders. As a result, the financial plans recommended to most countries did not leave enough room for contingencies.

Few analysts, if any, attempted to relate what was happening in Latin America to the rest of the world. The problem of the debtors was perceived as an isolated case with few ramifications outside the affected countries. A costly world precedent of recommending interest relief for the debtors was therefore not worth it; rather, a moderate amount of forced, involuntary lending was seen as a way of bringing countries to the point where they would be able to borrow in the financial markets again. However, since the debt problem was mainly one of paying the interest, the strategy of an extremely modest amount of new lending tended to put pressure on debtors to increase export volumes simply to pay interest. Logical and desirable enough on the surface, that strategy in time increased the oversupply in saturated commodity markets worldwide, compounding the problems of the debtors and spreading them to commodity producers around the world. From 1981 to 1985, the volume of Latin American exports rose about 25 percent, mostly in commodity exports, yet their value did not rise at all. The commodity depression was not just a normal cyclical phenomenon, as in the past, but was probably turned into a worse, longer-term one by the financial pressure upon debtors to expand production of exportable commodities in depressed world markets.

The objective of renewed access to financial markets by the debtors was another concept that was not studied in an international context at the time that the IMF and the bank lenders designed the debt relief strategy. At the time, it was hard to see that the crisis in Latin America would greatly accelerate major ongoing changes in international capital markets, including the flight away from syndicated bank loans made to lesser credit risks and the shift toward the sale of securities (such as bonds) on behalf of top-rated debtors (such as major international corporations and governments of industrialized countries, as shown in table 6-1.) The strategy for getting the Latin American debtors back to the market was thus not internally consistent; the crisis itself had dramatically altered the very financial markets to which the debtors were supposed to return.

The strategy articulated by the IMF cannot fairly be criticized in view of what happened later, although some of the changes in financial markets were already under way in 1982. It was on solid ground after the initial crisis, when what was needed was rapid belt-tightening. But the next step had not been thought through, and it was simply hoped that applying austerity measures, as in the past, would be all that was needed. After the IMF had expended much of its energy to secure emergency credits in 1983–84, it did not have enough resources to continue, nor did it have the financial clout to get other lenders, especially the multilateral development banks, to take over.

The scarcity of capital inflows after 1983–84 increased debtor resistance to IMF prescriptions. The inevitable measures necessary to cut budget deficits fed inflation in the midst of stagnation. Needed devaluations were in several cases accompanied by export taxes designed to capture the "windfall" to exporters; revenue measures such as these deprived the private sector of some respite from austerity, while the public sector continued to spend. Thus, the resulting adverse effect on employment was larger than it probably need have been. By 1985

Table 6-1 Publicized Gross International Bond Issues and Loans, 1980–1986 (in Billions of Dollars)

	1980	1981	1982	1983	1984	1985	1986
Bond issues	40	53	76	77	112	168	226
Of which developing countries	2	4	4	3	4	8	4
Syndicated bank loans	81	95	98	67	57	42	48
Of which developing countries	29	38	33	25	20	13	8
Other[a]	n.a.	53	5	10	29	47	27

Source: Organization for Economic Cooperation and Development (OECD), *Financial Market Trends* (May 1987, and earlier issues).

[a]Note issuance facilities and other back-up and stand-by credits.

major countries were looking to unorthodox solutions quite different from the standard IMF prescriptions; both the Austral Plan in Argentina and the Cruzado Plan in Brazil reflected this need to experiment with radically new ideas.

Mexico, the precedent setter in the debt crisis of 1982–83, illustrates well the strengths and the shortcomings of the IMF approach. On the one hand, in 1983 and the first part of 1984, Mexico was able to engineer an abrupt improvement in its financial fortunes well beyond the hopes of lenders. Public expenditures and the budget deficit were slashed, wages were drastically reduced in real terms, imports fell from 12 to 8 percent of GNP, a large trade surplus was built up, and foreign exchange reserves were rebuilt. The shock treatment to the economy, accompanied by a large one-shot injection of funds from the banks and the IMF, appeared to work. On the other hand, as inflation and economic stagnation persisted into 1984, the government was tempted to spend in order to rekindle economic activity; moreover, the gradual decline in oil income, which had been foreseen in the program agreed upon with the IMF in 1982–83, was nevertheless a powerful depressant upon the economy. Before the catastrophic fall in oil prices in the first quarter of 1986, the Mexican recovery program was already in deep trouble. The shock treatment had not been able to deal with the very large burden of debt in relation to exports and GNP, a fundamental problem that transcended the short-term financial recovery of 1983–84.

The IMF and Latin America

When a household runs out of money, expenditures must go down while new sources of income and finance are found. This simple fact is as true for countries as it is for households. Nevertheless, a number of commentators on the financial problems of developing countries seem to ignore this self-evident truth. The fact that belt-tightening is needed, they seem to suggest, is the fault of the IMF, and they imply that there is an alternative to cutting outlays and raising revenue. Indeed there is, in the form of a rich and generous uncle, but that alternative is not realistic in the 1980s. The rich uncle has virtually vanished, since the United States has generally withdrawn its support of multilateral financial organizations. What support there has been has increasingly taken the form of bilateral U.S. aid to countries that are considered to have special strategic value, such as Egypt, Israel, and some of the Central American countries. In those cases, the rich uncle has been willing to provide arms and budget support. But for most countries that is not the case.

The only international agency designed to help countries overcome their immediate financial problems is the International Monetary Fund. The fact that it is by definition a bearer of bad tidings does not make it a popular institution. When money runs out, countries have to take unpopular measures, with or without the IMF. More often than not, the IMF is a convenient prop for measures that finance ministers and central bank governors know full well must be taken but that do not have enough political support to be effectively enforced. Some of the political rhetoric against the IMF thus has to be taken with a grain of salt.

In order to understand the role of the IMF in the debt crisis, it may be useful to look briefly at its history. The IMF was originally conceived as an organization that would primarily help to correct temporary imbalances between the big players in world trade and capital movements, namely the industrialized countries. In the postwar period up to 1958, however, that role was played by the European Payments Union (EPU) and its predecessors, with large-scale support from the United States. The IMF was basically inactive in the industrialized countries and concentrated instead on its largest group of developing country members, namely Latin America. It provided considerable technical assistance to Latin American central banks in training and statistics and, because commercial credit was limited, was actively involved in developing and implementing standby credits to support stabilization programs in Latin America as well as some other countries in Asia and eventually Africa.

It was only in the 1960s that the IMF became active in industrialized countries. The EPU had been displaced by the IMF, which now played a major role in organizing and providing stabilization credits to Britain, France, and Italy, among others, and even the equivalent of $1.4 billion to the United States in 1971. However, with the abandonment by the United States of the gold exchange standard in 1971 and the shift to floating exchange rates away from fixed rates, the IMF largely lost its role in the industrialized world. Its role in Latin America was also diminished because countries found it easy to borrow from commercial banks instead of submitting to the tough stabilization programs required by the IMF.

In cases where the IMF was active, it did try to restrict the growth of loans from commercial banks by setting limits on such borrowing and by requiring minimum maturities, usually beyond those available in the market. Unfortunately, these programs were too infrequent to hold back significantly the growth of the external debt of Latin American countries in the 1970s and early 1980s.

Over the years, the IMF thus had a tradition of close association

with Latin America. Its annual detailed confidential reviews of economies of member countries gave its staff fairly continuous information.
The fact that it had and still has a deliberate policy of keeping its staff
small, with low turnover, and has emphasized the employment of citizens of the region, has given the Fund the most consistent source of
economic and financial information about Latin America among international organizations. The established employment pattern of the IMF
has also meant that the staff has been somewhat slow to experiment
and innovate.

Trust in the IMF by developing countries reached its peak during
the years when Pierre-Paul Schweitzer was managing director (1963–
73).[2] Later, commercial bank support for the IMF was enhanced by an
episode in the mid-1970s when the major commercial banks tried to
work out the financial crises in Peru and Zaire without the IMF. The
experiment was a failure, and the IMF came back to play an important
role during the Mexican financial crisis at the end of 1976.

The difference between the role of the IMF in the past and after
1982 was not only in the size of the problem but also in the fact that an
enormous effort was required to avoid a complete stoppage of bank
lending. Unfortunately, in the meantime the resources of the IMF had
declined in relation to the size of the likely financial problems of its
members.

Fund Policies

Even though the IMF was conceived at Bretton Woods as a response to the problems of the world economic system in the 1920s and
1930s, it has never had the systemic role envisaged at the time. This
failing is the inevitable result of the predominance of a few large
countries, such as the United States, Germany, and Japan, in the world
financial system; an international agency cannot therefore realistically
have an influence beyond its powers of persuasion. The IMF has been
far more influential when dealing with individual countries; again, naturally enough, the smaller and less powerful the country, the greater
the likely influence of the IMF.

It is therefore not surprising that after 1982 the IMF dealt with the
problems of each debtor country in turn rather than looking for wider
systemic solutions, such as a special credit facility for troubled debtors,
proposed by many observers of the debt crisis. Such a remedy would
have required far more resources than the IMF had, even after the
quota increase of 1983, and would in any case have been politically
impossible in the principal industrialized countries.

The so-called case-by-case approach to debtor country problems was, of course, logical in the sense that each debtor country had its own separate balance-of-payments problems. Yet the prescriptions were broadly similar. The debtor countries of Latin America as well as the Philippines all faced a similar immediate problem, namely, how to replenish their exhausted foreign exchange reserves. The prescriptions of the IMF for this ailment were as obvious and standard as aspirin is for a headache: reduction of demand by cutting back public sector deficits and domestic credit, stimulation of financial savings through higher interest rates, and promotion of foreign exchange earnings and cutbacks in foreign exchange demand through devaluation of the exchange rate. There was little that the IMF recommended to debtors that they would not have done on their own, had they had the political power to do so.

Thus, there is truth to the criticism that IMF policies are "devalue, deflate, and deregulate."[3] Nevertheless, in the immediate crisis of 1982–83, there was little alternative to such measures. The problems arose after the acute phase of the crisis had passed. After the initial emergency blood transfusion and treatment, there was unfortunately little thought given by the IMF and the banks to how to get the patient back on his legs and working. In short, there was no strategy for the restoration of economic growth in the context of a very heavy external debt burden combined with depressed commodity export prices.

The concept of "conditionality," in the sense that stabilization programs and reforms have to be enforced before IMF money is made available, obviously has to be part of the operations of a policy-based lender such as the IMF (or the Federal Reserve in the United States, for example), but the nature of the conditions is, of course, a matter for much discussion. Three aspects of IMF conditionality in particular stand out as problematic in the post-1982 period. First, public sector deficits were especially difficult to cut back when interest on the public debt in a number of countries was absorbing about 15 to 20 percent of total public outlays,[4] or about 4 to 5 percent of GNP, double the proportion of a few years earlier. With such a large part of expenditure devoted to interest and wages—the latter typically account for about half of central government expenditure—the room for effective spending cuts was limited indeed.

A second major obstacle was the control of state enterprises, which continued to spend. The IMF attempted to cut back public spending by holding back financing, namely, the expansion of bank credit; as a result, the continuing spending of state enterprises absorbed a higher proportion of a declining pool of domestic credit, severely squeezing out the private sector. As we have seen, total domestic banking credit fell as a proportion of GNP in the three largest economies—Argentina,

Brazil, and Mexico—between 1981 and 1983–84; but the proportion to the public sector went up, partly because of the state enterprises themselves and partly because of the burden of financing interest on the public debt. The result was that credit to the private sector was dramatically cut, probably aggravating unemployment more than if the credit cuts had affected the public sector in the first instance.[5]

A third major area of difficulty was the inevitable inflationary impact of increases in controlled prices. In Mexico and Peru, for example, where gasoline was marketed exclusively by the state petroleum monopoly at low prices in comparison with international prices, domestic sales led the state to forgo revenue in comparison with export sales, and large price increases had to be decreed. Because the items subject to regulation—basic staples, public transport, electricity, and fuel—account for the bulk of the consumer price index in most Latin American economies, increases in those prices automatically lead to inflation in a statistical sense. The first stages of an austerity program thus tend to lead to more inflation, until recession and the decline in real wages start to bring inflation down, as occurred, for example, in Mexico in 1983–84. The problem occurs when real wages do not go down but rather go up, as happened in Argentina in 1983–84, or when the inflationary psychology becomes so rooted that inflation accelerates, as was the case in Brazil and Peru in the period 1982–85. The fiscal squeeze that debtor countries found themselves in around 1982–83 led the IMF to press for sizable increases in controlled prices rather than a more gradual program, thus fueling inflation more than necessary.

The feeling of IMF staff over the years in Latin America, supported by their experience, was and is that corrective measures should be taken in one big step rather than spread over time; the gradualist approach, they feel, leads to no action. Unfortunately, the experience of a number of countries, such as Peru after 1984 and Argentina up to 1985, tends to show that this is a correct assessment. The other side of the coin, especially for increases in controlled prices, is that sudden large increases tend to feed an inflationary spiral unless they are neutralized by drastic real wage cuts and other painful income reductions that are politically very difficult to impose in an open society.

Some of the complexities of designing a stabilization program under extreme inflation are illustrated by the cases of Brazil and Argentina. In both cases, the traditional IMF-supported policies of cutting demand in order to attack inflation had not worked. The IMF would argue that the cause of the failure was half-hearted enforcement, but the facts suggest that the problems were far too complex for the simplified money-and-credit model, which the IMF has traditionally used in Latin America.[6] In the end, both Argentina and Brazil adopted unorthodox solutions, in the case of Argentina with strong financial support from the IMF. As of early 1987, the outcome of the Argentine plan was one of moderate success—lower inflation but only modest growth—while that of Brazil failed after an initial consumer boom fueled by fiscal deficits and consumer spending as well as by speculation against controlled prices.

In Brazil the bulk of inflationary pressure up to early 1986 came from the indexing of government debt. The public sector deficit, adjusted upward for the indexing of government domestic debt, hovered around 12 to 15 percent of GNP for several years. A gap of this size can be highly inflationary if no offsetting real resources are obtained.[7] Under the indexing of government debt, consumers, whose purchasing power often lags behind inflation, transfer resources to savers, who are usually among higher income groups and closely held corporations. The reversal of the process, deindexation, would probably imply a large transfer of income to consumers, away from savers, and would in the initial stages be highly stimulative, as happened in the first half of 1986, until capacity constraints rekindled inflation. But under indexation, squeezing more out of the consumer through increases in state-controlled prices may end up creating recession because demand is cut back and saving increases while inflation continues. Simply to squeeze more net revenue out of consumers thus becomes inflationary, while at the same time plunging the economy into recession. In a way, that is what happened in Brazil after 1981: more inflation, more recession.

Problems such as these led economists in various Latin American countries to explore ideas about cutting back inflation without causing economic depression. The idea of a temporary price freeze combined with deficit-cutting measures and followed by economic stimulation had been tried successfully in the Plan Pinay in France in 1952. Similar ideas were suggested by a number of economists, especially in Brazil.[8]

It was Argentina, however, pressed by an inflation rate of more than 1,000 percent in 1984–85, that first took a bold step with the Plan Austral of June 1985. Prices and nominal wages were frozen and real wages cut back after a major devaluation; drastic measures were taken to increase government revenues, including export taxes; and a new currency, the austral, was created. As of mid-1986, the plan had achieved the psychological and economic shock of choking off inflation, but the economy continued in recession partly because of the very high real interest rates needed to control credit demand. While an IMF standby credit successfully accompanied the Plan Austral, the plan itself was basically home-grown.

At the end of February 1986, the new democratic government in Brazil put into effect the Cruzado Plan, named after the new currency that replaced the cruzeiro. In general terms, it was similar to the Plan Austral in Argentina: a general price and wage freeze (although in Brazil a one-month wage bonus, approximately equal to an 8 percent salary increase, significantly boosted incomes) and the introduction of a new currency in order to discourage the inflationary mentality. Indexation of interest rates was eliminated, except for savings deposits. While the Brazilian plan was less drastic than the Argentinian one— there was no devaluation of the currency, and the wage freeze was moderated by the one-time increase—its initial chances of success looked greater because of the favorable change in the terms of trade in 1986 as a result of the collapse of oil import prices. The latter created the effect of a large capital inflow in the balance of payments and thus gave the authorities room to have a tight credit policy without causing sky-high interest rates.

The key to long-term success of the Cruzado Plan was the public sector and the unwinding of the price freeze. If public spending was not contained, the strong consumer demand created by the price freeze could turn into renewed inflation. Indeed, that is what happened in late 1986.

The other critical element was the exchange rate, which became increasingly overvalued in the course of 1986 as repressed inflation— higher real incomes facing frozen prices and stagnant supply—steadily gained momentum. By the end of 1986, the combination of an increasingly overvalued exchange rate and a consumer boom, itself fueled by the widespread belief that prices would not stay stable, led to a balance-of-payments crisis: imports boomed, the trade surplus evaporated, and international reserves plummeted. This sharp financial deterioration plus the need to maintain the domestic political standing of the government led it in February 1987 to declare a moratorium on interest payments to foreign commercial banks, except for short-term debt. Thus, almost five years after the Mexican moratorium on principal repayments to the banks, a potentially even larger Latin American debt crisis—because it affected interest payments—had arisen. The outcome is discussed in Chapters 8 and 9.

A highly positive but temporary side effect of the initial stages of the Cruzado Plan was the redirection of corporate investment toward real assets and away from the indexed government bond market. This was especially healthy after companies had virtually become banks, instead of investors, during the period of high inflation combined with indexation. On the other hand, for the investment boom to continue, timely price decontrol was especially important; without it, new investment in plant capacity would be discouraged by the prospect of meager returns. In fact, by mid-1986 it was already clear that the Brazilian economy was badly overstimulated: shortages developed as consumer spending ran into a lack of supply because of frozen prices.

As of November 1986, after parliamentary elections, selective increases in prices were allowed. By the first quarter of 1987, the fiscal deficit and an accelerated unwinding of price controls were leading to hyperinflation and a major balance-of-payments crisis. The long-range outcome of the Cruzado Plan, however, had already been increasingly doubtful in the course of the second half of 1986 as the combined objective of both rapid growth and low inflation proved elusive.

The Austral and Cruzado plans were both home-grown products. In the case of Brazil, which did not need IMF resources in 1985–86, the government was itself able to put the plan into effect and thus to avoid an agreement with the IMF. This was a highly popular stand with the Brazilian Congress and with the domestic press, and the results of the November 1986 parliamentary elections gave the government coalition a very large majority.

At the same time, the dismal outcome of the Cruzado Plan in 1987 showed that it is not possible to maintain a fixed exchange rate in the face of increasing inflationary pressures, a lesson that the IMF has preached for years; in Argentina, on the other hand, much slower growth combined with more timely devaluations made it possible to maintain the anti-inflationary policies of the Plan Austral much longer, an outcome consistent with IMF views.

The case of Venezuela illustrates different aspects. In 1983 and subsequently, the Venezuelan government refused to follow the approach suggested by the IMF: large-scale devaluation to a unified exchange rate. It did not need an agreement with the IMF because of its high level of international reserves. In a traditionally low-inflation economy, with a high propensity to import, a large-scale devaluation on the order of 300 percent—as suggested by the IMF in 1983—would have been highly inflationary. The Venezuelan authorities went instead to a partial, albeit large, devaluation and to a system of multiple exchange rates, anathema to IMF thinking, combined with tight domestic credit. The large existing speculative inventory of imported goods at the beginning of 1983, along with tight central bank credit, which held back consumer demand, restrained inflationary pressures. (Price controls imposed by the government in 1983 were largely cosmetic.) As a result of the 1983 strategy, Venezuela maintained until 1987 the lowest inflation rate of any of the major Latin American economies. Through these policies, and partly also by holding back foreign exchange for the service of the private sector external debt, which the authorities suspected was in part backed by large private deposits abroad, Venezuela was able to build up a high level of international reserves before the collapse of oil prices in 1986. This greatly strengthened its hand in negotiating the debt refinancing with the commercial banks in 1986–87.

In 1983 the banks were nearly at their wits' end with Finance Minister Arturo Sosa. A businessman who had been one of the joint presidents of Venezuela after the fall of dictator Marcos Pérez Jiménez in 1958, Sosa reluctantly agreed to serve in the last year of the Herrera administration up to February 1984. Behind his jovial personality, Sosa cannily set his own rules for negotiations with the IMF and the commercial banks, politely stonewalling them and refusing to be drawn into a rapid refinancing of Venezuela's external debt. More important, through an unorthodox combination of tight credit, multiple exchange rates, and a temporary slowing of payments on the private sector external debt, Sosa was able to engineer a relatively smooth transition to an economy devoid of external borrowing, without stimulating inflation at the same time. Real incomes, of course, did fall as a result of the world oil glut.[9]

The massive, across-the-board devaluation recommended by the IMF in 1983 would in all probability have been highly inflationary for Venezuela, not only on the side of costs, but also by creating pressures for looser domestic credit. The increase in revenues in bolívares in the oil sector would have created a "Please effect,"[10] with more revenue generating more public expenditure and quite probably a loss of foreign exchange reserves. In time, of course, Venezuela had to move to a unified exchange rate, or at least to a narrower range of exchange rates, as it did in part at the end of 1986 when it devalued the principal official rate from 7.50 bolívares to almost 15 per dollar, a major adjustment that reflected the long delay in adopting basic exchange measures after 1983. The devaluation and a fiscal deficit arising from lower oil prices led to inflation after 1986.

The argument between gradualism and radicalism in exchange rate policy was also at the root of the landmark dispute between Colombia and the IMF in 1966. In the end, the exchange system of Decree 444 established by Colombia at the time, which combined a "crawling peg" devaluation with gradually loosening exchange controls, served the country well.

Such cases do not argue against the need for stabilization or adjustment under IMF auspices but suggest that the circumstances of individual countries may vary greatly from case to case, so that a less generalized approach is needed. Simplified monetary models cannot cope with important variables such as expectations, inventory movements, and, most especially, outside forces beyond the control of individual countries. It is obviously impossible and no doubt also undesirable to insulate economies from the outside world, but neither the existing conceptual models used by the IMF nor its financing mechanisms themselves are sufficient to cope with the problems faced by its largest constituency, the highly indebted developing countries. For highly indebted commodity producers, the question posed by Ragnar Nurkse more than forty years ago still remains partially unresolved: what is a temporary as opposed to a fundamental balance-of-payments disequilibrium?[11]

Emergency Financing

The bulk of the emergency financing from the IMF took place in 1983, the year of immediate crisis for most debtors in Latin America. Net lending by banks, which accompanied IMF credit, was also strong in 1983 but then plummeted in 1984 (table 6-2). IMF credit continued at a strong pace in 1984 but fell off sharply in 1985 as the bulk of the credits contemplated in the standby arrangements of 1983 were disbursed.[12] New standby arrangements were hard to negotiate after 1983–84 because major debtors like Brazil and Mexico were close to the limits on new credits, set as a multiple of the quota of each country, so that new drawdowns would in any case have been small.

The decline in credit from the IMF and the commercial banks was not offset by the multilateral development banks—the World Bank, the Inter-American Development Bank, and, in the case of the Philippines, the Asian Development Bank. Even though the World Bank and the Inter-American Bank made a concerted effort to increase their disbursements of loans to major debtors, absolute amounts were too small to have a large impact on the balance of payments of major Latin American debtors.

Emergency financing from the IMF and the commercial banks in 1983 eased the transition away from the extremely high external borrowing of the past. But when financing dropped off in 1984 and again in 1986, there was nothing to replace it.

In the case of the IMF, even after the quota increase of 1983–84, the credit available for large developing country debtors was modest in relation to their new problems. First, the increase in IMF resources had restored their adequacy only a small part of the way to where they had been in relation to world trade in 1970. Quotas were equivalent to 10 percent of world exports in 1970 and only 5 percent in 1985, after the 1983–84 quota increase. Second, and more important, the possible swings in the balance of payments of developing countries that have been market borrowers are relatively much larger in the mid-1980s than they were fifteen or twenty years ago. This is so because of the

Table 6-2   Latin America and the Caribbean: Major Sources of Emergency Credit, 1983–1986 (in Billions of Dollars)

	1982	1983	1984	1985	1986
Net credit by IMF[a]	1.7	6.4	3.8	1.5	0.2
Argentina	0.2	1.4	—	1.0	0.2
Brazil	—	0.7	0.2	0.1	−0.6
Mexico	0.4	1.1	1.3	0.3	0.7
Net credit by commercial banks[b]	17.6	11.0	1.2	9.3	3.5
Argentina	0.8	1.1	−1.7	4.1	1.7
Brazil	7.9	0.5	4.6	1.3	2.7
Mexico	5.7	6.4	1.4	0.8	−0.8
World Bank net lending	1.4	1.7	2.1	1.9	1.7
Disbursements	2.0	2.5	3.2	3.2	3.1
Less repayments by countries	0.7	0.8	1.1	1.3	1.4
Inter-American Development Bank net lending	1.2	1.2	1.8	1.6	1.5
Disbursements	1.7	1.7	2.4	2.3	2.3
Less repayments by countries	0.5	0.5	0.6	0.7	0.8
Grand Total	21.9	20.3	8.9	14.3	6.9

Sources: Annual Reports of IMF, World Bank, Inter-American Development Bank, and BIS. BIS data underestimate bank lending in Latin America by about 10 to 25 percent, adjusted on a calendar year basis, because offshore banking centers are not included. However, BIS data for 1986 are not strictly comparable with those for earlier years because of the addition of bank lenders from Finland and Portugal and because the fall in the U.S. dollar makes it appear as if there is an increase in exposure in nondollar currencies, even though there was no such actual new lending.

[a]See note 12 of this chapter for an explanation of the concept of IMF net credit.

[b]According to the Bank for International Settlements. See source note above.

much larger size of external debts and the high proportion that is at floating interest rates.

In order to offset the potential cost to debtors of a rise in interest rates, one proposal has been to have an IMF Interest Rate Facility, which would finance the excess interest payments of debtors if interest rates went above an agreed-upon level.[13] If, for example, such a facility were to finance 3 percentage points of the excess above 10 percent— or only about one-third of the increase that took place after 1978 and until 1982—its budget would have to be about $9 billion annually for three years, or a total of about $25 to $30 billion. This compares to the quotas of Latin American and Caribbean countries in the IMF, as of 1986, of only about $8 billion equivalent out of total quotas in the IMF of $90 billion. Admittedly, because of the gradual increase in the amounts that countries can actually draw, which is a multiple of their quotas, as of early 1986 Latin American countries owed about $16 billion against their quotas and could, in theory, draw approximately another $8 billion. However, this additional borrowing would undoubtedly be subject to stiff performance conditions.

Thus, the size and distribution of IMF resources are inadequate in relation to the problems of debtor countries in the 1980s. Another example reinforces the point. In 1970, before the fifth general increase in quotas had been paid, Latin American and Caribbean countries had merchandise exports of $16 billion, an estimated external debt of $20 billion, and quotas in the IMF of about $2 billion.[14] Using this conservative point of comparison, quotas were thus about 13 percent of exports and 10 percent of external debt. By 1985 the eighth general increase in quotas had raised the Latin American and Caribbean share to $8 billion, but exports had risen to $92 billion, and debt to about $380 billion. Quotas had thus fallen to the equivalent of 9 percent of exports and only 2 percent of external debt. Because most of the external debt is at variable interest rates, the potential balance-of-payments swings caused by interest payments, as well as by the falloff in international lending to the debtors, are very large. IMF quotas have dramatically lost significance in relation to the biggest source of potential problems for developing countries, namely debt-related money flows.

The political fact that it would have been impossible to obtain a larger increase in IMF quotas from the industrial countries in 1983 does not change the judgment that today the IMF does not have the resources to give it clout with countries—except for small economies with no access to financial markets—on the scale it had fifteen or twenty years ago.

The IMF had exhausted much of its money by 1983 and early 1984. After that, the available resources that countries might have tapped would have required them to demonstrate a continuous slump in commodity prices over several years[15] or to agree to extended financial stabilization programs over three years, both difficult conditions to meet. At least most of the debtors thought the prize was too small to justify the effort.

The falloff in IMF credit to debtors was worsened by the decline of net lending from banks in 1984 and 1986. The decline had several causes. First, there was the inability of several countries to meet the financial performance conditions of standby agreements with the IMF. Thus, for example, of the $4.5 billion extended by means of a credit facility agreed upon in March 1983, only about $1 billion was actually disbursed to Brazil in 1983–84. Second, there was some erosion of the amounts available for short-term revolving trade finance from banks. According to the BIS, the short-term debt of the region, a reasonable proxy for the trend of trade-related finance, fell from $98 billion in June 1982 to about $83 billion at the end of 1985. The third and most important factor was, of course, the constant pressure of the market and the regulators upon banks to reduce their exposure to risky customers.

Nevertheless, a number of leading commercial bankers, especially in the United States, continued to envision a return within a few years to voluntary lending. This would be the reward for good behavior. By 1985, however, the objective of restoring voluntary lending looked elusive, to say the least. Mexico, the success story of 1983, was again in economic trouble.

The words of William Rhodes, the Citibank executive who chaired (and still chairs) the bank committees for Argentina, Brazil, and Mexico, and who has been among the most visible bankers in the debt question, are representative of the thinking of some leading U.S. bankers in 1983. Their disappointment at events in Mexico in 1985–86 must have been great. He closed his remarks at the Financial Times Banking Conference in London in December 1983 by saying:

> The crux of the issue is when we are going to return to voluntary lending, which spells the equivalent of normality in this situation. When will the debtors become customers again?
>
> I think Mexico will lead the way in 1985 for the reasons I mentioned earlier.
>
> When Hippocrates first coined the word "crisis," he meant it to describe a point in the treatment of a patient when his condition could take a turn for the better or worse.
>
> By that definition, I think the crisis point is past for Mexico, and I hope I can soon say the same for Brazil. Not that they aren't both troubled, but both have adopted policies, fiscal and monetary, which give them time to plan rationally for the future.
>
> In addition, the world economic recovery that has taken hold will be accompanied by an upswing in world trade, which should give them additional strength.[16]

The Multilateral Development Banks

The hope of many observers from the creditor countries, embodied in the Baker Initiative, that the multilateral development banks could somehow make up for these very large declines in emergency lending from the commercial banks and the IMF was evidently optimistic. There is no question that the World Bank in particular made a special effort to gear its disbursements toward the large debtors in Latin America and that it was especially successful in helping to put together fairly large packages of new money for medium-sized economies such as Colombia and Chile; but there is also no question that the multilateral development banks had only a modest impact in relation to the size of the problem, partly because they are not organized to provide emergency lending. Such a role would have been a drastic change from their original mandate.

Despite the inherent difficulty of altering their loan operations, which had in one form or another remained basically the same for decades, the World Bank, and to a greater extent the Inter-American Development Bank, adapted slowly to the fact that a major proportion of their borrowers were, in effect, bankrupt. The central problem, which should have been faced, was how to increase the disbursements of already committed loans at a time when borrowers did not have the local matching funds needed to make the disbursements possible.

If the multilateral lenders had been short of funds, their slowness to act would have been understandable. However, that was not the case. Cash reserves were high. In addition, as of the end of 1985, the World Bank and the Inter-American Bank together had about $23 billion of loans already committed to Latin American borrowers but not as yet disbursed. In the normal course of events, the loans would be disbursed in five to seven years, as the projects for which they provide partial financing are built (such as roads or electric works) or paid out (such as rural credit programs). The World Bank and the regional development banks modeled on it normally distribute money on the basis of work completed, paying a percentage of the verified bills.[17] In Latin America this has averaged around 30 to 40 percent of total project costs in recent years. However, since 1982, public investment budgets have often been cut under IMF programs. Many countries have not been able to come up with their share of project costs. Inevitably, this domestic shortage has limited the disbursement of loans from the multilateral development banks.

One way in which the financial gap faced by the debtors could have been alleviated was simply to raise, for a time, the percentage of each specific project which the development banks finance. The banks were reluctant to raise the percentage, except in a few cases, arguing—unconvincingly—that such a step would amount to balance-of-payments assistance, as if there ought to be a hard-and-fast rule to set one particular percentage of disbursements rather than another. The omission was especially visible in the case of the World Bank, which in the period from 1983 onward had particularly large cash reserves, averaging $17 billion, or in mid-1986, the equivalent of about two years of total disbursements to all borrowers.[18]

One reason why the World Bank had difficulty in responding to the special needs of some of its largest borrowers was the negative attitude of the U.S. government toward it and toward multilateral organizations in general. Other major World Bank and IMF shareholders, such as Japan, Germany, and Britain, went along with the U.S. attitude, which had been building up in the late 1970s and had intensified under the Reagan administration. There was a mixture of legitimate concerns about the emphasis of the multilateral development banks on investment by state enterprise and a general skepticism about multilateral organizations in general. The skepticism reflected fading support for internationalism in the United States, which had in any case been nurtured in the 1960s and 1970s by a relatively small constituency of intellectuals and some large multinational corporations.

The World Bank has for many years made a small volume of "program loans," especially to India and Pakistan. These loans are not project-specific and are designed to help the balance of payments by financing crucial productive imports, such as spare parts for industry. After the crisis in Mexico in 1982, the World Bank tried to raise the proportion of such loans beyond the world total of 10 to 15 percent which had been customary, but it received a clear negative signal from the U.S. Treasury. Nevertheless, through a "special action program" of fast-disbursing loans, the World Bank and also separately the Inter-American Bank were able to raise their disbursements to Latin America by about 50 to 60 percent between 1982 and 1984 (see table 6-2). After that, however, a plateau was reached, and, after counting repayments, net disbursements in fact fell off slightly in 1985 and in fiscal 1986. If interest payments are deducted, the net cash flow, or "transfer," from the World Bank to Latin America averaged only about $700 million per year in the period of the five fiscal years 1982–86 and dropped off sharply in 1986 as disbursements stagnated while loan repayments increased.[19] Disbursements picked up sharply in 1987, by about 40 percent, heralding a possible longer-term upward trend.

Overall, despite serious political difficulties and some disorientation in an institution that had been used to rapid growth under the presidency of Robert McNamara (1968–81), the World Bank showed that it could play an effective role in cases that are not overwhelmingly large. In Chile the World Bank was able to add $300 million to the $785 million in new loans put up by commercial banks in 1985, the third such new money package from banks in three years. Of the $300 million, half was jointly financed with commercial banks. In Colombia in 1984–85, President Belisario Betancur was unalterably opposed to any arrangement with the IMF; the World Bank stepped in, as a kind of "IMF with a heart," and played an important role in arranging $1 billion in financing from commercial banks, primarily for coal and oil development.[20]

The question of whether emergency financing is in principle a good idea or a bad one has been a hotly debated subject. The idea of pouring good money after bad loans is obviously unappealing. Detractors have argued that the very existence of potential emergency financing, such as that provided by the IMF, encourages irresponsible behavior by lenders and borrowers.[21] The increase in IMF quotas was seen by these critics as a negative development. On the other hand, the very fact that the IMF has been a tough taskmaster and that it has not disbursed its credits easily makes debtors think twice before going to it. The idea that the multilateral development banks can provide an alternative to the IMF should therefore be examined with care, since it would be counterproductive for debtors to think that there is easier money. Once the setting for financial order and stability exists, the present distribution of tasks, with the IMF helping with short-term emergencies and other agencies helping to provide funds for development, should be maintained.

There is an additional question, namely whether official development institutions, with their natural leaning toward state-sponsored projects, can make an effective contribution at a time when several Latin American and other debtor nations need to undo the excessive statism of the last fifteen years. To a significant extent, this excessive statism was supported by foreign lenders, both official and private. Although I shall return to this question later, it is clear that in a period of reform and reorganization in the debtor countries, the international organizations will also need long-term changes, not so much in the way they are organized internally but rather as a result of a review of what their function and mandate ought to be after more than forty years of existence.

Outlook: Moribund or Temporarily Incapacitated?

A key premise in the containment strategy spearheaded by the IMF was that the problem of the major debtors could be surmounted in a reasonably short period of time. The debtors were not insolvent, they were illiquid; the IMF has been an articulate proponent of this view in its periodic *World Economic Outlook* publication.[22] Its views have paralleled those of Morgan Guaranty Trust in its *World Financial Markets* monthly, as well as of a number of other bankers, the U.S. financial authorities, and other well-known observers.[23]

With minor variations, all these observers and participants—"the Collective" of lenders, in the words of George Soros[24]—have suggested the same remedies, namely austerity on the part of the debtors, renewed world economic growth, and the continuation of lending to the debtors; and all have visualized the same outcome by the late 1980s: a significant reduction of the burden of debt (measured as the ratio of external debt to exports) and a resumption of some voluntary, or "market," lending by commercial banks.

As of 1986–87 neither of these goals seems likely to be achieved within the period forecast. At the same time, however, the fact that the projections of the various observers have not materialized (table 6-3), largely because the value of exports has stagnated in comparison with the projections, has not meant that the economic problem of all the major debtors as a group is any the worse. Some, such as Brazil, have for a time been far better off than was predicted, while others, notably Mexico, are much worse off. That outcome shows that it is difficult and risky to generalize about the long-term future prospects of the debtors as a group.

To some extent, lender projections are the result of hopeful, if not wishful, thinking. It is true that the forecasts include "worst cases," but these usually comprise a relatively minor deterioration in the numbers, such as a one-point decline in the rate of growth of the industrial countries, a small change in international interest rates, or—for the oil exporters—no change in nominal oil prices.[25] The projections do show that the outlook could work out under various assumptions, as long as there are no major adverse changes—certainly a logical possibility, but a far cry from the real variability of international economic events seen in the last fifteen to twenty years. World economic events in that period have turned out to be sharply different than what was envisaged by the consensus of most forecasters.

As table 6-3 shows, major observers substantially overestimated Latin American export growth. The IMF was least optimistic, while the banks naturally were rather more optimistic. As a result, the burden of debt, which these observers projected to go down, in fact *increased,* not because the growth of the external debt was particularly rapid, but because the value of export earnings, despite a substantial increase in their volume, stayed flat.

Table 6-3 Summary Debt Projections: Major Debtors

	Base Year 1982	1985	1990
Morgan Guaranty Trust (6 countries)[a]			
Exports of goods and services (dollars in billions)	101	131	231
External debt (dollars in billions)	270	312	385
Projected debt-export ratio (percentage)	268	238	180
Actual ratio (percentage)[b]	268	308	—
	Base Year 1983	1985	1987
Cline (4 countries)[c]			
Exports of goods and services (dollars in billions)	76	111	137
External debt (dollars in billions)	258	273	282
Projected debt-export ratio (percentage)	339	246	206
Actual ratio (percentage)[b]	339	320	—
	Base Year 1982	1985	1990
IMF (total Latin America and Caribbean)			
Exports of goods and services (dollars in billions)	120	133	233
External debt (dollars in billions)	325	357	410
Projected debt-export ratio (percentage)	271	270	176
Actual ratio (percentage)[b]	271	297	—
	1982	1985	1987
Total Latin American—actuals (revised data)			
Exports of goods and services (dollars in billions)[d]	122	124	114
Merchandise exports (dollars in billions, f.o.b.)[d]	90	96	89
External debt (dollars in billions)	333	371	421
Actual debt-export ratio (percentage)	273	299	362

Sources: Derived from Morgan Guaranty Trust, *World Financial Markets* (June 1983); William R. Cline, *International Debt* (1984); IMF, *World Economic Outlook* (1985, 1986, 1987).

[a]Argentina, Brazil, Mexico, Chile, Colombia, and Venezuela.

[b]On basis of the definitions used by each entity.

[c]Argentina, Brazil, Mexico, and Venezuela as projected by Cline, who also has projections for all other major debtors.

[d]Total including interregional trade.

Commodity Depression: the Trade-Debt Link

The crucial neglected variable is the terms of trade. The terms of trade cut both ways, since they reflect the prices countries get for their exports and what they pay for their imports. First, they turned out to be a negative factor, as export prices, and thus exports, stagnated well below the projections of the lenders; then they turned out to be a positive factor for the oil importers, starting in 1984–85, and a negative factor for the oil exporters. For countries that are neither large oil importers nor exporters but rely on commodities for their exports, such as Argentina and Peru, the terms of trade were, on balance, a depressive factor.

It did not much matter if the world economy grew at 3 percent, as envisaged by lender projections, if the prices of the primary export products were steadily falling after the peak years of borrowing. The worldwide weakness of commodity prices in the 1980s has baffled observers. It was thought for a time that weak prices for raw materials were the result of the overly strong dollar in the three years of economic recovery up to 1985, since most raw material prices are quoted in dollars. Nevertheless, contrary to expectations, the decline of the U.S. dollar since September 1985 has not been accompanied by a broad strengthening of dollar commodity prices. In 1985 raw material prices, which on average account for three-quarters of the export earnings of Latin America and the Philippines, reached their lowest point, in real dollar terms, in the post–World War II period (table 6-4). A further sharp drop was evident in 1986, with a mild strengthening of prices in 1987 of petroleum and other products.

The weakness of commodity prices has been the result of causes which are not easy to disentangle. Two are foremost: the long-term decline in world economic growth since the 1950s and, since 1973, the gradual reshaping of industrial economies away from energy-intensive raw materials, such as metals, toward lighter products, such as plastics.

Also in the 1980s, the weakness of demand in Latin America and Africa has at the margin created further weakness in commodity markets. Even though changes in output and demand in developing countries may appear small in a worldwide context, it is precisely such marginal changes that cause wide swings in commodity prices. In the 1980s, the changes have been mostly in the direction of oversupply: not only has demand in major consuming nations such as Brazil and Mexico gone down but, in order to struggle out of their debt burdens, debtors have expanded production for export. The U.N. Conference on Trade and Development has estimated that exportable commodity output by developing countries has risen by about 7 to 10 percent in the 1980s, in what are essentially flat international markets.[26] Latin America, primarily a commodity exporter, expanded the volume of its exports in the 1980s but, as noted elsewhere, the value has remained stationary.

A few examples help to elaborate this point. Today the United States uses one-third less metals per unit of national output than it did in the early 1970s, and the average car and light truck made in the

Table 6-4   Weighted Index of Commodity Prices (in Constant U.S. Dollars, 1979–1981 = 100)

Annual Averages	Petroleum	33 Non-Energy Commodities
1948–49	28	113
1950–54	24	144
1955–59	23	128
1960–64	17	112
1965–69	15	115
1970–74	27	112
1975–78	61	109
1979	71	105
1980	107	105
1981	119	91
1982	109	82
1983	102	89
1984	102	92
1985	97	81
1986	42	69
1987[a]	55	75

Source: World Bank, *The Outlook for Primary Commodities, 1985 to 2000* (1985), and subsequent data.

Note: Weighted by 1979–81 export values of developing countries.

[a]Author's projections based on actual data as of June 1987.

United States uses 2,500 pounds of metal compared to 3,600 pounds in 1973. In the case of foods, especially grains, the increasing self-sufficiency of formerly large importers, such as China and India, has kept down the demand for internationally traded staples, while supply has overexpanded because of protection and subsidies by the industrialized countries to their small but politically vocal population of farmers. The best known but by no means the only offender has been the European Common Market, which, through its Common Agricultural Policy, provides massive subsidies to its tiny farm population. This enables European farm producers to dump their surpluses on the world market at a fraction of their full cost of production. Food aid by the United States has the same overall effect.[27] Chile has expanded by one-quarter its copper output and exports in the 1980s, and Brazil has increased its exports of iron ore by the same fraction. In both cases, weak markets and the expansion of production for export are related. The question, discussed in Chapters 7 and 8, is whether the debtors had a choice.

Low inflation in the industrial countries, largely in the wake of the wrenching economic adjustment that began in the United States around 1980, has also contributed to the lowering of commodity prices in real terms. During periods of high inflation, commodity prices have tended to outpace inflation and, conversely, since 1980 they have not kept up with it. This acceleration and deceleration is basically the result of stock-building in periods of inflationary expectations and destocking when prices are expected to be weak and the relative cost of financing is high. Such has been the case during most of the 1980s. In the case of copper, for example, prices remained depressed until 1987 despite very low levels of inventories, in contrast to past patterns of price behavior. Consumers knew that there was a sufficient supply, despite low inventories, both because of Chilean production and because of secondary copper coming from the replacement of copper telecommunications wiring by optical fibers.

Observers of the high-debt developing countries have not made enough allowance in their projections for the psychological and also the real effects of weak commodity prices upon the debtors. Just as a booming stock market in the United States generates optimism and tends to promote new investment, booming commodity markets in developing countries are the bellwether of investment and growth. The buoyant economic effect of the short-lived rise in coffee prices in several countries in 1985 is illustrative. The apparently reasonable prescription advocated by many, namely that the debtors export their way out of the debt burden, requires for its success a dynamic world economy. Otherwise, the additional exports risk flooding already weak world markets.

Oil has been the commodity price leader. This has continued to be the case in the 1980s, even though oil consumption receded in the wake of the artificially large oil price increases by OPEC in 1979. Other commodities were weakening even before the tough anti-inflationary policies of the United States started to be effective. High interest rates and the consequent recession further weakened collapsing commodity prices. For a while oil was artificially held up by OPEC production cuts, but in the end the post-1979 range of oil prices was not sustainable, and prices collapsed in 1986. While oil is bound to rise in time, the outlook for the demand and supply balance, short of war, makes a sharp rise in real prices unlikely until the 1990s.

This inevitable development probably augurs badly for other commodity prices. Higher energy consumption, due to lower energy prices, is unlikely to have much of an effect on other raw material prices, at least initially. Countries for which oil imports are a major item received in 1986 the equivalent of a windfall in their foreign exchange inflows. But for the bulk of commodity producers, the outlook for exports is problematic until their economies are reoriented toward industrial exports—a process that is not only difficult internally but faces formidable protectionist obstacles.

On balance, Latin America is a net exporter of energy, so that in the aggregate the region will be a net loser from lower oil prices, despite the significant gains for Brazil and other oil importers. It is clear, therefore, that whether the world economy grows somewhat faster or somewhat slower than the 3 percent annual rate used as a benchmark by several analysts, it is unlikely to make much difference to the debtors if commodity prices remain relatively depressed. In fact, the world economy in the 1980s is growing at a rate below 3 percent annually, further depressing the prospects for commodity prices. Whether the debtors face a temporary or a fundamental problem is thus not a question that can be decisively answered in a general way. Obviously, unpredictable economic windfalls or calamities can sharply change the financial viability of the debtors.

A key issue for the lenders and for the International Monetary Fund is whether the projections on which they based their strategy had enough of a margin to cope with the possible downward risks. These could include increases in international interest rates (which occurred, but only briefly, in 1984, and will no doubt occur again), a greater-than-expected reduction in international bank lending to the debtors (which has definitely occurred), depressed commodity export prices, protectionism in the industrial countries, and the ever-present risk of another worldwide recession. Did the outlook that the IMF and the lenders envisaged for the debtors leave enough room for these eventualities? The answer, clearly, is no.

However, the windfall from the oil price decline, which was not contemplated in most projections, for a time in 1985 and 1986 removed from the sickbed the largest of the debtors, Brazil, and will help a number of the smaller debtors, from Africa to Central America. Few can judge definitively whether lower oil prices are a phenomenon that will last several years or only a short while. If lower oil prices were to last into the early 1990s, the effect upon oil importers would be to dilute their external debt problems gradually, even if the prices of their exports remain depressed. If, on the other hand, oil import prices recover significantly, oil importers would lose a major economic stimulus, while oil exporters would only be back in the economic situation of 1984–85—not a buoyant one, even before the big drop in oil prices.

Thus, it can be argued that at least the large debtors face a fundamental problem: the size of their external debt in relation to their chief source of income to service it, namely exports. This burden exists in the long term, whether countries are oil exporters or oil importers, although the price of oil can obviously make a crucial difference. Just as the growth of debt can be attributed to diverse causes ranging from sharp increases in the price of oil to overexpansionary government policies but in the end is due only to one central cause—namely, the availability of money from the lenders—so the problem for the future is basically only one: the high level of external debt in relation to national economies and their ability to save and to export.

(7)

Outlook: The Political Economy of External Debt

Does the economic recession and the debt problem of most of Latin America matter to the world? Observers and participants have often wavered between optimism and pessimism; some have minimized the problem, while others have inflated its importance. A few consecutive headlines from 1985, in the months before U.S. Secretary of the Treasury James A. Baker announced his debt initiative, illustrate the changeability of perceptions about the debt problem:

"Latin America Moving Away from the Brink of Debt Crisis" (*Washington Post*, January 20).

"Debt Crisis Called All But Over" (*New York Times*, February 4).

"Third World Debt: The Bomb Is Defused" (*Fortune*, February 8).

"Debt Crisis Reappears in Latin America" (*Washington Post*, July 7).

"Under the Volcano" (*Economist*, July 13).

"Latin Debt Crisis Seen Intensifying" (*New York Times*, July 30).

"Three-Year Latin Debt Crisis: Gains, but Perils Persist" (*New York Times*, August 20).

"Debt Noose Tightens around Latin America" (*Washington Post*, September 29).

The central fact is that the debt problem is a continuing saga on a revolving stage, where the actors come and go but never disappear. Mexico is the most conspicuous case, with a crisis in 1982, financial recovery in 1983 and 1984, an accelerating deterioration later in 1984 and in 1985, a second major crisis in 1986, and a rapid second financial recovery in 1987—all the while with very slow economic growth. As of February 1987, Brazil and its creditors again faced a major crisis, greater than any past one because it involved prolonged nonpayment of interest. Small debtors, such as Costa Rica, Jamaica, Nicaragua, and a number of African countries, have generally stayed away from center stage. But the cast of major characters may expand if oil price weakness drags several oil-exporting countries deeper into difficulties.

A second important but sometimes forgotten fact is that the problems of the debtors do matter to the rest of the world, not just because of financial reasons, but because of the serious economic and political consequences as well. One major impact already has been the reduction of exports from the industrial to the developing countries. Had the annual economic growth rate in Latin America during the 1980s remained at a steady if modest 4 percent, exports from the industrial countries to the region would have increased from about $60 billion in 1980 to $85–90 billion in 1985.[1] Instead, there was zero growth, and exports from outside the region to Latin America declined to $45 billion. As a result, in depressed areas, such as the "rust belt" in the United States, and in the industrial belts of the Western European countries, perhaps about 1.5 million jobs were lost, amounting to around 8 percent of the total unemployment in the Western industrial nations.[2] Politically, slow economic growth and stagnation in Latin America and Africa are bound to further polarize the attitudes of both the industrial countries (the "haves") and the so-called Third World countries (the "have nots").

For the United States, the prospect of a growing immigration from Mexico is bound to have a sobering effect. While the debt strategy spearheaded by the Federal Reserve and the IMF since 1982 has given the larger internationally exposed U.S. banks time to strengthen themselves, its continuation unmodified into the late 1980s might place the Mexican economy and political system under great strain. It may seem far-fetched, but it is not inconceivable that, because of massive migration, Mexico could begin, in a sense, to recapture the U.S. Southwest, which it lost to the United States in 1848. The area of the U.S. Southwest forming an arc from Houston to Los Angeles has a population today of about 25 to 30 million; it is bound to be the first stop for the majority of immigrants from Mexico and Central America. If economic growth is not rekindled quickly, it is imaginable that perhaps one-third of the population growth of Mexico and Central America (about one million people per year) might spill over into the United States. Thus, it is at least a possibility that by the end of this century, recent Latin American immigrants could account for one-third the population of the

U.S. Southwest, a higher proportion than would be the case with a more prosperous Mexico. Furthermore, the implications for the United States of a radicalized and hostile Mexico would obviously represent a major adverse change.

The Politics of Debt

So far there has been no political explosion in the debtor countries. The conservative attitude of the governments of the creditors thus appears to have been justified: the debt problem, they have argued, is basically between the banks and the debtor governments. Nevertheless, creditor governments, led by the United States, have become increasingly involved in an effort to persuade banks to continue lending and thus have become increasingly responsible for the management of any future debt problems. At the same time, most governments of the debtor countries have, until 1986, shied away from radical solutions. Foreign ministries have been allowed to make radical pronouncements for domestic and international consumption, but, at least until the Brazilian default of February 1987, with the exception of Peru, most governments did not in practice seek to apply the innovations they were advocating, such as significant interest relief. However, just as the governments of the leading industrial countries are being gradually drawn into the debt problem, so the governments of the leading debtors are slowly abandoning their initial complaisance toward their creditors. The action by Brazil of suspending interest payments to the banks on all but the short-term debt represented a major change in attitudes, although the action was not so much the result of a deliberate policy as the consequence of the collapse of international reserves in the wake of the failure of the Cruzado Plan.

The reasons why there has been no political explosion in Latin America as incomes plummeted after 1982 are a matter of conjecture. It would be quite difficult to sort out the welter of explanatory social, economic, political, and psychological data. In fact, the little information that exists about social conditions tends to be somewhat general and conjectural.[3] The rise of farm incomes, as a result of devaluations as well as the impact of price decontrol, has acted as an important safety valve for social unrest: recent migrants to the cities have been able to return to the countryside without too drastic a reduction in their incomes. The return to democracy has been the principal political safety valve: the excitement of elections and of more open government has fueled hope of better times ahead.

Democracy, unfortunately, is not necessarily permanent or predictable. First, it may not last. Among Latin American countries, only Costa Rica, Colombia, and Venezuela, as well as Mexico with its special institutional political system, have reasonably long traditions of civilian elected governments. While increasing political maturity has greatly reduced the odds of a return to military rule in Argentina and Brazil, past history may well repeat itself in some countries if the economic strains of recent years do not ease significantly. So far, in 1985–86 only Brazil was able to show some real improvement in jobs and incomes, but much of the progress was lost in 1987.

Second, democracy does not necessarily mean successful government, any more than military rule means orderly government. The problem of rising social demands at a time of shrinking real revenues and ballooning outlays for interest service on the domestic and foreign public debts is almost intractable. Sometimes it is compounded by prejudice on the part of governments, especially against private initiative, and an innocent belief in economic rule by decree.

Nonetheless, the record of the major debtor countries in their international economic behavior was remarkable, at least until 1987. Until Brazil's unilateral moratorium in February 1987, only Peru, and to a more limited extent, Venezuela,[4] had unilaterally reduced debt service. The initiatives of the Cartagena Group, organized by debtor countries in June 1984 to promote a more aggressive and unified approach to the creditors, have not had significant practical impact. Brazil's action in 1987 was the result of its own internally induced economic problems, not of a desire to create a Latin American debt front. Undoubtedly, the Cartagena Group helped to focus opinion in favor of putting pressure on banks to ease their terms, but that pressure would probably have existed anyway. When the Cartagena Group leaned toward more radical initiatives, such as the proposal at Punta del Este in February 1986 to link debt service to exports—in effect a unilateral reduction of interest payments—Mexico, the most visible and needy debtor at the time, walked out of the meeting, and the initiative was left up in the air.

What explains the compliant attitude of most debtors in the period 1982–86? In 1982 Mexico set a pattern, followed a few months later by Brazil, which was at that point not easy to change. The idea that principal would be rescheduled, with some additional loans from banks, while interest would be paid as scheduled, seemed fair to politicians; finance ministers and economic technicians were left with the responsibility of working out the arrangements. Thus, a major reason for the attitude of debtors was the existence of a precedent and the fact that heads of state and politicians saw the arrangements as basically reasonable. This is confirmed by the fact that, with the exception of Venezuela in June 1986,[5] no Latin American parliament voted effectively to reduce interest payments to bank creditors.

The reasons for the moderate attitude of majority politicians are many. Certainly, political leaders did not do the type of calculus that some observers of the debt problem have described, under which a debtor calculates his payments and compares them to the inflow of new money: if the latter is at least equal to the former, then it would in theory be worth his while to keep interest payments current.[6]

If that sort of calculation had prevailed, even after a delay of a year or two most major Latin American debtors would have defaulted massively at some point after 1982, since, beginning in 1983, the outflow of interest from debtors to lenders was far larger than the inflow of new loans. The kind of highly rational calculus envisaged by economic observers appears to have had little influence on political leaders. The real views of heads of state are in any case masked by political rhetoric, but actual government policy speaks for itself: until 1986, other than Peru, no major Latin American debtor government unilaterally suspended interest service on the public sector external debt or even suggested it officially to its creditors.

Heads of state of the largest debtors, countries as diverse as Argentina, Brazil, Mexico, and Venezuela, were influenced by a general desire not to disconnect their economies from the world financial system. Even Peru's President García allowed the central bank to service short-term debt in the hope of maintaining bank trade credit lines. A related factor has been the desire to disassociate Latin America from "basket cases," such as some sub-Saharan African countries. While Third World speeches are considered suitable for the stage of the United Nations, in fact a typical middle-class Argentinian, for example, feels very uncomfortable, as a citizen of a sophisticated, advanced nation with a relatively high standard of living, at being lumped together with poor people of far-off miserable countries. That kind of attitude, which is reflected in middle-class voting strength, has probably been influential in tilting Latin American governments toward a "responsible" attitude on external debt. Even at low income levels, public opinion polls show a majority in favor of "paying one's debts."[7]

Thus, default would have lumped Latin American countries together with the poorest and least successful economies in the world. In the 1930s, when there were generalized defaults throughout most of the world, that might have been acceptable; but in the 1980s, most Latin American leaders have not wanted their countries to be singled out as unable to pay their debts.

A clearer influence upon most governments was their desire to disassociate themselves from the outspoken attitudes of Cuba, and also Peru, on the debt question. This desire was as much a matter of substance as of personalities. In his inaugural speech in July 1985, President Alan García of Peru, then thirty-six years old, roundly condemned the banks, the IMF, and the U.S. government for the depressive effect of their combined policies upon the debtors. He set down a general limit on Peru's external debt service of 10 percent of annual export earnings. The speech created a sensation in Latin America, especially among business groups, who see the burden of debt service as the major obstacle to growth. García was admired for his provocativeness, especially since U.S. Treasury Secretary Baker was at the ceremony and undoubtedly returned to Washington worried by his conversations in Lima with various Latin American leaders.

In fact, García was turning to his advantage a situation that he had inherited. In the last year of the preceding Belaúnde administration, Peru had already unilaterally limited interest payments on the debt to banks and to Paris Club creditors. In April 1984, Belaúnde had dismissed Economy and Finance Minister Carlos Rodríguez-Pastor, who had attempted to carry out a moderate program of austerity under IMF auspices.[8] As a result, in the year prior to García's inauguration, Peru's actual debt service payments were only about 9 percent of its merchandise exports, or about 30 percent of its total actual interest obligations.

García, a youthful and charismatic orator, appealed and still appeals to political opinion in much of Latin America. He seemed not only to provide a simple solution for a festering problem but also clearly upstaged Fidel Castro, who had earlier attempted to take the lead within Latin America on the debt issue. Early in 1985 Castro organized a conference on the subject to which he invited a number of leading Latin American businessmen. Contrary to the Cuban view expressed in previous international meetings,[9] Castro now advocated a moratorium. By endorsing a radical line, Cuba automatically foreclosed such options from consideration by the centrist and Social Democrat governments in most of Latin America.

The role of President García was more radical in the sense that he practiced what he preached. Both the context of his message and the way it was delivered upset his fellow Latin American presidents. The idea of unilateralism espoused by García did not appeal to chiefs of state such as Presidents Alfonsín of Argentina or de la Madrid of Mexico. They were spending a great deal of their political capital at home trying to keep trade union wage demands down and felt that the acceptance of unilateralism could have damaging consequences, leading to a breakdown of discipline at home. Another factor contributing to the negative reception of García's ideas was the way in which they were delivered. For example, on a state visit to Argentina in February 1986, García addressed the Argentine Congress, upstaging his host with a loud denunciation of the United States and of financial discipline under the IMF, which President Alfonsín was trying hard to carry out. As a small debtor, Peru could only hope to enlist others to its cause by first obtaining the political help of a major debtor such as Argentina, a traditional friend, rather than proclaiming its point of view loudly but alone.[10]

Ironically, therefore, Cuba and Peru separately may have done much to help the position of bank creditors by creating an atmosphere hostile to radical solutions. How long that atmosphere continues following the 1987 Brazil moratorium depends, of course, on what happens to the major debtors.

The efforts of the Cartagena Group have demonstrated that debtor countries have so far been unable to channel their common frustration into practical action. The formation of the group in June 1984, at a meeting in Cartagena, Colombia, hosted by President Belisario Betancur, awakened fears of a debtors' cartel.[11] The existence of the group may have backfired on the debtors in the sense that it has probably reinforced the reluctance of banks and regulators, especially in the United States, to consider special interest concessions to particular countries because of the fear of setting a precedent that would apply to a wide range of debtors.

Nonetheless, the Cartagena Group turned out to be a paper tiger. Most countries were unwilling to yield any sovereignty to a joint approach on the debt question. Foreign ministries, which were the leaders in Cartagena, in general did not have the technical skills to develop viable proposals for debt relief. Hence, at the various meetings of the group, including Cartagena in June 1984, Mar del Plata in September 1984, Santo Domingo in February 1985, Montevideo in December 1985, and Punta del Este in February 1986, only the usual calls for relating debt service to export income could be made.

The main stumbling block to the efforts of the Cartagena Group has been the position of the two largest debtors, Brazil and Mexico. Only if both countries see usefulness in a joint approach can the initiatives of a debtors' group begin to have clout. In the meantime, Mexico, with its proximity and financial access to the United States, has traditionally been reluctant to give more than rhetorical importance to Latin American regional groupings. The Sarney administration in Brazil, which has more internationalist proclivities than its military predecessor, is nevertheless far more interested in Brazilian rather than regional initiatives on debt. For the time being, the idea of a debtors' cartel is thus a little like Rip Van Winkle—perhaps alive but certainly in a deep sleep.

The Brazilian moratorium on interest payments to the banks, which began in February 1987, has clearly marked a change in the rules of the debt game. The new rules, however, will remain unclear until the outcome of the crisis. If the Brazilian action was making the best of a bad situation and also a tactic to pry new involuntary lending out of the banks, as many of the leading banks and official agencies suspect and as some of the Brazilian authorities stated after the moratorium, then the changes, if Brazil can stage an economic recovery before the end of 1987, might not be large. If, on the other hand, the moratorium is a concerted action to gain major interest relief, a long period of uncertainty and confrontation is likely between Brazil and its creditors; the confrontation may in that case spread to other major debtors.

Within Brazil, the task of controlling inflation after the abrupt demise of the Cruzado Plan is a daunting one; the fact that the reputations of President Sarney and his finance minister until early 1987, Dilson Funaro, were closely tied to the Cruzado Plan and have thus been seriously dented complicates the outlook, especially at a time of vocal political debate within the constitutional assembly. The fact that the assembly is dominated by Ulisses Guimaraes, the veteran politician with declared presidential ambitions, makes tough economic decisions, already difficult to make, even more complicated. The return of a period of high inflation combined with unclear policies would make a prolonged confrontation with creditor banks a distinct possibility. A lengthy confrontation between Brazil and the banks, most of which insist on an IMF-sponsored program of needed economic measures, stretching over the duration of 1987, would have a substantial probability of spreading to other countries. Such an event would accelerate the advent of some interest relief formulae, to be addressed in Chapter 8.

The Economics of Debt: Commodity Depression Again

In a period of stagnating export earnings caused by the decline of commodity prices as well as declining inflows of external capital, the only way in which the Latin American debtors as a group have been able to pay interest on their external debt has been by keeping their economies depressed and thus building up large trade surpluses made possible by a low level of imports. To some degree Brazil has been an exception: about half its exports are manufactures and, despite protectionist hitches and a weak U.S. economy after 1984, have grown enough to offset commodity price weakness; while on the payments side, the decline in oil prices has given the Brazilian economy the equivalent of a significant capital inflow which has offset the dearth of actual capital inflows.[12] However, countries that have gained only from the lower cost of oil imports, such as Chile or the Central American nations, have not benefited significantly because of the parallel stagnation of export earnings. In Latin America most countries have paid for the interest on their debt by cutting back imports and economic growth.

Thus, since 1982 Latin America has been able to transfer out resources, mostly interest on the external debt, because of its trade surplus. The problem of meeting interest payments, the crux of debt servicing, eased considerably after 1984 as international interest rates fell gradually to relatively modest nominal levels by mid-1986. However, total exports have, by and large, stagnated—volume increased, but commodity prices fell—and interest payments have been met only because of the low level of imports. This is especially striking after oil imports are netted out (table 7-1); low imports are directly tied to stagnant domestic economic activity.

As economies expand, imports, and hence the need for external capital, will also expand. This happens either directly or because governments attempt to finance the gap through inflation, and hence by increasing demand for imports, as happened in Brazil toward the end of 1986 and early 1987, and in Peru in 1986 and 1987. Efficient investment can reduce the degree to which imports and external capital are needed, but it cannot dispense with the need for more imports and external capital as investment and economic activity recover. Nevertheless, some observers, enamored of the large trade surpluses of most Latin American countries, continue to believe, against most historical evidence, that the debtors can continue to live with negligible import growth.

In simplified form, from 1982 to 1986 the trade surplus of the debtors paid for the interest on the external debt, given the dearth of capital inflows. Table 7-1 gives an idea of how the inflow of outside capital fell drastically after 1982. Overall, there was a negative "resource transfer" from the debtors to the creditors, if interest paid out is deducted from capital inflows. Even if the concept of a resource transfer can be debated, since there is no intrinsic reason why the bulk of interest payments should be covered by capital inflows, two points remain clear: first, without capital inflows, imports, and hence economies in the process of development, cannot grow; and second, as shown in table 7-2, the bulk of the interest on the external debt was owed to banks, and beginning in 1983, the net flow of funds between banks and debtor countries was negative. It is true that interest payments to banks have gradually receded since 1982, except for the run-up in interest payments in 1984; nevertheless, given the dearth of capital inflows, the only way in which countries have been able to finance debt

Table 7-1 The Resource Transfer from Latin America and the Caribbean (in Billions of Current Dollars)

	1980	1981	1982	1983	1984	1985	Prelim. 1986
Trade balance[a]	−3.2	−5.5	5.5	28.4	37.0	32.7	16.3
Exports, f.o.b.	93.6	99.7	90.3	91.9	101.6	96.3	79.0
Index of export volumes[b]	100.0	106.0	103.5	112.0	121.5	121.5	111.7
Imports, f.o.b.	96.8	105.1	84.8	63.6	64.6	63.6	62.7
Of which non-oil imports	71.0	78.4	61.1	43.6	45.2	46.8	50.0
Net services	−28.1	−38.7	−49.1	−41.1	−41.7	−40.1	−35.8
Of which interest on debt and profit remittances	−26.0	−37.7	−45.5	−40.5	−44.1	−41.3	−35.6
Net capital inflows: transfers, net foreign investment, and net borrowing (incl. short-term)	49.3	69.4	37.7	15.0	18.5	11.1	6.2
Implied resource transfer[c] (minus sign = net outward transfer)	23.3	31.7	−7.8	−25.5	−25.6	−30.2	−29.4

Sources: Derived by the author from International Monetary Fund, World Economic Outlook (April 1987), tables A36 and A41, and International Financial Statistics.

Note: Cuba is excluded from this analysis.

[a]IMF data on trade differ from UN data shown in table 5-2 but are used here for consistency with capital account data. Trends under both definitions are similar.

[b]The Inter-American Development Bank, in its annual Economic and Social Progress in Latin America, shows higher export volumes, totaling a 33 percent increase in the period 1980–85 (1986, p. 13).

[c]Net services less net capital inflows. See text for reservations about this definition.

Table 7-2   Estimated Flow of Funds between Commercial Bank Lenders
and Latin American and Caribbean Debtors (in Billions of Dollars)

	1980	1981	1982	1983	1984	1985
1. Net new loans from banks	34.0	33.7	17.6	11.0	2.0	−3.0[a]
2. Less estimated interest paid to banks	24.5	35.2	33.4	26.0	29.5	23.7
3. Plus estimated interest paid by banks on official reserves of debtors	5.0	5.7	3.3	2.5	4.1	2.7
4. Net transfer from banks (1 − 2 + 3)	14.5	4.2	−12.5	−12.5	−24.2	−18.0

Sources: Bank loans and interest on debt: author's estimates, based on basic data from Bank for International Settlements. See table 4-3 for explanatory note on BIS data, which underestimate total exposures. For 1985, because of the addition of banks from Spain and Finland, the BIS shows a small increase in net lending. However, if the series is adjusted to cover the same country definition throughout, based on individual country data (see, for example, quarterly *Country Exposure Lending Survey* [Washington, D.C.: Federal Financial Institutions Examination Council]), the estimate above for 1985 would be more accurate, after counting exchange rate movements. Interest on reserves: derived by author from IMF, *International Financial Statistics.*
[a]BIS data after adjustment for changes in statistical coverage.

service has been to keep their economies depressed so as to cut back imports.

Thus, a key economic question is whether the pattern of large trade surpluses after 1982 is consistent with the renewal of economic growth. The answer is definitely no. But that does not mean that capital inflows on the scale of the breakneck borrowing of 1979–81 are needed. More efficient growth requires, in time, the elimination of capital flight as well as less state expenditure on subsidies and Pharaonic "investments." This type of growth will require less investment—and hence fewer imports—than the inefficient growth of the late 1970s and early 1980s.

It is thus conceivable to imagine growth restarting with only modest capital inflows, as long as there is excess productive capacity so that capital goods imports can be kept down. For a while, growth could then be consistent with continued trade surpluses. However, the idea that growth can resume with large trade surpluses for a long period—other than the surpluses corresponding to windfalls such as lower oil prices—and hence continuing capital exports to the outside, seems overly optimistic, as does the idea of "exporting one's way out of debt" without taking into account the capital needed to do so.[13]

The prospect that more efficient growth can be achieved with less external capital than in the past, and that for a few years growth can be achieved even if Latin America transfers more resources out than it receives, depends on what happens inside economies and internationally. Domestically, the need for new capital can be limited as long as there is plenty of spare capacity in industry and in basic public services such as electricity, water, and transport. Once capacity limits are approached, as they were in Brazil in 1986, one way or another capital needs will increase and imports will go up.

The other domestic issue is whether savings can increase so that the dependence on imported savings or capital can decline. With governments having to devote such a large part of net income to paying interest, public sector savings have plummeted in most of Latin America since 1980; even if the inflation-indexing component of interest is excluded, public savings are low, and private savings have fallen.[14] A huge effort will be needed to rebuild savings, but this may be difficult, at least for a time, because private savings are likely to be under attack as governments raise taxes in order to cut back budget deficits. Thus, there is likely to be a contradiction between raising taxes, the kind of measure often advocated in stabilization programs, and at the same time increasing private savings. The solution, which is extremely difficult in a period of recession, may be to shrink public expenditure or find new sources of external capital.

The international outlook is as difficult as the domestic one. Two issues in particular stand out: the real burden of debt at a time of depressed commodity prices, and the market prospects for Latin American and other developing country exports in light of protectionism and slow growth in the industrialized countries.

As noted earlier, the real burden of debt ought to be measured against the prices that affect the income of debtors. As any farmer in Kansas or any oilman in Houston knows, it is not the general U.S. cost of living that affects the real cost burden of his debt; rather, it is the price of what he sells. The same is true for the debtors in Latin America and elsewhere. Despite major cyclical downturns in 1974 and 1978, commodity prices important to developing countries held up during most of the 1970s.[15] Although external debt did rise by about one-third as a proportion of exports, rising commodity prices did help to hold back the growth of the real debt burden. In the 1980s, however, commodity prices declined, and this has sharply pushed up the real value of the debt by about 80 percent, in terms of the prices of the commodities which Latin American debtors export (table 7-3). Even though nominal international interest rates have declined steeply since

Table 7-3 Value of the Outstanding External Debt of Latin America and the Caribbean, Adjusted for the Purchasing Power of Exports (in Billions of Dollars)

	1980	1981	1982	1983	1984	1985	1986	Est. 1987
Total outstanding external debt, end-year	242	294	331	355	374	384	395	421
Adjusted for prices in industrial countries	242	270	287	301	302	298	299	310
Index of wholesale prices in industrial countries, 1980 = 100	100	109	115	118	124	129	132	136
Adjusted for purchasing power of Latin American exports	242	288	338	390	411	452	506	507
Index of unit values, L.A. exports, 1980 = 100	100	102	98	91	91	85	78	83

Source: IMF, *World Economic Outlook* (April 1987). These data differ slightly from those derived by the author in table 2-5. Deflators used by author from IMF, *International Financial Statistics.*

Note: Other possible deflators can be selected, but they are not available on the same consistent basis as the above IMF data.

1982, and especially after 1984, the real interest burden continues to be onerous because the value of Latin American exports has gone down.[16] From 1980 to 1985, the volume of Latin American exports rose at least 20 percent, but the value stayed constant.

As noted earlier, this squeeze is the result of an extremely slow-growing world economy in the 1980s, combined with the demise, at least for the time being, of world inflation. Another long-term force at work is the gradual loss of worldwide economic momentum after the reconstruction of Europe and Japan after World War II. In addition, two other neglected factors are important. First, the depression in most of the high-debt countries which began in 1982 is, at the margin, sharply reducing worldwide growth of raw material consumption. For example, Latin American steel consumption in 1985 was at the same level as eight years earlier, contributing to the stagnation of the world iron ore and steel market. Second, the inevitable pressure upon debtors to boost commodity production has flooded world supply in already weak and glutted markets. This is especially so in metals and grains. What happens in Chile or Argentina can therefore have a major impact on producers in Arizona or Kansas.

Given such a setting, one has to ask whether the debt containment strategy is actually worsening the problems, not only of the debtors, but of other producers around the world as well. It is not enough to project, as many observers have done, that *when* world growth resumes and commodity prices rise again, *then* the real debt burden will decline. The point is that such an eventuality is unlikely, at least for several years, not only because of slow world economic growth, but probably also because of the debt strategy itself. Economic life with a high debt burden and with limited prospects for its reduction becomes very difficult in such a setting.

To export one's way out of debt seems a logical remedy, and the objective is by itself sound. But to put it into practice is difficult, since success would itself create major problems, especially greater protectionism in the industrialized countries and an even larger glut of commodities. As seen in Chapter 6, there is a possible contradiction between expanding commodity exports in order to reduce the debt burden and actually reducing it; increasing the oversupply of certain commodities may in fact *increase* the real debt burden as the purchasing power of exports declines.

The logical alternative is to industrialize for export, as Brazil has done, as well as to develop services such as tourism and processing. Implementation, however, requires two major adjustments: lower overall wage costs in manufacturing (not necessarily lower take-home pay, but the rationalization of nonwage benefits as well as the elimination of restrictions on dismissals and labor mobility) and a sharp reduction in the role of the government in private business. The changes would be difficult under any circumstances, but they are particularly difficult for small economies where the concessionary style of private enterprise has been entrenched since Spanish colonial days. Thus, the message of the U.S. government in the Baker Initiative for debtors to open up their economies is generally correct; in the short term, however, debtors do not feel they have the necessary foreign exchange reserves, and more important, in the long term, it contradicts the way societies are organized and the way business has been done for centuries.

The growing protectionism in industrialized countries is well documented.[17] Exaggerated changes in the relationship between the U.S. dollar and other major currencies have intensified protectionism. Two arguments are used to minimize the likely impact of protectionism upon Latin American exports: (1) the East Asians have succeeded despite protectionism; and (2) the share of manufactured exports from developing countries is very small in the final demand for manufactures in industrialized countries. It is true that the East Asian exporters have succeeded, but this is partly because of extremely low costs, which enabled them to replace maturing exports from Japan; if they had relied simply on adding new supply, and if this supply had competed against similar products from Latin America, protectionist pressures would have been much stronger. Indeed, that happened in textiles, shoes, and specialty steels, all of which face import quotas in the United States and in which Latin American exporters, especially from Brazil, are important suppliers. Where newly industrializing countries from Asia and Latin America have competed head-to-head in the same markets, protectionism has often resulted. This is especially so for products in which developing country suppliers have a very important share of the markets in industrialized countries. In the Western industrialized countries, for example, according to Bela Balassa, 74 percent of clothing imports in 1981 came from developing countries, and those imports accounted for 14 percent of consumption.[18]

In a sense, therefore, the success of East Asia is partly possible because of the lack of challenge from Latin America. Where such a challenge has existed, especially in crowded markets such as textile and specialty steels, protectionism has inevitably resulted. This does not mean that Latin American economies should not attempt to reorient their economies more toward exports of manufactures and services than in the past, but it does mean that the job of reorientation is complex. Heavy fixed investments should be minimized; they reduce the flexibility needed for industries to shift from one product to another as saturated markets create pressures for protection. This new type of more flexible industrialization, of the type that has been followed by a number of export industries in Taiwan and Hong Kong, for example, is difficult in a setting where governments have had a large role in industry and where tax and monetary policies, through subsidies, encourage capital-intensive investment. Of course, this is the case in much of Latin America. A wholesale, extremely difficult, but nonetheless healthy change in policies is needed.

Thus, escape from the stranglehold of debt requires a complex web of policies, both within the economies of the debtors and internationally. The difficulty of putting into place such policies cannot be underestimated. If slow growth persists in the industrialized countries in the remainder of the 1980s, not only will demand and prices for commodities remain stagnant, but the markets for new industrial exports from developing countries will become increasingly protected. For debtors, policy reform, desirable as it is, strikes at old patterns of behavior and social organization; while a shortage of capital inflows in effect slowly mandates reform, there is always the hope that the shortage of resources will end and that the days of easy money will return. The role of the international agencies is important here; if they give the impression that easy money will follow vague commitments for reform, this will tend to assure that reform does not take place. More than anything else, rapid world economic growth would help to dilute the debt problem. That prospect, however, is at present most unlikely. There is thus no panacea, but only a variety of palliatives for the debt problem.

Panaceas and Palliatives

Many interesting proposals have been made in recent years to "solve" the debt problem. If the frequency of proposals is any guide to the urgency with which the problem has been viewed, then it reached its peak in 1983 and 1984 and has since then gradually been seen to recede. Because payment of interest is the crucial issue, the most vocal proposals tended to coincide with the run-up in interest rates in 1984; as nominal interest rates fell sharply after 1984, so did the degree of attention paid to proposals to reduce the debtors' interest burden. The events in Brazil in early 1987 are bound to lead to new proposals and the dusting off of old ones.

The debtors' problem, as has been argued throughout this book, is not simply one of indebtedness. Although it reflects the large size and unsuitable conditions of debt, it is also a development problem. Its significance results from the pattern of development followed by the debtors and the substantial changes in international economic conditions since the late 1970s. Most of the debt proposals pay little attention to this general context; they tend to look at part of the problem and are presented as a solution rather than as part of a comprehensive program.

There have been hardly any proposals from the governments of creditor nations, since their strategy has been, by and large, the one followed since 1982. The initiative of U.S. Secretary of the Treasury James Baker in Seoul in October 1985 was not so much a specific plan as an expression of concern. The Baker Initiative was nevertheless important in signaling a change in the attitude of the U.S. government. Governments of the industrialized countries seemed more willing than in the past to get involved in helping the debtors and creditors out of their problems.

Proposals from the debtor governments have also been scarce, with the exception of that of Peruvian President García. As already mentioned, the Cartagena Group has avoided specific proposals; its periodic resolutions have always called for limiting debt service to the ability to pay without disturbing development prospects and for interest rates below commercial ones—both rather vague concepts. The Sistema Económico Latinoamericano (SELA),[19] the regional organization that includes Cuba, made a specific interest reduction proposal at its conference in Quito, in January 1984. The proposal would have cut the interest paid to creditor banks in half, a huge reduction that was supposed to be made up as export earnings increased in later years.

The most prolific proponents of schemes to reduce debt service have been financial observers and bankers in the industrialized countries. The schemes range from radical to conservative, but all of them face two major obstacles: who pays, and how to limit benefits to certain debtors—the most indebted developing countries—and not to extend them to other hard-pressed debtors of all kinds around the world, the so-called moral hazard problem. A further problem with some schemes is that they would have relatively little impact on the debtors. For example, at the prevailing international interest rates in 1986, if the World Bank or taxpayers in the industrialized countries guaranteed the debt—as several observers have directly or indirectly suggested—the reduction in the interest bill for the debtors would be modest or, under certain assumptions, insignificant.

Felix Rohatyn, the well-known New York investment banker, has suggested a general debt consolidation under the aegis of a new financial institution, guaranteed by various industrialized country governments. This institution would acquire the loans of commercial banks to developing countries in exchange for long-term bonds of its own, and it would pay a rate of interest similar to what the industrialized country guarantors would pay.[20] A related proposal is that of Peter Kenen of Princeton, under which an International Debt Discount Corporation would buy up the debt at a 10 percent discount.[21] Percy Mistry, a World Bank economist, in 1987 suggested that governments of the industrialized countries fund, within the World Bank, a Debt Restructuring Facility: the Facility would borrow in the capital markets, using capital of one-tenth of its obligations, and would use the proceeds to buy up Third World debt from banks at a discount, passing on to the debtors the benefit of the discount. The substantial discount would help the debtors, but it would also mean that the capital needed would be far larger than envisaged. Richard Weinert, another U.S. investment banker, had earlier proposed a World Bank-based facility to buy up a proportion of the loans. In all these cases, the lending banks would obviously face large losses. Minos Zombanakis, former vice-chairman of First Boston, has suggested a rather more complex and perhaps more feasible arrangement under which the IMF would guarantee the later maturities of rescheduled loans in exchange for acceptance by the bank creditors of a long-term U.S. or comparable government paper rate on the whole loan.[22]

George Soros, the well-known New York-based fund manager, has proposed a sophisticated system under which an International Lending Agency would collect the loans and assume a new flow of lending, but the agency would clearly require the guarantee of industrialized country governments in order to get off the ground.[23] In March 1987, with the support of their government, the Japanese banks set up a similar central agency to collect debts, but it was not clear whether the new agency would have authority to provide new loans: rather than a vehicle to overcome past problems with future action, the agency seemed to be a way to maximize tax benefits for the creation of reserves under the Japanese tax system. As of mid-1987, the system was used only for Japanese bank loans to Mexico. Lord Harold Lever, in his book with Christopher Huhne on the debt crisis, has proposed a two-pronged scheme: lending banks would agree to gradually write off and forgive debt so as to reduce the burden of interest upon debtors, while at the same time, under IMF guidance, they would make new lending available with the guarantee of the export credit agencies.[24] As with several of the other proposals, this one would require a major—and most unlikely—political commitment by creditor governments to guarantee the banks' new loans and, by implication, to be heavily involved in their past loans. A less ambitious proposal, which should elicit interest if and when interest rates rise, is that of the co-chairman of Deutsche Bank, Alfred Herrhausen, to create an interest Compensatory Fund that would stabilize interest rates at, say, 7 percent and would use contributions from banks, multilateral development banks, and also governments during periods when market rates were above the fixed rate.[25]

All of these proposals, and many other similar ones, require major political commitments from industrialized countries. These commitments do not exist at present and are unlikely to materialize in the next few years, especially in the case of proposals to use government funds to repurchase debt: why, it should be asked, should the taxpayer provide funds to buy up something that can already be traded in the market? The fiscal cost is likely to be considerably higher than if banks incur the losses directly—reducing their profits and hence their taxes— by creating reserves and selling off loans at market prices.

Since the mid-1980s so far are a period of relatively moderate nominal international interest rates combined with a positive yield curve (higher interest rates for longer maturities) because of expectations about future inflation, proposals to change the debt from a renewable short-term rate basis (LIBOR plus a spread) to a long-term fixed rate basis, such as the U.S. government pays on its bonded debt, may well in practice leave debt service unchanged or increase it in the immediate future. Taking late 1986 as a point of reference, the calculation is simple. Assume that the six-month LIBOR rate is 6 percent, the equivalent maturity U.S. Treasury bill rate 5.8 percent, and the thirty-year Treasury bond rate 7.5 percent. Thus, on average, Latin American debtors paid in late 1986 slightly more than 7 percent (LIBOR plus approximately 1.25 percent). If the debt were guaranteed by industrialized country governments, the U.S. portion would cost the debtors the base rate (5.8 or 7.5 percent, depending on whether a short- or long-term base rate is used) plus a premium, since guaranteed paper is slightly more costly than straight government debt (probably another 0.25 percent). In addition, there would have to be a guarantee fee to be charged by the debt refinancing agency of the type proposed above. A guarantee fee of less than 1 percent seems unlikely, given the risk. The total cost to the debtor would thus end up at about 7 percent (i.e., no significant reduction in cost, if the Treasury bill is taken as the base) or 8.75 percent (if the long-term fixed rate is the base), the latter representing a significant increase in cost for the short-term future. Taking end-1987 interest rates changes the calculation upward but not the basic conclusion, except that a U.S. Treasury bill base would in this case represent a net saving.

Because there is no overriding cost advantage, the major Latin American debtors have not been interested in these types of market-based interest relief schemes. They make sense only as insurance against future interest rate increases—if bank debt is converted into long-term fixed rate debt—but in the present environment there is no cost saving and hence a difficult job of selling the plan to parliaments and to the public.[26] For the governments of the industrialized countries, the political difficulties of providing guarantees on such a scale, even if only on a contingent basis, are insurmountable and, in any case, are not worth the battle for a negligible economic result.

For these reasons, the only interest relief schemes that are attractive to the debtors require a significant subsidy from some source. The cost of such a plan, however, is likely to be politically unmanageable for those called upon to provide the subsidy. Economist John Makin has suggested that in the case of Mexico, banks should defer part of the debt, which, in effect, would then be assumed by creditor governments.[27] The indirect result would be that governments would become by far the largest shareholders in a number of large international banks. Writing off debt, as some have suggested, does nothing for the debtors: the full amount is owed; only its recovery is in doubt. Senator Bill Bradley, Democrat from New Jersey, has suggested a straightforward system: banks would forgive 3 percent of the principal for three years, and for the same period would take 3 percent off the interest rate charged.[28] The cost to someone—either banks or their governments or both—would be very high. A 3 percent annual interest subsidy would amount to almost $9 billion for the whole of Latin America, or six times the cash contribution of the U.S. government since 1945 to the capital of the World Bank.[29]

Difficult as it is to find a practical and economical form of interest relief, the subject is nevertheless very important. In 1984, as interest rates flared for a few months, even Chairman Paul Volcker of the Federal Reserve, a strong enemy of any subsidy scheme, did not rule out the possibility of interest concessions, although it was a subject to be discussed between borrowers and their creditors.[30] At the same time, Anthony Solomon, then president of the Federal Reserve Bank of New York, had organized a closed-door seminar of various experts where he floated the idea of an interest rate cap, in which the portion of the interest above the agreed limit would be capitalized.[31] Had interest rates continued to rise and the idea been developed, it is possible that some of the regulatory constraints might have been eliminated; but the bankers at the meeting were against the idea, and it remained a dead letter, despite much general support for special interest rate concessions from such authorities as Henry Wallich, a long-time governor of the Federal Reserve, and Arthur Burns, its former chairman. An IMF Interest Compensatory Facility was another idea discussed at the time, but the cost would have been high, and there is little likelihood that industrialized country governments would have supported such a scheme.

Markets provide examples that could be adapted to design some practical form of relief against future increases in interest rates. First, when interest rates are declining, there is an opportunity for countries in a reasonably strong position to renegotiate part of their debt from a floating to a fixed-rate basis in order to limit the damage from possible future increases in interest rates. There would be a cost, of course, in order to provide an incentive for the lending banks to switch to a mortgage loan type of interest arrangement. Brazil in 1986 might have been able to convert part of its debt to a fixed rate base, but it did not seize the idea at the time. The interest rate swap market, where borrowers and lenders convert obligations from fixed to floating rates and vice versa, provides the practical basis for a conversion, although it could not begin to cope with the size of the transactions in cases such as Brazil. Major bilateral negotiation would thus be necessary, but the opportunity should not be missed.

Second, capital markets have in recent years pioneered ways in which capital can be raised with part of the interest deferred until the fortunes of the debtor improve. An unusual example of this, in the sense that it depended in part on a U.S. government guarantee, was that of Chrysler. Creditor banks and the U.S. government were given warrants to buy Chrysler stock at what turned out to be bargain prices in view of the turnaround engineered by Lee Iacocca. In 1986 oil companies were able to raise cheap money in the U.S. capital market by giving bondholders a share of future oil price increases.[32] At the time, these borrowers were able to get funds at a cost *below* the U.S. Treasury, in exchange, of course, for a considerable premium if oil prices rose above a certain level ($25 per barrel) within a certain period (five years). Such an example could be studied in the case of Mexico or other oil producers, but was, unfortunately, ignored in the discussions of Mexico with the banks in mid-1986. Chile in 1987 saved some interest payments by converting to an annual as opposed to a more normal semiannual payment basis, but such a change is marginal over a longer period.

Another market example is that of the adjustable-rate mortgage (ARM) market in the United States, which had about $250 billion in outstanding mortgages at the end of 1985. Under an ARM loan, the borrower has the option of a below-market interest rate for an initial period (one to five years). If actual rates turn out to be higher during the initial period, the debit balance is capitalized and the higher level of payments is applied to the next interest period, thus avoiding a possibly unmanageable final payment, as would be the case in a simple capitalization scheme.

The point about these market arrangements is not that they can be applied directly to the cases of developing country debtors; rather, it is that they provide interesting real-life examples in which debt burdens are shifted to future periods when debtors should be better able to handle them. Because it is market-based, interest deferral or relief along these lines has a greater chance of eliciting favorable accounting and regulatory treatment than untested arrangements. So far the regulatory hurdle has been the main stumbling block for most types of interest relief. Designing arrangements that take this obstacle into account ought to be a high priority.

Interest relief is only one possible component of plans that will meet the needs of debtors. The circumstances of each debtor are different, so that any general formula would be very difficult to design and apply. For instance, as of 1986, an oil-related sliding interest rate formula could apply to part of the debt of Mexico, Venezuela, or Ecuador, while for Brazil, the need is additional capital and protection against future interest rate increases.

Obviously, to the extent that nominal interest rates fall, the justification for interest relief fades. It would be hard to place the major burden of relief on interest rates when the problem, as of the mid-1980s, has more to do with the depressed level of commodity prices. Admittedly, depressed prices for the debtors' export products magnify the real burden of debt, but there is very little that can be done about commodity depression. The only palliative is a comprehensive program for each country, comprising policy reform at home, new inflows of private and public capital, restructuring of external debts in order to minimize the possible impact of future increases in interest rates, and, in a number of cases, market-inspired forms of interest relief. Second best? Indeed. There are no panaceas, only partial remedies.

Market Systems

Despite publicity in the financial press, market mechanisms designed to deal with the debt problem are imperfect and unlikely to have any large-scale impact on the balances of payments of the debtors, although they could be important for lenders in a position to absorb the losses of getting out.

Since 1983 a market has slowly developed in which banks have sold off or traded their participation in loans to various countries. The main suppliers to this market have been so-called regional U.S. banks and smaller banks in Europe, both of them with limited exposure and therefore able to absorb the losses from selling loans at prices well below their nominal value. Such write-downs, however, would be very costly if not catastrophic for the large international banks, so that they have not been suppliers of saleable loans, although some, especially Citibank and Bankers Trust, have traded others' loans actively. While automatic write-downs of remaining loans are not required in the United States when part of the loan exposure in a country is sold, the reality is that the remaining loan exposure, whether written down or not, weakens the stock price of exposed banks and hence their ability to raise additional capital.

From 1983 to mid-1986, perhaps $20 billion of Latin American and other troubled international loans have changed hands or been sold off, mostly to other banks and to a few international institutional investors. European banks have been the principal sellers. The main attraction for the buyers has been the very high discounts below book values, which thus permit a very substantial interest premium to be earned. That is also the main source of difficulty for the market. Because discounts are unpredictable, very few participants have been willing to maintain significant inventories of saleable merchandise, a basic requirement for a functioning market. The Latin American loan market is thus a little like a supermarket with bare shelves: buyers put in their order, since they believe that there may be some supply, but they do not know what will be available or when. Each transaction is carefully negotiated and there are no standard prices, so that the quotations discussed in the press are usually only indicative (table 7-4).

This limited secondary market is unlikely to change as long as the

Table 7-4   Illustrative Price Ranges on Latin American and Other High Debtor Loans Bought and Sold in New York (Percentages of Nominal Value of 100 Percent)

	March 1986	*June 1987*
Argentina	63–67	55–56
Brazil	74–76	62–63
Chile	65–68	68–69
Colombia	80–83	84–86
Ecuador	68–70	51–52
Mexico	59–63	58–59
Poland	48–53	43–46[a]
Venezuela	76–81	71–72
Yugoslavia	78–81	77–81[a]

Sources: Shearson Lehman Brothers loan transactions group and Latin American Information Services, Inc.
[a]April 1987.

outlook for the debtors remains unpredictable. In any case, the development of a market in loans does not affect the obligations of the debtors. The investor who bought a Mexican loan in mid-1986 at 60 cents per dollar fully intended to get interest and principal on the 100-cent piece of paper owed by the debtor. Otherwise he would not have bought the paper. The result for the buyer in mid-1986 was an effective interest rate of 12 percent for what is basically a short-term piece of paper, instead of the 7 percent the debtor is actually paying on the nominal value. The market is thus saying that the effective interest rate on such debts ought to be 5 or 6 percent over LIBOR instead of the approximately 1 percent debtors are paying. The large discount is the main reason why debtors such as Brazil and Mexico have been cool toward the development of a secondary loan market. A market write-down of their obligations would simply raise the interest rate and maintain the interest payments due. The debtors would gain little or nothing from it. Large banks have also been unenthusiastic because loan sales by smaller banks reduce the number of participants in new involuntary loans. Furthermore, there is a temporary but complex problem in identifying who the ultimate holders of the debt are.

Since the process of selling loans in the secondary market is slow and uncertain, a number of New York and London investment bankers have studied ways to sell off troubled Third World loan exposures as securities. Such sales are likely in 1988, especially on behalf of banks with strong capital positions with middle-sized exposures: the banks would be able to take the losses arising from the sale, while their exposures are too large to be sold on a piecemeal basis in the secondary loan market. It is clear, however, that the discounts on the loans in order to make their sale as securities possible would have to be large, and doubtless larger than in the loan market. The reason is that securities require liquidity; liquidity cannot be obtained without a broad spectrum of international institutional investors, who will require a substantial return for the risk. As an illustration, at a discount of at least 55 to 60 percent on the loans of the larger Latin American government debtors, it is conceivable that fairly large issues might be placed, although the total market appetite for such paper remains highly uncertain. Again, however, these securities could only be placed if there was at least some chance of recapturing the full value of the debt: if "securitization" is seen simply as an avenue toward debt forgiveness, the discounts would have to be even larger for the market in the securities to clear.

Thus, while capital markets have been inventive in dealing with the complex problems faced by marginal borrowers, especially in the United States, those techniques are not easily adapted to the problems of the large debtors in Latin America. The basic reason for this is the volatility in the prospects of these debtors. For example, the leading dealer and underwriter of below investment-grade paper, Drexel Burnham Lambert, announced in August 1985 that it was forming a new unit to adapt its pioneering "junk bond" techniques to Latin America. Two years later a deal had yet to be made. While there is no doubt that an oil-linked issue could probably be done for Mexico or Venezuela, for example, there is also no doubt that the cost would be so high that borrowers would not be much interested; nor would the existing bank lenders accept it at a time when they are being forced to cut back the interest margins to the debtors.

Another much-publicized development has been the conversion of debt into equity, a technique pioneered in Chile and also being used in Mexico. The available data show that the amounts are small, totaling perhaps $3 to $4 billion altogether up to the end of 1987. A domestic or foreign group of investors or a corporation buys up the debt of a country at a discount; they then present these claims to the central bank of the country, which buys the debt back in local currency at full value or at a slight discount, giving the investors a substantial exchange subsidy. The cost to the country is the exchange subsidy and the ensuing monetary expansion (although foreign investment not linked to imports generally creates some monetary expansion), which may lead to higher domestic interest rates—and thus may create a disincentive to investment—as the central bank tries to offset the increase in the money supply. The benefit is an increase in the amount of investment above what would have taken place otherwise, although this effect is quite difficult to quantify, especially when some of the investment would have taken place anyway.

Before 1982 foreign direct investment into Latin America was running at an annual rate of about $5 to $6 billion; after 1982 the flow was halved, and much of what remains has been in the form of reinvested earnings in Brazil and Mexico. By 1986 net direct foreign investment was down to almost nothing. There is thus at least a theoretical potential of increasing the volume of foreign direct investment above what it would have been through debt-equity swaps to perhaps $7 to $8 billion annually in the immediate years ahead (i.e., the previous peak level of inflows adjusted for inflation). The sum would, by itself, seem large, but even so it would have only a small impact on the debt burden of the major debtor countries. Moreover, whether such sums can be reached in the next few years is debatable, especially if the swaps are to be channeled to new investment rather than to acquisitions: the levels of investment from abroad in the late seventies, years of rapid economic growth in Latin America, were driven by buoyant incomes and high effective demand. Those are the factors that will revive investment, both foreign and domestic. Debt-equity swaps, properly constructed, can be one useful instrument to revive dragging investment from abroad, but the concept is not a panacea for the debt problem.[33]

Another mechanism that received publicity, especially in 1984 and 1985, was barter and countertrade, a long-established form of import payment by countries in the Eastern Bloc, which are usually short of foreign exchange. Peru proposed to its bank creditors in the fall of 1986 a scheme to pay for part of the interest due in products. Although the volume of debt repayment via trade has undoubtedly increased since 1982, such schemes face a basic difficulty, which often makes them costly for the debtor. The problem is that creditors, if willing at all, will only take standard products (e.g., copper concentrate of certain characteristics) that can be placed in commodity markets, which the debtors are in just as good a position to access on their own. Debtors therefore prefer to exchange nontraditional, nonstandard products (e.g., shirts and shoes) for debt, a trade that most banks cannot carry out, except at huge discounts. The result is that a majority of potential countertrade and barter negotiations do not lead to concrete transactions.[34]

In the end, the fundamentals count. Foreign and domestic investment will recover as prospects for economies improve. There may be a case for subsidizing the initial impetus through existing debt-equity swap mechanisms, but the eventual costs could turn out to be significant, since swaps put governments back in the business of subsidizing private enterprise. Most importantly, the case that clearly exists for equity investment as opposed to debt should not be oversold. Clearly, the debtors would not today face the same burdens if they had relied more on market-related foreign investment and less on large-scale public sector borrowing. There is thus a strong case for encouraging equity investment, both foreign and domestic, mostly because of economic efficiency arguments. The merit of foreign risk capital is that if it is unsuccessful, there is no burden on the exchange system; however, a foreign exchange obligation arises if the investment is successful and generates profits and dividends.[35]

Interlude: Mexico and Brazil Again

In June 1986, almost four years after its first debt crisis, Mexico faced another crisis. In the wake of collapsing oil prices, which began to be felt by March, Mexican foreign exchange reserves were said to be down to $4 or $4.5 billion, or the equivalent of only three months of payments for imports and interest. Although major international banks were much better prepared than in 1982 to deal with the problem, some were still badly exposed. For the already weakened Bank of America, in particular, with an exposure to Mexico of about $3 billion, or about half its primary capital, a Mexican default would have been catastrophic and would surely have required U.S. government intervention.

Fear of a Mexican default, which had been a topic of conversation since 1985, intensified in early June 1986 when U.S. officials and bankers heard that the rumor of a moratorium plan might have substance. The plan had been prepared at the request of President de la Madrid and then-Finance Minister Jesus Silva Herzog; it consisted of depositing the peso equivalent of external debt service in an escrow account in Mexico until reserves had increased enough to warrant a resumption of interest payments in foreign exchange. Although it was never entirely clear whether the payment-in-pesos plan was designed mainly as a negotiating tool with the banks, Paul Volcker rushed to Mexico on June 9 to dissuade the Mexicans and work out a rescue package. The key to the rescue package was in effect a financial fig leaf, a more lenient definition of the Mexican public sector deficit—to exclude the inflation component of the interest on the public domestic debt[36]—so that the IMF could accept what was in effect a large but inevitable public sector deficit of about 10 to 12 percent of GNP and proceed with a standby arrangement. This, in turn, opened the door to renewed bank lending plus a package of U.S. government loans, as in 1982. The commercial banks were quite reluctant to come up with the $6 billion needed, especially at low interest spreads: only strong pressure from the Federal Reserve made the loan possible. Within Mexico, the basic inflationary pressures from the budget remained, casting doubt on whether the IMF program would succeed in lowering inflation, which was still running at an annual rate of 100 percent in 1987 and increasing rapidly.

In the middle of negotiations, Silva Herzog resigned on June 17, and the creditor banks were thrown into disarray. His forceful and attractive personality, which, up to 1986, clearly made him a front runner for the presidency in 1988, combined with a longstanding dispute over public spending with Carlos Salinas, the then-expansionist budget minister, led to Silva Herzog's resignation.

The Mexican rescue package totaled $12 billion over two years, including $1.7 billion from the IMF, $1.9 billion of new loans from the World Bank (part of which would have been made anyway), only $400 million from the Inter-American Development Bank, $1.5 billion in debt relief from the Paris Club, U.S. food import credits of $800 million, and most important, $6 billion from commercial banks. In addition, $1.7 billion of contingent loans from commercial banks were to be provided; of this total, $1.2 billion would be allocated to support investment expenditures in case of an unforeseen reduction in public revenues, and $500 million, partially guaranteed by the World Bank, would be linked to economic performance during the first quarter of 1987. As of early 1987, Angel Gurría, the Mexican director of public credit, was still globe-trotting to line up banks to complete the $6 billion bank loan, but it was signed in the end, in May 1987.

By the end of August, a bridge loan of $1.6 billion had been committed in principle under the steadying hand of a new finance minister, Gustavo Petricioli, another long-time Banco de Mexico official. Roughly one-third of the total came from the U.S. Treasury and the Federal Reserve, another third from European governments and Japan plus Brazil, Colombia, and—incredibly—Uruguay,[37] and the remainder from fifty commercial banks. The negotiations with the banks were quite tense and dragged on into September. The banks, supported by Chairman Volcker, rejected outright a partial interest capitalization scheme proposed by Mexico.

Under the IMF standby arrangement, Mexico agreed to some fiscal tightening over the period. In addition, outside the IMF standby, declarations were made to sell off state enterprises and open up the economy further to imports (which Mexico was in no position to afford) and to foreign investment.

The Mexican arrangement, an emergency combination of debt relief and new funds, does not overcome the fundamental problem: how can a country with an external debt five to six times its annual exports make ends meet, let alone develop? With its major exports depressed— total merchandise exports fell from $24 billion in 1984 to $22 billion in 1985, and about $16 billion in 1986—it was in any case unlikely that the Mexican economy could grow. The 1986–87 stabilization program was, nevertheless, a relative success, except on the inflation front. Because of a rapid real rate of devaluation, non-oil exports again started to grow rapidly (by 41 percent in 1986), and the strong growth continued in 1987, since a favorable exchange rate and commercial policies were maintained; devaluation plus high domestic interest rates stimulated a reflow of flight capital, at an annual rate of probably $3 billion in 1986 and the first nine months of 1987, until the stock market crash of October 1987. Still, according to preliminary estimates, real GDP decreased by 3.8 percent in 1986. The economic decline reflected the drop in oil revenues that represented close to 6.7 percent of GDP, the amortization of external debt by the private sector, and the effect of the grave deterioration of the terms of trade.

Unlike the crisis in Mexico in 1986, the Brazilian moratorium, which began in February 1987, was not provoked by external circumstances. Basically, the freezing of prices by decree in March 1986, the essence of the Cruzado Plan, should have been accompanied by fiscal restraint and wage moderation so as to eliminate inflationary expectations. It was not. The one-time general wage bonus granted on March 1, 1986, together with continued subsidies to state enterprises—the source of a major part of the public sector deficits in much of Latin America— fueled inflationary expectations in the midst of a massive consumer boom. With prices frozen, shortages began to appear and, in time, significant pressures to postpone export shipments and accelerate import payments—the traditional and inevitable results of an increasingly overvalued exchange rate. As the trade surplus shrank and external payments accelerated, foreign exchange reserves collapsed and Brazil had no choice, given the uncertainty of whether it could conserve the remaining foreign exchange reserves, but to postpone payments on all the interest due banks other than on short-term debt. The postponement was thus clearly intended as a tactic to force the banks into new lending or interest relief, or both.

As described earlier, the outcome of the Brazilian moratorium was uncertain as of mid-1987. The longer the moratorium continues, the more likely it is to spill over into other debtor countries. The creditor banks thus have a strong interest in reaching an accommodation with Brazil, even if it is at the cost of sacrificing their insistence upon an IMF-sponsored program and replacing it with a watered-down set of austerity measures, perhaps under World Bank sponsorship. Brazil also has an interest in reaching an accommodation with the banks, since the alternative, hard as it is to visualize, may well be a period of costly internal financial disorder.

By July, the new finance minister, Luiz Carlos Bresser Pereira, a São Paulo businessman and retailing executive, had put together a program of moderate fiscal austerity and price adjustments. At the same time, he had worked out a more conciliatory approach to the IMF. For the new chief of the Fund, Michel Camdessus, a former governor of the Banque de France and head of the French Treasury, a man sympathetic to developing countries from his days as secretary of the Paris Club of export credit agencies, Brazil is likely to be the first major test. Just as his predecessor five years earlier was instrumental in coaxing the banks into involuntary lending, so for Camdessus the test may be to prod regulators to help banks establish a selective system of capitalization of interest. For Brazil, which owed about $4.5 billion in interest arrears at the end of 1987 at a time of low foreign exchange reserves, the only alternative to capitalization would be new credits, unlikely to be forthcoming in such amounts in 1988.

Conclusion

Since 1982, governments of the creditor banks as well as of the debtors have pondered whether debt relief was a feasible or even a desirable alternative. More than anything else, because of the political difficulties involved, they evidently decided that it was not. It is possible that time will show that they were correct. However, in an era of depressed commodity prices, that prospect is more unlikely. The further negative consequences of the debt problem, including a far larger involvement of the leading industrial country governments, could well continue for at least several years.

The payment of interest is the key issue for debtors and creditors alike. Although the burden of interest eased in 1985–86, it still remained high in real commodity-adjusted terms for most debtors. As a result of the decline in commodity prices, by 1986 the average commodity-adjusted debt-to-export ratio in Latin America was four-and-a-half to one and was considerably higher in Mexico as well as in the Philippines. To service such a debt with very limited capital inflows is possible only with low imports and hence low economic growth.

The experiences of Mexico in 1984 and of Brazil in 1986, when faster economic growth quickly led to increase in imports, strongly suggest that it cannot be otherwise. Furthermore, although it is too early to provide conclusive evidence, it appears that the strategy of "exporting one's way out of debt" exacerbates the world commodity problem and thus leaves the debtors with only slow or no growth in new export income. The evolution of the commodity boomlet of mid-1987 will signal whether the commodity depression of the mid-1980s is over, although that prospect is unlikely.

In such a setting, the only way to break out of the vicious circle may be a sharp reduction, at least for a time, in the interest burden. The biggest obstacle to interest relief is not institutional or economic; there are many market precedents, and the mechanical aspects of particular schemes are not the central issue. The obstacle is primarily political. Until the governments of the industrialized countries convince themselves that the political cost is bearable, they will prevent their banking systems from considering relief except at unreasonably high cost to the bank shareholders and, ultimately, to taxpayers. This is especially so in the case of the United States, whose financial authorities have played the leading role in convincing others to follow the debt crisis containment strategy.

In his initiative in Seoul in October 1985, Secretary of the Treasury Baker recognized that growth was urgently needed. However, the proposal supposed a reasonably dynamic world economy and sufficient capital inflows into the debtor countries, neither of which materialized. The contingency of interest relief was not considered (see Appendix 1 for the text of Secretary Baker's speech of October 1985). The Baker Initiative approach was used in coping with the Mexican crisis of 1986, when more lending was thrown at the problem in order to cover part of the interest payments. The approach was not unsuccessful, but two of the major underlying problems of the Mexican economy continue—inflation and low economic growth.

Another possible U.S. approach was embodied in the proposal of Senator Bradley in July 1986 to provide some debt forgiveness and substantial interest relief for three years. While the proposal was not fully fleshed out,[38] it had the significant merit of recognizing the link between depression in the debtor countries and world trade, particularly in the form of lost markets for U.S. exports. The loan forgiveness aspect of the proposal could be very costly for lenders but would, in fact, provide little real interest relief, the crucial aspect for the debtors. Here, significant regulatory changes would have to be introduced, especially in the United States, if interest relief is to be a real option for the banks: under present U.S. regulatory practice, deferral of interest can be accepted by banks without necessarily reserving against the loans in question, as long as the loans are deemed "collectible" by the regulators, a standard that is hard to meet in the case of countries that have rescheduled their principal repayments.

Baker's stress on reform and creating the conditions for capital inflows, especially investment inflows, and Bradley's espousal of interest relief in order to get trade and growth moving again both emphasize important aspects of working out the debt problem. While measurable progress has been made on creating the preliminary conditions for financial stability, no progress has been made beyond that. Thus, uncertainty and the prospect of further stagflation continue to cloud the economic prospects of the debtors and, to a more limited degree, their creditors and the economies of their creditors.

(8)

Outlook and Prescription:
Is Development Dead?

————————

The debt problem will eventually fade, both for the debtors and for the creditors. The question is how long the process will take and what is the price of delay. On optimistic assumptions, it would take at least until the early 1990s for the majority of the highly indebted countries of Latin America plus the Philippines to make up the income declines of the 1980s. The 1980s thus represent a "lost decade." However, the process of catching up involves a mixture of policies and events—such as reform within the debtor countries, the renewal of capital inflows, and a more buoyant international economy—which would be beneficial not only to the debtor countries themselves but also to the world economy at large.

A key test for the shape of the future will be when and how Brazil, today the largest single debtor to the international banking system, resumes interest payments to the banks on a steady basis. To do so will require compromises both on the part of Brazil, which would have to accept some sort of international monitoring of its economic program, a difficult concession in political terms, and of the banks, which would probably have to settle for something less than full IMF monitoring and a formula on the interest deferred in 1987, both significant precedent-setting concessions. If no agreement is obtained within a reasonable period, far-reaching consequences would likely ensue: other debtors would be tempted to default, and lenders would face major write-offs. Even though the major international banks have greatly strengthened their capital and lessened their exposure to troubled debtors since 1982 (see Chap. 5), such write-offs could be costly indeed to some banks.

Banks will obviously want to avoid such an outcome, but so should debtors. Some observers have argued that banks would soon return for more lending, even if they had to write off a major part of their loans.[1] That is most unlikely to be the case after a major systemic shock. After the large-scale defaults in the 1930s to international bondholders by most major Latin American countries, the flow of international credit to them, other than official funds, did not resume on a significant scale until the late 1950s and early 1960s, well after the disruptions of the depression and World War II.

It is therefore important to have a workable international debt strategy. The debt containment strategy designed in 1982 had already run its course by the spring of 1987. In May Citicorp, the largest international bank lender, both worldwide and in Latin America, announced the creation of an additional reserve of $3 billion—equivalent to almost one-quarter of its loans to troubled developing country debtors, the bulk of them in Latin America. Other major banks promptly followed its example. These actions confirmed the end of the containment strategy, or at least its first stage. Thus far, no new scheme has taken its place. The question now is not only whether the big debtors in Latin America will pay but also where the money will come from.

No long-term solution to the debt question is possible without a mixture of economic reform in the debtor countries and additional fresh capital, both of which are needed to revive economic growth. Both were important in the original debt strategy, but neither was forthcoming in sufficient amounts despite considerable differences among debtor countries.

The coming year is likely to be one of major decisions as several debtor countries face fundamental choices. There is not only the question of Brazil. Mexico has to decide on the shape of basic national policies once the successor to President Miguel de la Madrid, former budget minister Carlos Salinas, takes office at the end of 1988. Argentina has to decide whether it should further intensify its effort at economic reform after two years of slow economic growth associated with the struggle against inflation and a growing budget deficit, or whether it will have to suspend debt service payments. Only Colombia, of the major Latin American countries, has avoided a debt-induced crisis, because of past conservative borrowing policies, although the economic depression of its neighbors affected it also.

A scenario of a gradual economic "Albanianization," or autarky, is conceivable if more highly indebted countries pursue unilateral defaults, as have a few of the smaller debtors in Latin America and elsewhere. Following this path means that their economies would gradually become disconnected from the international financial system;

credit would be difficult if not impossible to obtain, and foreign trade would be reduced to bare essentials. While the largest debtors—including Brazil, Mexico, Argentina, Venezuela, and the Philippines—are unlikely to take this step, the creditors' financial systems are put under increasing strain with each default, manageable perhaps, but very costly in terms of eventual write-offs of loans and ensuing higher domestic credit costs.

Leadership in the industrialized world is now essential to convince governments and legislatures to support viable new plans and innovative financing mechanisms. Otherwise an opportunity will be lost, and the damage to world trade, employment, and international finance could be large and lasting.

The Banks after Citicorp

The basic objective of the containment strategy begun in 1982 was for the major debtor countries, notably the larger economies of Latin America plus the Philippines, to continue interest payments on their external debts (see Chap. 4). The means, in the absence of major capital inflows, was to build up large trade surpluses. These surpluses were achieved by tough austerity measures, including those recommended by the International Monetary Fund, which led to domestic economic recession for the debtors (see Chaps. 5 and 6). The average decline in real personal incomes in Latin America exceeded 10 percent between 1982 and 1986. However, there was no follow-up to the initial success of the containment operation; no new sources of capital flows were developed, export earnings of the debtors stagnated despite significant increases in volume, and sustained growth has not been rekindled.

The weakness of commodity prices, in the wake of a slow-growing world economy, is a key reason the debt problem lingers on. Although the volume of exports from Latin America has gone up by about one-quarter since the early 1980s, their value is lower. As of mid-1987, Latin America owed about $400 billion abroad, against exports of about $80 billion in 1986 and perhaps $90 billion in 1987; before the crisis broke in 1982, Latin America owed $325 billion against average exports in 1981–82 of $94 billion. The relative debt burden has thus not declined, as a number of observers and officials had hoped in 1982 that it would. Only the sharp decline in international interest rates until 1986 has made the debt service manageable. As the upturn in interest rates in the first half of 1987 has once again made clear, however, the debtors remain highly vulnerable to these increases, since virtually the whole of their debt to commercial banks—three-quarters of the total—is at floating interest rates.

Involuntary lending by the banks, lending carried out in order to finance part of the debtors' interest payments, was an important element of the original strategy. This lending declined sharply after 1984, however, as market obstacles increased. In most European countries, for example, each dollar of new lending to troubled debtors requires a mandatory reserve against possible future losses of part or all of the amount lent—a prescription that obviously constrains lending. In the United States, bank stockholders have reacted negatively to significant lending exposure to Latin America. Smaller banks, and even some larger ones, have therefore done what they could to sell off their loans, if they could do so without too much of a loss. The volume of such sales has been relatively small—perhaps $8 billion worldwide in 1986 out of total international commercial bank exposure in Latin America of about $300 billion (including trade finance), of which about one-third belongs to U.S. banks. The trend toward selling loans accelerated in 1987, with increasing discounts on the loans as the result.

In sum, up to 1987 the commercial bank lenders gained time by making some involuntary loans to the debtors to avoid the danger of default, but also by gradually building up reserves against doubtful loans. They also increased their capital from other sources and in general strengthened their balance sheets against another rainy day (see Chap. 5). That day came on February 20, 1987, when Brazil, the largest debtor among the developing countries, announced that it would not pay interest, for an indeterminate period, on the approximately $68 billion medium-term debt that it owed to international commercial banks, including $8 billion owed to Brazilian banks. (Short-term debt was excluded.)

The reaction of the banks was, predictably, one of great concern. The fifteen largest U.S. banks placed the loans on a nonaccrual basis, so that the income from interest cannot be counted unless actually received. Most major banks registered some first-quarter weakness in net income. Even though a special effort was made to establish a dialogue with Brazil, the collapse of Brazilian foreign exchange reserves made any rapid resolution difficult. At the end of 1987, Brazil was negotiating an interim agreement to pay up the interest arrears of 1987 to the banks, about $4.5 billion. While some sort of agreement was probable on this score, as described in the Postscript, debt servicing problems were likely to continue into 1988, a presidential election year. Clearly, Brazil is likely to continue to use further rounds of debt negotiations to seek substantially easier terms for its bank debt.

Concern over the poor results of the debt strategy became officially visible in April 1987 at the regular semiannual meeting of the International Monetary Fund's Interim Committee, a kind of ministerial superboard. U.S. Treasury Secretary James A. Baker called on the commercial banks to develop a "menu of alternative new money options."

In retrospect, the fact that some lending continued, even though on a declining scale, was the real financial news. In the spring of 1987, after lengthy negotiations, commercial banks agreed to two large new loan packages—$6 billion to Mexico and $1.9 billion to Argentina, plus contingent credits in case outside economic conditions were to deteriorate. But the large reserve increases by all major commercial banks in the United States and several in Britain and Canada, coming on top of previous gradual increases, in effect put a damper on further larger general-purpose commercial bank loans to sustain the balance of payments of the debtors.

After Citicorp announced its $3 billion one-time increase in reserves against loans to troubled developing country borrowers on May 19, Chase Manhattan followed with $1.6 billion, BankAmerica and Chemical with $1.1 billion each, and Manufacturers Hanover with $1.7 billion. These large increases in reserves, which led to the largest losses by large banks since the depression[2]—even if they will in time be partially offset by a lower future tax liability—signaled the banks' decision to take losses in earnings now rather than at a possible future date when actual write-offs of loans might be necessary. Many observers saw the actions as an overdue acknowledgment that the service on the loans is unlikely to be paid in full.

These actions may well improve the banks' negotiating strength with the debtors—Citicorp's stock price rose the day after its announcement—but they do not change the basic ingredients of the debt question. The banks' actions do, however, clarify a number of changes that were already under way. The most important one is the greatly increased reluctance on the part of the banks to provide general-purpose balance-of-payments loans to troubled debtors.

From the point of view of the debtors, life is no easier. The banks' actions do not change their obligation. Lenders may be more willing to consider interest concessions, but not necessarily. For the debtors, the increasing difficulties in obtaining new loans from commercial banks may well revive the temptation to default on interest payments, especially if fresh capital cannot be obtained from other sources. It is too early to judge whether large syndicated loans such as the recent ones for Mexico and Argentina can still be put together, but it is clear that an increasing number of banks with small and medium exposures will not want to participate.

Several results are likely to emerge, with implications both for the debtors and for the creditor banks. First, each bank will increasingly look individually at its options, which will make it difficult to hold together the large syndicates of the past. The administration of debt will thus become more complex. Banks will henceforth look to the so-called menu of new options, perhaps including a limited amount of new lending by the largest banks, but also conversions of debt to equity, notes, or securities, and so-called exit bonds for lenders that do not want to provide new money.[3] The menu offers increased flexibility but does not go to the heart of the problem of providing fresh capital. That is a problem, as far as the banks are concerned, of security for their loans combined with returns that are attractive internationally. If the banks become equity holders, with the attendant risks, they will in time expect proportionately higher returns, difficult as they may be to obtain.

Second, credit decisions are likely to become even more concentrated in the larger banks, which in any case already hold the bulk of the debt. Therefore, the large banks will be in a position to be firmer in their negotiating positions, both because of their increased reserves and because of the reduced number of players. The reserves may make it possible for U.S. banks to look into new formulas such as partial capitalizations of interest, which would have been too costly for them to contemplate before they created the additional reserves.

The banks' action could thus lead to more complex negotiations, but with the possibility—as yet untested—of greater flexibility. On balance, most of the options on the menu that may be available to banks are likely to result in less fresh money from them than in recent years, when it was already difficult to obtain. It is quite unlikely that the larger banks would be willing to shoulder the additional burden caused by the refusal of smaller lenders to participate.

Creating substantial reserves strengthens the banks' financial position, but the banks still need to shore up their own finances further. The reserve levels now reached by major U.S. banks, including the reserves gradually created in the past, are in the range of 25 to 30 percent of the total loans to most of the major debtors and are comparable to those achieved over several years by most European banks. The publicity given to the one-time action of major U.S. banks, however, is leading many of the smaller U.S. banks to sell their loan positions. As more banks seek to sell their loans, the supply of loans in the secondary market is increasing, but the demand is not. This means that the average prices of the loans have fallen in recent months, and banks are forced to take a greater loss when they sell. For example, a typical portfolio of loans to the governments and public sector agencies of the four largest Latin American debtors—Brazil, Mexico, Argentina, and Venezuela—had an approximate market value in mid-July 1987 of 58 cents on the dollar, admittedly in a rather thin market, compared to 66 cents in February. Brazil's partial suspension of interest payments was the trigger that eventually led to the decline in value.

Another key issue for the banks is whether public recognition of problem loans helps their ability to raise capital for themselves in the most economical way, namely through equity. Most banks need to strengthen the quality of their capital. The creation of reserves has shifted capital out of bank shareholders' equity and put it into reserves. While undoubtedly a prudent move, the resulting decline in common equity now has to be made up in the case of most large banks, especially since the reserves built up in recent months would decline if loans are written off, which occurs if they are sold at a discount. Selling additional bank stock is undoubtedly a challenge; only a few of the largest banks, including Citicorp, have succeeded in recent years. In August 1987, Citicorp announced a $1 billion stock offering, a record for a U.S. bank: not all major banks may be able to follow this example. Greater regulatory flexibility may therefore be needed in the definition of what constitutes useful capital in order for the banks to strengthen their finances in the next couple of years.

In the end, of course, what matters is the quality of the banks' assets. To the extent that the quality of the loans to troubled debtors in Latin America improves, the banks' position improves. But to improve the quality of these loans, what is needed is a more buoyant international economy, further progress toward economic reform within the debtor countries, and, especially important at present, new sources of funds.

The International Economic Setting

Unfortunately, among the governments of creditor banks, there appears to be little sense of urgency. The June 1987 economic summit of Western and Japanese leaders in Venice brought no new or clearcut ideas on the subject. Yet the Baker Initiative of October 1985 clearly needs to be refurbished; its success was dependent on renewed economic growth, which has not occurred. It also called for $29 billion in lending over three years to the fifteen most indebted developing countries, $20 billion from commercial banks and $9 billion additional net lending from multinational financial institutions over and above their projected net lending of about \$3 to \$4 billion annually. These levels have not been met, and the banks' recent action makes it clear that they will not meet these targets any time soon.

The international environment for the recovery of the major developing country debtors, most of them in Latin America, is uncertain. The growth of the world economy in the period 1983–86, spurred by an unusual combination of forces—namely a Keynesian fiscal stimulus in the United States, financed to a substantial degree by foreign savings—was already running out of steam by the end of 1985. The imbalance between relatively fast U.S. and Japanese growth and virtual recession in Europe was evening out, mostly because of a gradual cyclical downturn in the United States. The most rapidly growing major economy in Europe, that of Spain, grew at about 3 percent annually in 1985 and 1986; most European economies are suffering from unusually high, persistent levels of unemployment. The likely prospect is for only modest growth in world trade and continuation of generally high unemployment worldwide.

Such an international setting means that there is little reason to expect a sustained commodity boom for quite some time, short of a war—the usual precursor of commodity booms—or a sustained revival of inflation. Commodity-producing developing countries (including Latin American countries except Brazil, a major industrial exporter) rely on commodities for about 80 percent of their exports. The decade of the 1980s could turn out to be that of the slowest economic growth since the 1930s (table 8-1). The combination of sluggish growth worldwide, lagging purchasing power of commodity exports, and the high burden of servicing the interest on external debt spells a sobering and perhaps bleak outlook for commodity exporters in general, and for the highly indebted among the developing countries in particular.

The depression in most of Latin America not only bodes ill for the political prospects of the new democracies in the area, but it has also cost the traditional suppliers of Latin America, especially the United States. For example, the United States exported about \$42 billion to Latin America in 1981, a record year, mostly in machinery and farm products. In the period 1984–86, these sales fell to about \$30 billion annually. Even moderate growth in Latin America, instead of depression, might have pushed those sales to perhaps \$50 billion today, making a measurable contribution to reducing the U.S. trade deficit and helping some of the distressed areas in the Midwest (see Chap. 7).

The restructuring of inefficient industries, needed in the advanced industrial economies as well as in the state sectors of many developing

Table 8-1   Comparison of Economic Growth and Exports (Average Annual Percentage Changes)

	1950–59	1960–69	1970–79	1980–86	1982–86
GNP growth					
OECD	6.0	5.1	3.2	2.2	2.5
Developing countries	6.0	5.6	4.9	2.7	2.8
Latin America	5.9	6.4	6.2	1.8	1.3
Terms of trade of developing countries					
Oil exporters	−0.5	1.5	4.0	−0.1	−11.2
Oil importers	5.0	0.5	−2.0	−1.6	−0.3
Merchandise export growth (in real terms)					
OECD	10.3	8.5	5.8	3.6	3.6
Developing countries	7.5	7.0	5.0	0.2	2.4
Latin America	5.6	3.1	3.5	1.8	1.1
Interest as percentage of annual merchandise exports (estimated)					
Latin America	5	8	18	40	45
Memorandum: net					
resource transfer[a]					
$ billion, annual average					−24.0

Sources: Derived by author from World Bank, *World Development Report,* various issues; International Monetary Fund, *World Economic Outlook,* various issues; plus author's estimates.

[a]See table 7-1.

countries to improve global economic prospects, is difficult for everyone. The prospects for shifting successfully into new ventures are made even worse by the fact that in the late twentieth century the natural tendency for maturing industrial products to behave increasingly as commodities has accelerated. The easy entry of new competitors—because of increasing access to technology and the large role of developing country governments in industry and mining—has created oversupply in products such as petrochemicals, copper, and steel, without effective incentives to correct the imbalance. Everyone loses: the old industries, which can no longer compete because of older equipment and high labor costs, and many new industries because of the high cost of amortizing expensive new plants and servicing the debt.

The free trade system is now threatened. It flourished after World War II partly because of bad memories of the 1930s. A key underpinning of free trade was that there were very few important participants in international trade in the two decades after the war. In the last fifteen years, several new and increasingly important players have emerged. While it is true that the recent decline of the U.S. dollar will, after a lag, reduce protectionist pressures in the United States, the underlying protectionist trend has long-term causes that are not easy to uproot.

In sum, the relatively upbeat and comfortable setting of the world economy has changed. This outlook need not spell doom for economies that have shown flexibility and adaptability, such as those of East Asia, but it is disturbing for countries and industries that are already in trouble.

Reform in the Debtor Countries

A new strategy is needed for the debt problem. It includes (1) economic reforms in debtor countries, (2) a new inflow of capital, and (3), if the first two are inadequate, viable formulas for partial and temporary interest deferral.

Two immediate issues loom on the horizon. First, letting the debtors rely on large trade surpluses and low capital inflows is unlikely to work. Trade surpluses are impermanent; either they will erode as domestic growth and demand for imports resume, or exports could decline if there is a weakening in the world economy. Second, the debtors remain highly vulnerable to increases in international dollar interest rates, as occurred on a massive scale in the period 1979–82 and to a lesser extent in 1984. Rates looked like they might be rising again in the spring of 1987. A rise in dollar interest rates, induced by the collapse of orderly exchange rates among key currencies, might by itself precipitate the default of both Mexico and Brazil.

Even with the lower interest rates prevailing in 1986, debtor countries were not able to rekindle significant economic growth (except for Brazil, where a price control-induced spending boom stimulated a short-lived growth spurt). Domestic product statistics, often quoted as evidence of some renewed growth, omit the negative effects of declining terms of trade on incomes. It is incomes that matter: their lack of dynamism is reflected in the stagnation of investment, which is the harbinger of growth prospects.

The lesson is clear: substantial capital inflows are needed. If there are no inflows, the international banking system will be dragged into unilateral or possibly negotiated interest relief.

As part of the debt strategy, it is imperative that the debtors put their own houses in order. The problems of domestic economic restructuring in developing economies, however, are at least as complex as those facing older industries in Europe and the United States. These problems are even more difficult in poor countries, which lack the resources to absorb change. In addition, while there is a significant private sector in virtually all the economies of Latin America, the Spanish colonial tradition of special concessions and monopolies for particular enterprises, as well as other protected economic privileges, dies hard. There is thus a big difference between what is apparently private business and truly effective entrepreneurship.

The debt crisis has made it clear that the past emphasis in Latin America on state enterprises was excessive. The public in the debtor countries correctly perceives that much of the excess external borrowing was due to the profligacy of state-run companies. In many Latin American countries, "privatization" has become a topic for lively debate. But actual progress in this direction has been slow, except in Mexico, where there has been a reprivatization of the industrial assets of the commercial banks taken over by the state in September 1982, and the subsequent sale of minority interests to the public in the state-owned commercial banks in February 1987.

Privatization is not easy. Moreover, enthusiasts sometimes forget that many developing countries lack the most elementary services, and that therefore the governments must assume some responsibility for providing them. If privatization is presented as a panacea, it could become just another fad, such as land reform in the early 1960s or regional economic integration a few years later.

The careful opening-up of economies is another obvious high priority. It would foster entrepreneurship, efficiency, and a greater long-term ability to compete with imports and to expand exports on a realistic competitive basis. It would also attract foreign investment and stimulate the reflow of flight capital. This is not disputed, and a number of countries, notably Chile, Colombia, and Mexico, have in recent years moved in this direction. The important point is that a more open trading system cannot be pursued unless there is a well-established and consistent policy of realistic exchange rates. The long-term success of Brazil from the mid-1960s onward in expanding its industrial exports almost as rapidly as have the East Asian countries is testimony to the benefits of a realistic exchange-rate policy over a long period. Without such a policy, liberalization of trade merely stimulates a speculative import binge. Such an event would imperil the already feeble debt-servicing capacity of the most highly indebted countries.

Reform is difficult in any setting, and in the Latin America of today there are many obstacles. The new democracies are naturally cautious about radical economic changes, especially if they are likely to cause higher unemployment in the short term, even though there would be longer-term gains. Just as there are political pressures against free trade in the United States, so there are in developing countries. In the latter, private sector leadership is often opposed to freer trade and is cozy with state enterprises, which are major buyers of their products and services. Trade unions, which cover the uppermost tier of the labor force, are naturally also the defenders of established patterns of economic behavior.

Nevertheless, there are strong forces for change: everywhere a younger generation of managers and entrepreneurs, in some countries strong national leaders who believe in change, the example of the outside world—always a powerful force in Latin America—and an increasingly young labor force (although high unemployment could well turn the latter into a volatile political element). The outlook for the region as a whole is uncertain, but there is likely to be significant progress in several countries, notably Mexico, Argentina, and in time Brazil.

Liberalization and privatization of economies are urgent priorities for the debtors. The task has to be undertaken in full awareness of the considerable historical, political, and economic obstacles. To the extent that their balance-of-payments constraints can be eased, at least partially, the chances of their new economic policies succeeding are greater. But the case for interest relief and for greater capital inflows cannot be made unless the governments of the debtor countries at the same time put their own houses in order. There is a growing consensus in many of these countries on the need to do so.

The Burden of Interest

For most Latin American countries, the burden of paying interest on their external debt is the major economic issue. There are several reasons for this: the shortage of external capital flows, which has made it necessary to maintain large trade surpluses and to keep imports and thus economic growth down; the lack of growth itself, combined with persistently high inflation in several major economies; the unfavorable outlook for traditional exports as well as the increasing threat of protectionism to more recent manufactured exports; and the very large fiscal burden of servicing the debt, which puts pressure on governments to raise taxes, most of which are indirect and thus inflationary in their initial application.

The interest owed to commercial banks by Latin American debtors in the period 1982–85, virtually all at variable rates, averaged slightly under $30 billion per year, of which about one-tenth was for trade-related credit. That sum was equivalent to about 30 percent of merchandise export earnings, and to it must be added another $10 billion or so for fixed-rate obligations to bondholders and official creditors. Altogether there has been a net cash outflow of about $24 billion annually from 1982 to 1986, as interest payments regularly exceeded the inflow from loans and investments. Aside from the internal pressures that could erode trade surpluses, there are international developments that might make it necessary for some debtors to delay interest payments: for instance, a slowdown in the world economy and a further drop in international commodity prices (which looks unlikely at present), an increase in international interest rates, always a possibility, and increasing protectionism.

The likelihood of declining bank lending to the debtor countries, unless it is offset by a sharp expansion in official lending, would mean that there would be little incentive for countries to keep up interest payments. Unless there can be rewards to the debtors in the form of continued funding, it would be especially important to have in place before the next crisis the main points of an acceptable scheme for facing the demand for deferral of part of the interest burden.

Deferral is not forgiveness, which would encourage profligacy. A relief scheme would not necessarily have to be put into effect, but its outline would at least have to be ready. It was difficult enough for hundreds of banks to defer principal repayments by debtors in 1982–86; it would be far more difficult and complicated to face the sudden deferral of interest—as happened in 1987 in Brazil—even if many banks were in a stronger capital position to face the ensuing losses.

Under normal accounting and banking regulatory practices, the nonpayment of interest after a time entails, first, charges against the bank's income (because of the need to create reserves against possible losses) and eventually, if nonpayment continues, writing off loans. Any formula that partially defers interest must therefore as a first step be sufficiently credible economically to be acceptable to the bank regulators. Otherwise it cannot be considered by the lenders. The focal point for thinking about any future arrangements thus has to be within the key three or four central banks in the financial capitals of the world, as well as a few of the very largest international commercial banks. There also needs to be an informal group among debtor nations that could speak for them and convince them to support a multilateral debt strategy. Unfortunately, so far there are no clear signs that such a process has begun.

Many types of deferral schemes have been proposed. None has managed the feat of combining in one package three key requirements: political viability in the creditor countries, financial viability for the major bank lenders, and real cash-flow relief for the debtors. The first requires that the need for deferral be generally accepted; regrettably, a crisis may be necessary to bring about this recognition. The second requirement is particularly difficult for the largest bank lenders, especially in the United States, because a very large proportion of their income still comes from interest on past loans to the troubled debtors.

As for the third requirement, a major deferral in interest payments might be possible if it were selective enough that not all debtors would want to participate. Otherwise, countries that have been cautious and have managed to avoid payment problems, such as Colombia, would be penalized for their past careful behavior. For the present, debtors seeking relief would have to agree to an IMF stabilization program and to economic reforms supported by lending from the multilateral development banks. Of course, debtors do not have to accept these conditions, but then creditors do not have to give temporary relief either. Thus, there must be some generally accepted standards of assistance that give lenders confidence in the future of borrowers. Otherwise there would be a legitimate fear that interest relief would be used to finance an expansion of public spending.

A plan to defer interest payments would work only if it were monitored by a widely trusted international agency and subject to reasonably objective standards of application. In this way deferral could be granted to those needing it, thus meeting the fear of creditors that all debtors would demand the same privileges. Those needing relief are the countries with a big debt service—both because of the size of the debt itself and because of depressed commodity export markets—and which are taking measures to put their financial houses in order. The various special facilities organized within the International Monetary Fund over the last twenty years provide a useful precedent in the design of a selective and controlled interest plan.

To illustrate: countries wishing to participate would have to show that interest on their external debt would absorb, for example, at least 30 percent of their current foreign exchange earnings for a period of at least one year. They would have to demonstrate that existing and foreseeable foreign exchange reserves would be inadequate to cover minimum payments of, say, four months of imports and interest payments. It is not necessary for an IMF "Interest Facility" to lend to countries, as has been proposed in the past, because that would simply expand short- and medium-term debt. Rather, the facility's role should be to provide credibility to a deferral or capitalization program, so that banks and bank regulatory agencies can have confidence that deferred interest would not simply fund fiscal profligacy. Plenty of examples exist in the market, such as the adjustable-rate mortgage system in the United States, under which some $300 billion of mortgage loans are outstanding.

Several more advanced interest relief schemes have been suggested. One variety would have an international public authority, under the aegis of the World Bank, offer to buy back debt at a discount and pass on the benefits to the debtors. The obligations would decline and so would the interest payments. For this scheme to function, substantial guarantees would be required from creditworthy industrial countries, given the likely fluctuation in the underlying debt service from the borrowing countries. Such guarantees would far exceed the contingent capital that the industrial countries have provided over forty years to the multilateral development banks. As a more economical and practical alternative, George Moore, former chairman of Citibank, has suggested a facility run by the IMF, which would borrow with the guarantee of the developing country debts themselves, suitably discounted.[4] This scheme would probably require the banks to sell debts at substantial discounts, at least initially, a step most large banks are understandably reluctant to take.

Such repurchase schemes have a substantial cost, which someone has to bear. In addition, they tend to reward debtors whose debt sells at the biggest discount and to penalize those whose economic performance maintains their debt at high values. Their implementation, an unlikely eventuality, would lead to a significant erosion of international financial discipline.

New Sources of Funds

No single scheme will solve the debt problem; there is no alternative, however, to some mix of reform of debtor economies and fresh capital. Unfortunately, time is running out, and progress on new action has been limited. Among the debtors, the siren song of default is gaining new supporters. There is the example of Peru, which practically ceased debt service in 1985 and 1986. After several years of depression Peru enjoyed strong economic growth in 1986, and this has encouraged admirers, both in the public and private sectors, who do not realize the one-shot nature of the growth spurt, which was encouraged by large salary increases made possible by the temporary buildup of foreign exchange reserves once most debt service was suspended.

Making the interest burden bearable is not enough; there must be more funds for development. If all the elements of the program—a stronger international economy, restructuring of domestic economies, and more capital inflows, plus a contingent policy on the interest burden—can come together, then there is a chance of improving an otherwise gloomy trend for debtors. Additional capital may be the hardest element to obtain.

The largest reservoir of funds that is in theory available to the debtor countries is the capital that left these countries during the period of high external borrowing. Much of the money borrowed from commercial banks fled because overvalued exchange rates, themselves made possible by the borrowing, made such flight attractive. The $80 to $100 billion or so that fled Latin America after 1974 (see Chap. 2), and which are undoubtedly worth a lot more today, are the single largest resource that could help the balance of payments of the region. But the money will not begin to return until there is a period of consistent and realistic economic policies accompanied by visible economic growth.

The repatriation of capital is a necessity; without it, foreign direct investment will be slow to revive from the low levels it has reached. The reason is simple: foreign corporations are understandably reluctant to put money into countries from which their local partners are withdrawing. In net terms, foreign direct investment into Latin America fell to almost nothing in 1986, and inflows in many cases resulted in bargain-hunting purchases rather than additions to productive capacity.

Special insurance arrangements, such as the Multilateral Investment Guarantee Agency approved two years ago by the World Bank, can help speed up the process of changing debt into equity; however, results will not be visible for some years, and they will not be forthcoming unless the overall economic outlook improves. Therefore foreign investment is likely to be a follower rather than a leader in recovery.

One idea that has gained many supporters among banks and Western governments is to exchange part of the debt for equity in enterprises and projects in the debtor countries. The basic concept is sound. The fixed burden of interest would be replaced by the more variable and usually lower outflow of dividends derived from production and profits; this would encourage private investment and the privatization of government enterprises.

In its actual application, however, the debt-equity swap idea has to be treated with care (see Chap. 7). It does not mean that new funds come into the debtor countries; it is only a substitution of one form of obligation for another. If Japanese investors were to shift their holdings of U.S. Treasury debt into U.S. real estate, as they are doing to some extent at present, the debtor position of the United States vis-à-vis Japan would not change, only the nature of the obligation would be altered: the same is true in the case of Latin America and the Philippines vis-à-vis their creditors. Admittedly, dividend outflows are likely to be less than interest payments, at least initially, but investors fully expect to be able to repatriate their equity and profits.

In order to encourage banks to sell off their debt at a loss and trade it for equity, the debtor countries (such as Chile and Mexico, the most active swappers so far, for a total of about $3.5 billion by mid-1987) have had to make up the loss by giving the investors the equivalent in local currency of full nominal value (or close to it) of the debt. This can lead to excessive domestic money expansion, the assignment of domestic credit for the single purpose of prepaying debt, higher domestic interest rates, and thus the choking-off of domestic investment. Properly managed, debt-equity swapping is one among several ways to make the debt burden more manageable. But it is no panacea.

How much can be realized in debt-equity swaps? In theory and at the outside limit, perhaps as much as was invested in Latin America from abroad in the boom years of the late 1970s, which at today's prices means perhaps $8 billion annually. But those were days of burgeoning investment opportunities due to rising incomes. The first task is therefore to provide the setting for economic growth.

Given the current limited outlook, and the fact that commercial banks are unlikely to provide new large general-purpose lending, real capital inflows must thus come initially from public sources. Such a statement no doubt will generate strong ideological reactions in an age of deregulation and privatization; yet, as the case of U.S. aid to Central America demonstrates, creditor governments are likely to put up large amounts of public funds in official aid to governments if they perceive an emergency.

The one source of capital flows with so far unrealized potential is multilateral development banks. They must begin to play a significantly larger role than in the past. Does this mean using U.S. and other taxpayers' money? Not necessarily. First, the multilateral development banks have relatively large cash reserves, particularly in the case of the World Bank, which could support larger disbursements in the short run, as was the case in 1987. Since 1984, the World Bank and the Inter-American Development Bank have increased their disbursements somewhat, but the overall sum remains relatively modest, a combined total of about $4 billion net of amortization in Latin America in the 1986–87 fiscal year, after falling in the previous year.

Second, the multilateral banks need capital increases to expand their long-term lending for development. But the capital they need to continue expanding their borrowing from private markets can be supplied almost entirely in the form of noncash guarantees by their shareholding governments. In its forty years of existence, the World Bank has never had to rely on the guarantees, or "callable capital," supplied by its shareholders and, like the Inter-American Development Bank and the Asian Development Bank, it has never faced major defaults.

Such callable capital, specifically the portion from highly creditworthy countries such as Japan, the Western European countries, Canada, and the United States, is what gives the multilateral development banks their financial clout, enabling them to borrow funds in the capital markets of the world at the lowest possible costs without the governments of the industrialized countries having to put up more than symbolic amounts of taxpayers' dollars.

Last, the institutions have the experience and knowledge necessary to play an effective role. Since the Baker Initiative of October 1985, which predicated a mix of reform plus official and commercial bank lending, the psychological responsibility for developing some sort of plan for new capital inflows has been laid squarely at the door of the World Bank. While much useful institutional innovation has taken place, the World Bank responded slowly in 1986 to Baker's expectations, partly because it was in a management transition. The major problem, however, concerned the discussion over the next increase in callable capital. Without some assurance from the United States, the World Bank has been reluctant to draw down its considerable cash reserves as it gears up lending. In addition, the bank has yet to define what role it can take in a new attack on the debt problem.

The next step in developing a new debt strategy is therefore to build up the capital (and hence the lending) of the multilateral development banks, which has in fact stagnated in recent years. This involves going to parliaments and congresses, always a thorny and politically difficult process. Given the demand from major emerging borrowers, in particular China, and the potential role of the bank in the major debtor countries, a doubling of its total capital—from the equivalent of $85 billion to at least $170 billion, mostly guarantees, not cash—would be needed. The decline of the U.S. dollar since 1985, because the bank has borrowed in stronger nondollar currencies, makes such an increase all the more pressing.[5] An equally difficult requirement will be improving the multilateral institutions' operational capacity, streamlining them so they can more effectively foster the economic reforms that debtor countries have to make if the original causes of the debt problem (especially bloated public sectors and state enterprises and the ensuing inflated fiscal deficits) are to be rooted out.

Barber Conable, an experienced former U.S. congressman who became head of the World Bank in 1986, has completed a major internal reorganization of the institution. Another reorganization is likely at the Inter-American Development Bank, where the United States, the largest provider of its capital, has felt that greater emphasis should be placed on economic reform within borrowing countries.[6]

Much of the debate about the roles of the World Bank and the Inter-American Development Bank has focused on the need for general-purpose sector loans, as opposed to specific project loans of the type that both institutions have traditionally made. Sector loans, which have existed in various guises for quite a few years, are used to encourage broad policy reforms. There is no doubt that such loans are indeed needed; however, policy problems that have been around for years will not disappear because of one or even two large loans. A long-term persistent effort should therefore be envisaged.

One idea that has frequently been mentioned in the United States is for Japan, today the largest capital exporter, to put some of its money into the debtors. While it is likely that Japan will take a special interest in the Philippines, both directly and through the Asian Development Bank, it is unlikely that it would take the leadership in an area such as Latin America, which is not a major trading partner, unless the United States takes the initiative first. Japan would undoubtedly act in part through international institutions; for this to become a practical possibility, Japan would have to be given a larger voice in the capital of these organizations and greater representation on their staffs, both difficult but not unattainable aims. The special loan collection company that Japanese banks organized in early 1987 for some of their Latin American loans was primarily the result of domestic tax considerations and does not so far represent a major international contribution to alleviating the debt problem.[7]

A reasonable estimate is that the Latin American countries would need approximately $20 billion per year in the next three or four years in net capital inflows in order to permit moderate growth.[8] Foreign investment, which declined to almost nothing in 1986, can be expected to recover to perhaps $4 to $6 billion annually with some help from debt-to-equity swaps. The key will be the repatriation of flight capital, which totaled about $3 billion in the case of Mexico in the last year. That represents a real inflow, as does lending from official multilateral institutions, which in net terms could reach $6 to $7 billion per year, if there were a major effort within those institutions and, internationally, at a political level. The multilateral development banks are thus crucial.

Official export credit agencies such as the U.S. Export-Import Bank, the Japan Export-Import Bank, and similar agencies in Europe are another important source that has been dormant since 1982. The Nakasone recycling plan announced in early 1987 promised untied lending by the Japan Export-Import Bank of up to $3 billion over several years. The part destined for Latin America is as yet unclear. An enhanced role on the part of export credit institutions could help commercial banks provide some of the balance, with some form of parallel or joint financing with official institutions. The overall outcome will be difficult to achieve, but it is plausible, as long as the political will is there on both the side of the debtors and especially that of the governments of the creditors.

How can the three parts of this new approach—economic reforms, interest policy, and new capital inflows—be put together? Unfortunately, there are several complicating factors. First, retrenchment will be the top priority of money-center banks for some time. Bank stock prices are at relatively depressed levels, preventing banks from adding to their capital in the most economical way, through the equity market.

Second, the banks have been the subject of conflicting signals from their regulators, especially in the United States. On the one hand, the Federal Reserve has been telling them to expand lending at concessional terms to those troubled countries that try to get their affairs in order. On the other, the Federal Reserve itself, as well as the Congress, the Securities and Exchange Commission, and the Comptroller of the Currency, has imposed disclosure and tighter capital requirements that make it very difficult for banks to ease troubled customers back to health, domestically or abroad. Additional regulatory demands are likely, including calls to expand bank capital. Capital is to a large degree a matter of providing financial confidence, and ways exist to make the expansion of capital more flexible.

Third, the industrialized countries face serious tasks at home. In Europe, stagnation and sick industries, and in the United States, the political difficulties of reducing the budget deficit, naturally receive priority attention. The debt crisis appears to be a more distant issue, even though it has undercut a major U.S. export market.

It is thus difficult for policymakers in the major creditor countries to focus on preventive action. The Baker Initiative fortunately broke this pattern. But it has faced serious difficulties: neither the economic growth nor the credit flows have materialized to the extent envisioned. The clear support of industrialized country governments for an expanded initiative is essential. The major debtors, especially Brazil and Mexico, could play a key role in tilting the balance in the direction of an internationally accepted set of initiatives. It is important to get clear agreement among the principal creditors and debtors—perhaps eight to ten key participants altogether—on a few basic working assumptions, without which the design of further action would not be possible. A large conference could not achieve the consensus of a small group. Among the basic precepts on which agreement is needed before any specific schemes can be broached are the following:

- The problems of the heavily indebted countries, most of which are very dependent on commodity exports, are long term and cannot be alleviated only through financial stabilization programs accompanied by modest lending from abroad.
- Most of the debtor governments have made major efforts to adjust to the new austerity, but external financial support for these efforts has been inadequate. The continuation of financial discipline and the beginning of fundamental economic reform require more external support in the next few years, especially from international public sources.
- This support can be obtained with minimum funds from taxpayers by substantially expanding the disbursement, lending, and, of course, the callable capital of the multilateral development banks.
- To the extent that capital inflows can be effectively stimulated, the need for large-scale interest relief will be less; but it is still desirable at least to plan some interest relief, in case major debtors cannot pay interest. Existing market mechanisms provide examples that might be helpful.

Agreement on these working assumptions will not by itself restore the high-debt countries to economic health—a plan has to be fleshed out in detail—but it would provide a ray of hope to alleviate the increasing strains of 1986 and 1987. Certainly, after the Baker Initiative of October 1985, there is no turning back. The only question is how to turn general proposals into concrete action and with all deliberate speed.

(9)

Postscript and Update: December 1987

As 1987 was coming to a close, it was clear that the Latin American debt question would still be present for several years to come. It was equally clear, however, that there is likely to be increasingly rapid evolution in the next year or two. This is because of growing fatigue by large bank creditors, whose stockholders and managements are tired of the uncertainty surrounding a large part of their international assets, and by debtors, whose electorates are tired of the combination of austerity, stagnation, and inflation, which they associate primarily with the debt problem. As in the past, different countries will be on center stage at different times, but the overall problem is likely to fester until the fundamentals change: a very high debt burden in relation to depressed export income, a political atmosphere not conducive to basic economic reforms among the debtors, and thus a setting that discourages the capital inflows essential to spark the revival of economic growth.

The dichotomy of views about the debt outlook for Latin America had been vividly illustrated in October 1987 at the annual Interamerican Dialogue, which includes moderate business and political leaders from the Americas. Leading U.S. bankers argued that the debt problem was on the wane and that the economic prospects for the major debtors were distinctly improving. The unanimous view of the Latin American group, including several conservative former ministers of finance, was

An abridged version of this postscript appeared as "Debt Update" in *The International Economy* 1, no. 2 (January 1988).

that the outlook is increasingly uncertain; short of substantial and immediate additional capital inflows—an unlikely eventuality—this group argued that more radical debt relief in 1988 was a virtual certainty.

On the same day that the Dialogue was discussing debt, the U.S. stock market came crashing down in the largest percentage fall ever recorded in one day. In the next few days, virtually all of the stock markets of the world were dragged down by widespread pessimism after several years, in most cases, of euphoria. In Mexico, where the small stock market had the fastest growth in the world in real terms in 1987, the ensuing crash, a total reduction in market capitalization of more than 60 percent, was caused in large measure by the flight of hot money, including Mexican capital that had been attracted back from abroad by high interest rates and a buoyant stock market. The lesson for Latin America is that the capital inflow needed to help overcome the debt crisis has to rest on solid foundations, namely upon a recovery in the demand for real investment.

Does the question matter, anyway? As of 1987, the evidence shows that it does. While the Latin American debt question has been a sideshow, although a well-publicized one in the international press, at least in comparison with the crises of the U.S. dollar and the U.S. stock market, it has been harmful to the U.S. economy and its major banks as well as to other industrial economies and their banking systems, and has been a disaster for most Latin American economies and their rapidly growing and highly urbanized populations. A reversal of the still-festering crisis is therefore highly desirable. A sample of facts:

- Latin American economies have on average barely grown since 1981; per capita income has fallen 10 percent overall between 1981 and 1987.
- The labor force in Latin America is growing at about 3 percent annually, or about 30 million in the last five years: a number at least equivalent to that has been added in the same period to the unemployed, because of economic stagnation.
- On conservative assumptions, the belt-tightening and import cuts in most of Latin America since 1982 have cost U.S. suppliers and farmers a total of at least $75 billion in lost exports between 1983 and 1987. There has been a similar loss to other suppliers around the world, including the Latin Americans themselves.
- For the biggest U.S. banks, as well as a few of their British and Canadian colleagues, 1987 will be remembered as a year of record losses since the onset of the depression, because of the general move to create large additional reserves against possible future losses on LDC debts, basically in Latin America plus the Philippines.

The statistics of the International Monetary Fund, in its *World Economic Outlook* of October 1987, certainly do not give a cheerful picture of the evolution of Latin American debt as a whole. No doubt countries differ greatly, but the regional totals still show rising debt, declining export earnings, and a growing debt service burden. The twin requisites of greater capital inflows from the outside and more meaningful reform at home are the only solid ways out of the prolonged problem. If either falters, a not unlikely eventuality, major unilateral or negotiated debt relief will become inevitable. In the end, however, only capital inflows and reform can rekindle sustained economic growth.

The Outlook for 1988

As in 1987, which was marked by reserve-taking by U.S. and other banks in the wake of Brazil's suspension in February of interest service on its $68 billion medium-term debt to international banks, so in 1988 there is likely to be change and evolution. This will come from two sources: the debtors themselves, and the increasing attempts by a growing number of banks to get rid of, or at least drastically reduce, their exposures, a process that can loosely be labeled "securitization."

The international economic outlook for 1988 is difficult to predict. On the one hand, the U.S. stock market crash and the related international exchange rate problems have created the view that an inevitable recession is at hand in the United States and in other industrial nations. On the other hand, the U.S. economy—as well as that of Japan—continues to be strong, partly due to the depreciation of the dollar, and domestic U.S. inflation continues to be low because of the import boom and continued weakness in the international oil market. For the debtor countries, which are largely—with the exception of Brazil—commodity exporters, what matters most is world inflation, the dominant influence on commodity prices. The period 1982–87 was a time of slow to moderate growth in the industrialized world, but with low and declining commodity prices, a combination that turned out to be calamitous for the debtors. Thus, a recession would by itself not necessarily be devastating, unless it was accompanied by further commodity price weakness. While that prospect appears unlikely, the obverse, namely world inflation and a sustained increase in commodity prices, which would be favorable to developing countries, looks equally unlikely. In any case, such a setting would include higher interest rates most unfavorable for debtors. The international economic setting is thus unlikely to provide much relief to the debtors.

In the debtors themselves, there was some improvement in 1987, especially in Mexico up to October, but large uncertainties remain. For

Table 9-1   The Latin American Debt Story: 64 Numbers from the IMF

	1980	1981	1982	1983	1984	1985	1986	Est. 1987
Real per capita GDP (% change)	3.7	-1.9	-3.2	-5.0	1.3	1.4	2.2	1.6
Inflation (CPI % change)	54	59	68	106	128	149	87	118
Terms of trade (% change)	7.2	-4.1	-5.4	-2.7	3.5	-1.9	-12.2	-2.5
Exports (f.o.b., $ bn.)	94	100	90	92	102	96	80	89
Imports (f.o.b., $ bn.)	97	105	85	64	65	63	64	70
External debt outstanding ($ bn. year-end)	231	288	333	344	362	371	391	421
Debt as % of exports of goods & services	183	210	273	292	277	299	361	362
Debt service ratio as % of exports of goods & services	34	42	51	45	42	43	51	55

Source: IMF, *World Economic Outlook*, October 1987, statistical appendix tables. These data differ in amount, but not trend, from those in the earlier chapters of the book, largely because of different definitions.

1988, as in the past, the key will be what happens in the three major debtor countries. In Argentina and Brazil, governments have recently been weakened. Even in Mexico, the stock market crash and increasing inflation sparked a crisis of confidence in the last two months of 1987, with a massive devaluation in December signaling that the healthy return of flight capital, which had taken place in 1986 and most of 1987, was being reversed. The devaluation, inevitable though it may have been, will further stoke the fires of inflation.

In Argentina, the Alfonsín government in October 1987 lost mid-term congressional elections to the Peronists, not a good omen for further austerity. Fiscal discipline had in any case increasingly been breached by large-scale central bank financing of public enterprise deficits, the key cause of inflation, while foreign exchange reserves had fallen to a bare minimum. Despite the election results, financial realities were leading the economic team at the end of 1987 to make a determined attempt in December to put into place tax increases and expenditure cuts to reduce the budget deficit. In Brazil, the financial picture was somewhat better, although the level of international reserves in November was just about equivalent to the accumulated interest arrears to the banks—about $4.5 billion. A tentative repayment plan for the arrears was worked out in early November. The committee of banks agreed in principle to finance two-thirds of the bill as long as Brazil paid the other third and reached an agreement with the IMF. The package needs to be confirmed by the seventy-five banks that would provide the $3 billion in new money, a process that is likely to be difficult, given the uncertainties about the economic program in Brazil. In mid-December, the resignation of Finance Minister Luiz Carlos Bresser Pereira, the architect of the transition from the Cruzado Plan, created uncertainty, but it seemed to dissipate under his successor.

A key factor in determining the feasibility of a stronger fiscal and anti-inflationary program will be the political strength of the Brazilian administration in 1988, after the mid-November vote in the constituent assembly that, at least for the time being, shortened President Sarney's term to four years ending in March 1989. The elections that would have to be called by the end of 1988 are hardly a propitious setting for tough fiscal medicine, although there are some who believe that the new finance minister will take tough fiscal action.

The short-term outlook in Argentina and Brazil is thus mixed. Combining political democracy with economic austerity is most difficult. A key economic problem, for all major debtors in the region, is the fiscal burden of service on the debt, both domestic and foreign, which probably absorbs close to one-quarter of central government outlays. That, plus public enterprise deficits, which in the short run can be cut only by raising controlled prices, means that inflation becomes almost inevitable: governments are damned if they take the measures—which immediately raise prices—and damned if they do not, as the fiscal deficit keeps pumping up demand because investors switch out of devaluing financial assets into spending.

In Mexico, international reserves of about $15 billion at the end of 1987 augur well for debt service in 1988, as long as oil prices do not fall too much, but inflation of about 130 percent annually rages on, threatening the progress made in 1986 and 1987. In Venezuela, the fourth largest debtor in the region, an increasing public sector deficit, partly in anticipation of the November 1988 elections, is driving inflation past 30 percent, well above its normally moderate range of about 15 percent. On the other hand, Chile, which was doing financially well, will now benefit from the strength of copper prices, which passed $1 per pound in November for the first time in five years. Colombia, which has not rescheduled, also looks strong, with solid economic growth and modest inflation.

Commodity prices, which affect three-quarters of Latin American exports from the outside, strengthened about 10 percent in 1987, adding to the fairly depressed level of exports in 1986 of $80 billion, still well below the 1981 level of $100 billion. Nevertheless, about two-thirds of the 1987 gain was eaten up by higher international interest rates during most of the year. It is noteworthy that 1987 export values are still below those of 1981, despite a 20 percent gain in volume.

This mixture of good and bad provided the backdrop to the Acapulco meeting of eight Latin American presidents in November. Differing viewpoints on specifics, ranging from the more orthodox views of Colombia and Mexico to radical Peru, nevertheless had one strong common denominator: debt fatigue. All presidents agreed to the general idea that the debtors must somehow benefit from the market discount on their debt to banks, although they did not suggest any action to follow up their idea. After five years, debt frustration also extends to the largest of the bank creditors, who do not see the problem going away in the next few years.

Securitization

This type of at best mixed outlook is leading a growing number of banks to look for a way out. For the large banks, the continuation of the debt crisis is eroding profits and making it difficult to find the resources to enter new areas of profitability, such as investment banking, which are seen by some, including the U.S. Federal Reserve, as the way out of the financial burden of past bad loans.

The secondary loan market, where perhaps $8 to $10 billion of Latin American, Philippine, and Polish paper were sold and bought in 1986, essentially collapsed in 1987 in the wake of the Brazilian partial suspension of interest payments. An average portfolio of Latin American sovereign debt, which was worth about 68¢ per dollar of loans on the books at the beginning of 1987, had fallen to less than 50¢ at year-end, with few buyers in sight. The major buyers of paper in 1987 have been bargain-hunting corporate investors, to take advantage of the debt-equity swap schemes in Chile and Mexico, where about $2 billion of equity investments were approved (although not necessarily disbursed) during the year. Unfortunately for creditors, debt-equity swap schemes simply do not provide a large enough exit. Finding the right investments in a constricted setting is difficult enough, but making them prosper is yet another and even more daunting task.

In mid-December 1987, the question of banks' future attitudes came up again when the Bank of Boston, the largest in New England and also a force in domestic banking in Argentina and Brazil, announced large additional reserves and a 20 percent write-off on its exposure in Latin America. Even though the additional amounts involved—about $400 million out of a total exposure of about $1 billion—were modest in comparison with those of the large money-center banks, and the action was motivated primarily by the bank's desire to be perceived as a U.S. "superregional" rather than an international bank, the action undoubtedly put pressure on larger banks to do the same. With few exceptions, they could hardly afford to do so on a large scale. Substantial write-offs and reserves undoubtedly open the door to securitization, under which heavily discounted loans would eventually be sold off to investors as tradable securities.

Securitization is so far untested, although a few large issues (in the $500 billion to $2 billion range of gross loans each) might be possible in 1988. The first point is that before a portfolio of Latin American and other LDC loans can be rearranged and turned into a package attractive to investors, the selling bank has to take a deep breath and be willing to take a large write-off. If a 50 percent discount is evidently not enough to clear the market, as the secondary loan market shows, deeper discounts will be needed to package salable and tradable securities catering to various types of investors. Few banks are, at least so far, willing and able to face such write-offs, unless they have relatively small exposures. The fact that discounts are in part the result of delays by the debtors themselves reinforces the banks' reluctance. Second, the virtual collapse of the U.S. high-yield or "junk" securities market in the wake of the stock market crash makes it difficult to unwind high-interest debt through stock issues. This has added to the skepticism of investors about risky paper, no matter how high the potential return. The third point, assuming that the seller can get by the many legal and administrative complications, concerns the effect that securitization, if successful, would have on the debtors' view of the nature of their obligation to service debt.

Securitization and write-offs by themselves do little for the debtors. While the write-offs and the possible subsequent repackaging of a portfolio of loans of many countries grouped together conceal the individual discount on each country, there is at least some risk that write-offs and securitization would strengthen the political resolve of some countries unilaterally to reduce their debt service. So far, however, the big discounts in the secondary loan market have not been emphasized by debtors as an overwhelming reason to justify a unilateral reduction in debt service, although most debtors are busy exploring how to translate at least part of the market discount into lower debt service.

Despite the obvious difficulties, there is little doubt that 1988 will see major developments in securitization. From the side of the debtors, there will also be attempts in the same direction, although the objective is quite different: to lower the medium-term interest burden and to make it fixed. This means that an exchange offer of loans for securities would most likely have to give the securities—basically more easily tradable loans—some special features in order to make them halfway attractive to even the most jaded lenders. The crucial ingredient is credibility of future debt service. At a minimum, lenders would, in exchange for a fixed below-market rate on a long-term piece of paper, require an agent such as an international institution, which can be expected to try hard to pry out the debt service due on the new instruments. Exclusion from new money packages as well as easy tradability are other key ingredients. But even with these and other additional features, such exchanges would involve large write-offs. "Securitization" by the debtors is therefore likely to be a negotiated and lengthy process.[1]

The case of Brazil, which was working at the end of 1987 with outside advisers on a tentative proposal to convert part of its bank debt into low fixed interest rate bonds, looked as if it might be the first major test of securitization. But, as in the past, Mexico took the lead. With the help of Morgan Guaranty, one of its major creditors, Mexico in the days between Christmas and New Year announced a bold plan to try to convert up to $20 billion of its bank debt into hopefully no more than $10 billion of bonds to be taken up voluntarily by its bank creditors. The plan, officially backed by the U.S. Treasury, would, if successful, mean a major reduction in interest service, of about $1 billion annually; in exchange for the very large write-offs of loans involved, the bank creditors would be guaranteed final repayment in twenty years through a "zero coupon" U.S. Treasury bond to be purchased by Mexico. With this form of advance repayment, which would accumulate interest while in escrow, Mexico would in time pay off the principal, although there would be no special guarantee on the interest due in the intervening years. The resulting securities are thus likely to trade at a substantial discount: bank creditors would then suffer a double loss, albeit palliated by tax benefits: the write-off of part of the debt itself, plus the discount on the bonds themselves.

The really novel aspects of the Mexico-Morgan Guaranty proposal were, first and most important, that the U.S. government officially endorsed it, marking a major and sudden break from its steadfast past attitude against any major debt relief and, second, that Morgan Guaranty, as the commercial arranger, believed that there would be enough takers at the large discounts envisaged. In any event, the results of the exchange at the end of February 1988 were disappointing to Mexico, with $3.6 billion of debt converted to $2.5 in bonds, or a discount of 31 percent. Nevertheless, the stage has been set for new attempts at similar conversions for all troubled sovereign debtors. The question remains, however, why the U.S. government at the end of 1987 suddenly changed the view it had held so staunchly for so long. The change of attitude is bound to raise questions among the debtors of whether the austerity efforts they made in the intervening years since 1982, while their external debt went up by one-third—in large part to pay off interest—were in fact in vain. The possible consequences in political attitudes toward the United States could be worrisome.

Is "securitization" likely to be more than a fashion, as debt-equity swaps have been for the last couple of years? In the end, these and other are palliatives to a problem that is likely to wax and wane for several years. A longer-term solution requires at least three ingredients, all of them hard to find: clearer market signals, capital from outside, and reform by the debtors.

Market Signals

The idea of involuntary lending by banks, when it was started for Mexico in 1982 at the behest of the IMF, was designed to help ease borrowers back to the market over time. That process is taking much longer than expected. Banks of all sizes are most reluctant to participate in new money packages, even for countries that have behaved well. In the case of Colombia, for example, a $1.06 billion loan was under negotiation for the better part of 1987: the loan would enable Colombia to recoup 1987 amortization payments, mostly already made to the banks, so that the exposure of the banks would not increase. Banks would have preferred to tie the loan to specific projects, as was done in 1985, but the fact remains that the opposition in Colombia saw the difficulty of getting the loan agreed in 1987 as a sign that good behavior does not pay. In Venezuela, on the other hand, banks substantially expanded short-term and trade-related lines of credit after the country amortized $1 billion of sovereign debt in the last two years, the only sovereign debtor to pay off bank principal since the onset of the crisis. The Mexico-Morgan proposal would, if it succeeds and is extended in time to other debtors with economic rehabilitation programs, represent a major positive market signal.

In the meantime, however, market signals for "good behavior" have not been clear. Governments are under attack from opposition politicians and even from their own parties, who argue that orthodoxy has no reward. International agencies have not filled the void. The International Monetary Fund, a medium-term balance-of-payments lender, is not adding new money because it is not being paid back the credits it granted at the beginning of the debt crisis. The two multilateral development banks have tried to increase disbursements of loans, but the results have been modest so far. In 1986–87 their net cash inflow into Latin America—namely disbursements less amortization and interest—averaged less than $1 billion annually. Part of the problem has been the reluctance to expand lending until there was a clearer U.S. commitment to increase their capital, something that has happened for the World Bank but not for the Inter-American Development Bank. The other, equally important problem has been that countries are often unable to meet the conditions for using the money, such as increasing electric tariffs to draw down electric power loans—a problem in several countries. The result in most debtor countries is widespread skepticism about where the external capital is going to come from.

Reform and Capital

Capital inflows into the high-debt countries have simply been inadequate to jump-start the engine of growth. As savings-poor countries, the debtors need to import capital. The problem is how to foster investment flows rather than more borrowing. Private capital will simply not move unless prospects for more growth improve. In turn, the prospects depend on reform to free economies from the shackles of excessive and capricious government regulation as well as the asphyxiating competition in most countries from subsidized state industrial and commercial enterprises. Despite enormous difficulties, rooted in tradition and habit, progress is possible. In the years ahead, several factors are likely to favor the move to reform: among them are gradually decreasing demographic and labor pressures in the cities, reflecting the decline in the growth of the labor force and the retention of more people in rural areas as a result of the debt crisis, and also the emergence of a younger and more internationally minded group of entrepreneurs. Mexico showed the way in the last three years with the elimination of many trade restrictions and the reprivatization of enterprises which had been nationalized along with the banks in 1982. Money that had fled returned, perhaps $3 to $5 billion up to mid-1987. But the fragility of this capital reflow was shown up by the stock market crash. For efforts at reform to persist, continuity is needed: that is where a modicum of support from international public sources is important, especially in the difficult transition from depression to recovery.

The keys are thus greater multilateral development bank involvement, especially in the early transition years, and the reflow of private capital on a sustained basis. The perhaps $100 billion that left Latin America from 1975 to 1983 is probably worth at least $250 billion today, even with conservative money management. Even if only one-third of the annual interest on this sum were to return—or about $8 billion annually—the immediate problem would be defused. It is up to the international community to make one more big push, especially the governments of creditor countries, along with the major debtors, to create the conditions for this to happen. Relief from debt fatigue is within reach. But if no effort is made and capital is not forthcoming in sufficient amounts, then major and financially painful debt relief will become hard to avoid.

Appendix 1.
The Baker Initiative

Statement of the Honorable James A. Baker III, Secretary of The Treasury of the United States, before the Joint Annual Meeting of the International Monetary Fund and the World Bank, 8 October 1985, Seoul, South Korea

Chairman Touré, Managing Director de Larosière, President Clausen, fellow Governors, and distinguished guests:

It is a pleasure to be here for the 40th annual meeting of the International Monetary Fund and the World Bank. Strong, effective international financial institutions are as essential to our economic well being today as they were 40 years ago.

Our host country, Korea, is a nation whose economic success is surpassed only by its warm hospitality. Korea's market-oriented approach and strong emphasis on private initiative are a lesson for us all.

Foundation for Growth

I would like to focus my comments today on policies for growth within the context of the international debt strategy. Sound policies and sustained, low-inflation growth in the industrial countries must provide the essential foundation for a successful debt strategy, and are a prerequisite for stronger growth in the debtor countries.

The major industrial countries have already made considerable progress in this direction. Two weeks ago in New York the Finance Ministers and Central Bank Governors of the Group of Five industrial nations underscored the progress which had been achieved, particularly with regard to the convergence of economic performance toward sustained, low-inflation growth. They also announced a set of policy intentions that will help to consolidate and extend that progress and to improve and sustain growth for the longer term.

We emphasized, for our own countries, the central importance of reducing structural rigidities, strengthening incentives for the private sector, reducing the size of government, and improving the investment environment. We also rededicated our governments to resisting protectionist pressures that threaten our own prosperity and the opportunities for others. We must jointly accelerate our efforts to launch a new round of trade negotiations within the GATT.

These industrial nations agreed that the significant progress already achieved in promoting a better convergence of their economic performance had not been fully reflected in exchange markets and that some further orderly appreciation of the main non-dollar currencies against the dollar was desirable. We expressed our willingness to cooperate more closely to encourage this when to do so would be helpful.

This package of measures had an immediate, significant impact on exchange markets which continues to be positive, and reflects the importance of the commitments made.

I am convinced that if each of the major industrial nations fulfills its policy intentions and maintains or improves access to its markets, we will have taken a major step toward more balanced and sustainable growth, while providing a solid framework for improving the debt situation in the developing world.

Strengthening the Debt Strategy

Fellow Governors, it is essential that we begin the process of strengthening our international debt strategy.

Three years ago the international financial community developed a flexible, cooperative, case-by-case strategy to address the debt problem and lay the basis for growth in the debtor nations. In three years:

- Aggregate current account deficits in developing countries have been sharply reduced from $104 billion in 1982 to $44 billion this year.
- Growth in developing countries has been restored to about 4 percent, compared to less than 2 percent in 1982.
- This growth has been fueled by sharp increases in developing nations' exports, including a 21 percent increase in their exports to the United States last year.

These developments reflect improved growth and sharply lower interest rates in the industrial nations, as well as adoption of improved policies within most debtor countries. These policies have been given important support by reschedulings and rollovers amounting to approximately $210 billion, and by net new commercial bank lending.

The international financial institutions have also played an important role in the progress that has been achieved. The IMF in particular has very capably played a leadership role, providing guidance on policies and temporary balance of payments financing, both of which have catalyzed commercial bank flows.

Despite this progress, some serious problems have developed. A number of principal debtor countries have recently experienced setbacks in their efforts to improve their economic situations, particularly with regard to inflation and fiscal imbalances, undercutting prospects for sustained growth. Bank lending to debtor nations has been declining, with very little net new lending anticipated this year. The sense of increasing reluctance among banks to participate in new money and debt rescheduling packages has introduced serious uncertainties for borrowers, in some cases making it more difficult for them to pursue economic reforms.

These problems need to be addressed, promptly and effectively, by building upon the international debt strategy in order to improve the prospects for growth in the debtor countries. This is an enterprise which will require, above all, that we work together and that we each strengthen our commitment to progress.

If the debt problem is to be solved, there must be a "Program for Sustained Growth," incorporating three essential and mutually reinforcing elements:

- First and foremost, the adoption by principal debtor countries of comprehensive macroeconomic and structural policies, supported by the international financial institutions, to promote growth and balance of payments adjustment, and to reduce inflation.
- Second, a continued central role for the IMF, in conjunction with increased and more effective structural adjustment lending by the multilateral development banks (MDBs), both in support of the adoption by principal debtors of market-oriented policies for growth.
- Third, increased lending by the private banks in support of comprehensive economic adjustment programs.

I want to emphasize that the United States does not support a departure from the case-by-case debt strategy we adopted three years ago. This approach has served us well; we should continue to follow it. It recognizes the inescapable fact that the particular circumstances of each country are different. Its main components, fundamental adjustment measures within the debtor nations and conditionality in conjunction with lending, remain essential to the restoration of external balance and longer-term growth.

We need to build upon the current strategy to strengthen its ability to foster growth. There must be greater emphasis on both market-oriented economic policies to foster growth and adequate financing to support it.

In essence, what I am suggesting is that adequate financing can be made available through a combination of private creditors and multilateral institutions working cooperatively, but only where there are reasonable prospects that growth will occur. This will depend upon the adoption of proper economic policies by the developing countries. Financing can only be prudently made available when and as effective policies to promote economic efficiency, competitiveness, and productivity—the true foundations of growth—are put in place. We cannot afford to repeat the mistakes of the past. Adjustment must continue. Adjustment programs must be agreed before additional funds are made available, and should be implemented as those funds are disbursed.

These efforts should be mutually reinforcing. Sound policies in the principal debtor countries will not only promote growth, but will also stimulate the needed private bank lending. And it will be important that these policies be supported by the IMF, complemented by the MDBs. These institutions can help encourage and catalyze both needed policies and financing.

In today's highly interdependent world economy, efforts at economic isolationism are doomed to failure. Countries which are not prepared to undertake basic adjustments and work within the framework of the case-by-case debt strategy, cooperating with the international financial institutions, cannot expect to benefit from this three-point program. Additional lending will not occur. Efforts by any country to "go it alone" are likely to seriously damage its prospects for future growth.

I would like to elaborate on the actions that will be required by each participant in this three-point program.

Structural Change in the Principal Debtors

The essence of the need for structural change in the principal debtors is captured in two quotations I would like to share with you.

First: "The only way to overcome our economic crisis is to tackle at their root the structural problems of our economy to make it more efficient and productive."[1]

And second: "Economic growth will have solid foundations only if we reestablish trust and stimulate private enterprise, which must be the flagship of our economic development. . . . We will promote authentic institutional change in the economic sector."[2]

These are not the words of a U.S. Secretary of the Treasury. They are statements made in July of this year by the Presidents of Mexico and Brazil. I believe they reflect a growing sentiment in Latin America.

It is essential that the heavily indebted, middle income developing countries do their part to implement and maintain sound policies. Indeed, without such policies, needed financing cannot be expected to materialize. Policy and financing are not substitutes but essential complements.

For those countries which have implemented measures to address the imbalances in their economies, a more comprehensive set of policies can

1. President de la Madrid at Mexican Bankers Association Annual Meeting, July 22, 1985.
2. President Sarney in a televised address to the nation, July 23, 1985.

now be put in place, which promises longer term benefits from stronger growth, higher standards of living, lower inflation, and more flexible and productive economies. These must not only include macroeconomic policies, but also other medium and longer term supply-side policies to promote growth.

We believe that such institutional and structural policies should include:

- increased reliance on the private sector, and less reliance on government, to help increase employment, production and efficiency;
- supply-side actions to mobilize domestic savings and facilitate efficient investment, both domestic and foreign, by means of tax reform, labor market reform and development of financial markets; and
- market-opening measures to encourage foreign direct investment and capital inflows, as well as to liberalize trade, including the reduction of export subsidies.

This broader approach does not mean that policy areas that have been the focus of efforts to date—in particular fiscal, monetary, and exchange rate policies—can receive less attention. Indeed, macroeconomic policies have been central to efforts to date and must be strengthened to achieve greater progress. These policies should consist of:

- market-oriented exchange rate, interest rate, wage, and pricing policies to promote greater economic efficiency and responsiveness to growth and employment opportunities; and
- sound monetary and fiscal policies focused on reducing domestic imbalances and inflation and on freeing up resources for the private sector.

The cornerstone of sustained growth must be greater domestic savings, and investment of those savings at home. Macroeconomic and structural policies which improve economic efficiency, mobilize domestic resources, and provide incentives to work, save, and invest domestically will create the favorable economic environment necessary for this to occur. Such an environment is also critical to attract supplemental foreign savings.

As a practical matter, it is unrealistic to call upon the support of voluntary lending from abroad, whether public or private, when domestic funds are moving in the other direction. Capital flight must be reversed if there is to be any real prospect of additional funding, whether debt or equity. If a country's own citizens have no confidence in its economic system, how can others?

There are essentially two kinds of capital inflows: loans and equity investments. Foreign borrowings have to be repaid—with interest. Equity investment, on the other hand, has a degree of permanence and is not debt-creating. Moreover, it can have a compounding effect on growth, bring innovation and technology, and help to keep capital at home.

We believe that the debtor nations must be willing to commit themselves to these policies for growth in order that the other elements of a strengthened debt strategy can come into place.

Enhanced Effectiveness of the International Financial Institutions

The international financial institutions must also play an important role in strengthening the debt strategy to promote growth. However, we must recognize that the international financial institutions cannot have sufficient resources to meet the debtor nations' financing needs all by themselves. An approach which assumes that the IMF and the World Bank are the sole answer to debt problems is simply a non-starter. For most developing countries other sources must play a more important role. These include private sector borrowing, increased export earnings, foreign equity investment, and repatriation of capital which has fled abroad. All these routes should be pursued.

Among the international financial institutions, the IMF has played a major role in advising member nations on the development of policies necessary to promote adjustment and growth. There has been a particular focus on monetary, fiscal, and exchange rate policies, although increasing attention is being paid to other areas such as trade liberalization, pricing policies, and the efficiency of government-owned enterprises.

Emphasizing growth does not mean deemphasizing the IMF. Through both its policy advice and balance of payments financing, the Fund has played a critical role in encouraging needed policy changes and catalyzing capital flows. It must continue to do so. But it must also develop new techniques for catalyzing financing in support of further progress. "Enhanced surveillance," for example, can sometimes provide an effective means of continued IMF involvement.

The Fund should give higher priority to tax reform, market-oriented pricing, the reduction of labor market rigidities, and to opening economies to foreign trade and investment. This will help assure that Fund-supported programs are growth-oriented. It will be particularly important for the Fund to work closely with the World Bank in this effort.

I would now like to turn more directly to the role of the MDBs, which need to be brought into the debt strategy in a stronger way, without diminishing the role still to be played by the IMF.

The World Bank, and indeed all MDBs, have considerable scope to build on current programs and resources, and to provide additional assistance to debtor nations which is disbursed more quickly and targeted more effectively to provide the needed stimulus to growth.

There is ample room to expand the World Bank's fast-disbursing lending to support growth-oriented policies, and institutional and sectoral reform. An increase in such lending can serve as a catalyst for commercial bank lending.

A serious effort to develop the programs of the World Bank and the Inter-American Development Bank (IDB) could increase their disbursements to principal debtors by roughly 50 percent from the current annual level of nearly $6 billion.

Increased disbursements would require greater borrowing by the MDBs in world capital markets. Their ability to borrow at low rates is a precious asset which must be preserved. Therefore, their lending must be in support of sound economic programs that enhance the borrower's ability to service its debt and grow.

It should be possible, with a concerted effort by both the World Bank and borrowers, to streamline World Bank operations in order to reduce considerably the time period required to formulate and implement such assistance programs. This will expedite the actual disbursement of funds.

The value and role of an indigenous, competitive private sector needs to be recognized and developed more fully than it has in the past. The Bank, for its part, should actively promote the development of the private sector and, where appropriate, provide direct assistance to this sector. In addition, the Bank should seek to assist, both in a technical and financial capacity, those countries which wish to "privatize" their state-owned enterprises, which in too many cases aggravate already serious budget deficit problems.

Given the importance of increasing commercial bank flows to the principal debtors, there is also an urgent need for efforts to expand the Bank's co-financing operations. These efforts should be pursued vigorously to increase the effectiveness of the Bank in helping its borrowers to attract private finance, and should have substantial potential in the context of this three-point program.

The enhanced program of the International Finance Corporation, with an expanded capital base, and the recently negotiated Multilateral Investment Guarantee Agency (MIGA) are two important Bank Group initiatives in support of developing countries. Both organizations can do much to assist their members in attracting non-debt capital flows as well as critical technological and managerial resources. We urge all Bank Members and particularly the principal debtors to give their full support to establishment of the MIGA.

If developing countries implement growth-oriented reform; if commercial banks provide adequate increases in net new lending to good performers; and if increased demand for quality IBRD lending demonstrates the need for increased capital resources, we would be prepared to look seriously at the timing and scope of a general capital increase.

We believe the World Bank's efforts can be supplemented actively by the regional development banks. Since some of the most serious debt problems are found in Latin America, special emphasis should be placed on strengthening the IDB's policies to enable it to be a more effective partner in support of growth-oriented structural reform.

In the case of an IDB capital increase, it will be critical to assess the extent to which the institution strengthens its lending policies. There must be well-defined economic and country strategies tailored to enhance economic reforms which encourage growth. Given a firm commitment by the IDB to move in this direction, we believe that it should be permitted to introduce a major program of well targeted non-project lending. In the meantime, such lending could be associated with World Bank programs until the IDB has implemented the necessary reforms.

Increasing Lending by the International Banking Community

The international banking community has played an important role during the past three years. I am, however, concerned about the decline in net bank lending to debtor nations over the past year and a half, particularly those nations which are making progress. All of us can appreciate the commercial banks' concerns, but we believe these concerns would dissipate if the banks were confident that new lending is in support of policies for growth in the developing nations.

If creditor governments, in an age of budget austerity, are to be called upon to support increases in multilateral development bank lending to the debtor nations, and if the recipient nations are asked to adopt sound economic policies for growth to avoid wasting that financing, then there must also be a commitment by the banking community—a commitment to help the global community make the necessary transition to stronger growth.

Our assessment of the commitment required by the banks to the entire group of heavily indebted, middle income developing countries would be net new lending in the range of $20 billion for the next three years. In addition, it would be necessary that countries now receiving adequate financing from banks on a voluntary basis continue to do so, provided they maintain sound policies.

I would like to see the banking community make a pledge to provide these amounts of new lending and make it publicly, provided the debtor countries also make similar growth-oriented policy commitments as their part of the cooperative effort. Such financing could be used to meet both short-term financing and longer-term investment needs in the developing countries, and would be available, provided debtors took action and multilateral institutions also did their part.

Appendix 2.
Select Statistics

Table A-1 External Debt Outstanding of Latin America and the Caribbean, 1973–1986 (Gross Outstanding Debt, Including Short-term, at End of Years Shown, in Billions of Current U.S. Dollars)

	1973[b]	1975	1979	1980	1981	1982	1983	1984	1985	1986[b]
Gross outstanding[a]	48.0	98.9	196.8	241.5	293.5	331.3	355.0	374.1	383.9	395.0
of which:										
Argentina	4.5	6.0	20.9	27.3	33.7	43.6	45.1	46.8	48.4	49.2
Brazil	12.0	25.0	60.1	70.0	79.9	91.3	97.8	103.5	106.7	110.6
Chile	3.4[c]	7.5[b]	9.4	12.1	16.6	17.3	18.2	19.9	20.2	20.7
Colombia	2.7[c]	5.4[b]	5.9	6.9	8.7	10.3	11.4	12.3	14.0	14.8
Ecuador	0.6[c]	2.9[b]	4.5	5.6	7.3	7.6	8.1	8.3	9.2	9.9
Mexico	9.5	16.9	42.8	57.1	77.9	86.1	93.0	97.4	97.4	98.3
Panama	0.7[c]	1.3[b]	3.5	3.0	3.3	3.9	4.4	4.4	4.7	5.0
Peru	2.4[c]	7.2[b]	9.2	10.0	10.3	12.3	12.4	13.1	13.7	14.4
Venezuela	6.0	17.2	24.1	29.6	31.9	31.8	32.3	34.3	32.1	33.6
Others	6.2	9.5	16.4	19.9	23.9	27.1	32.3	34.1	37.5	38.5

Sources: United Nations, CEPAL, Balance Preliminar de la Economía Latinoamericana 1986 (December 18, 1986); Inter-American Development Bank, Economic and Social Progress in Latin America, 1987 Report, and earlier issues; World Bank, World Debt Tables, various issues.
[a]Excluding Cuba, which has an outstanding debt of about US $13 billion.
[b]Estimate.
[c]Public medium- and long-term debt only.

Table A-2 Gross Domestic Product of Latin America and the Caribbean, Total and per Capita, 1970–1986

	Total GDP (Billions of 1986 Dollars)					Per Capita GDP (1986 Dollars)		
	1970	1980	1984	1985	1986[a]	1970	1980	1986[a]
All countries	430.0	780.0	783.4	812.3	843.0	1,615	2,288	2,140
Consumption	344.6	630.2	630.5	640.9	655.0	1,295	1,849	1,663
Gross domestic investment	92.3	187.1	123.8	127.7	125.7	347	549	319
Exports[b]	53.6	96.6	119.6	119.6	114.4	200	283	290
Imports[b]	60.6	135.2	91.7	85.7	95.6	228	397	243
Major debtor countries								
Argentina	60.1	77.4	72.6	69.3	73.3	2,531	2,752	2,361
Brazil	128.7	296.0	297.4	322.0	348.4	1,382	2,486	2,525
Chile	21.3	27.3	26.2	26.8	28.3	2,275	2,463	2,306
Colombia	11.6	19.4	33.1	35.9	36.8	926	1,277	1,330
Mexico	96.9	183.6	193.6	199.0	191.5	1,940	2,734	2,407
Peru	16.9	23.8	22.8	23.3	25.2	1,264	1,374	1,250
Venezuela	34.2	51.2	47.9	48.0	49.5	3,066	3,408	2,762

Sources: Inter-American Development Bank, *Economic and Social Progress in Latin America, 1987 Report*; and United Nations, CEPAL, *Balance Preliminar de la Economía Latinoamericana 1986* (December 18, 1986).

[a]Estimate.

[b]Goods and services.

Table A-3 Balance of Payments of Latin America and the Caribbean, 1975–1986 (in Billions of Current U.S. Dollars)

	1975	1976	1979	1980	1981	1982	1983	1984	1985	1986[a]
Current account balance, of which:	-13.9	-11.1	-19.3	-27.4	-39.9	-39.0	-8.0	-0.8	-2.8	-13.6
Exports, f.o.b.	36.2	41.7	71.2	93.9	100.7	86.3	91.5	100.9	95.3	80.0
Imports, f.o.b.	-42.2	-43.6	-71.0	-95.5	-102.9	-78.9	-61.4	-63.1	-62.9	-62.0
Capital account, net balance, of which:	16.4	16.2	26.7	35.0	49.1	27.6	6.0	10.5	3.4	6.2
Private sector	9.7	4.6	16.2	21.8	24.6	7.6	-12.1	-9.5	-2.5	n.a.
Public sector	3.8	6.7	7.2	5.2	5.8	17.6	19.7	21.7	10.8	n.a.
Monetary sector[b]	2.8	4.9	3.2	8.0	18.6	2.4	-1.6	-1.4	-2.3	n.a.
Errors & omissions	-1.8	-0.8	2.2	-5.5	-11.5	-8.9	-3.5	-2.5	-4.7	n.a.
Net change in reserves[c]	-0.7	-4.3	-9.6	-2.1	2.3	20.3	5.5	-7.5	1.5	8.0

Source: Inter-American Development Bank, Economic and Social Progress in Latin America, 1987 Report.
[a]Estimate.
[b]Basically short-term financing.
[c]Minus indicates an increase in international reserve holdings.

Table A-4 Summary Balance of Payments of Four Major Latin American Countries, 1975–1986 (in Millions of Current U.S. Dollars)

	1975	1976	1979	1980	1981	1982	1983	1984	1985	1986[a]
Argentina										
Current account	-1,287	655	-497	-4,787	-4,633	-2,241	-2,439	-2,391	-953	-2,641
Capital account, net	203	488	4,491	2,465	1,791	1,979	410	2,759	397	516
Change in reserves[b]	1,081	-920	-4,231	2,628	3,058	641	2,474	-265	556	2,125
Brazil										
Current account	-7,007	-6,549	-10,465	-12,793	-11,762	-15,388	-6,798	55	-338	-2,849
Capital account, net	6,418	8,744	6,333	9,682	12,828	10,792	5,543	4,951	311	-780
Change in reserves[b]	1,016	-2,683	2,908	3,462	-673	4,952	1,874	-5,411	524	3,629
Mexico										
Current account	-4,054	-3,410	-5,453	-8,162	-14,020	-5,700	5,321	4,238	1,237	-1,270
Capital account, net	5,482	5,861	5,121	12,897	23,433	7,446	-2,356	-1,074	-1,527	2,271
Change in reserves[b]	-179	595	-315	-958	-1,097	3,342	-2,022	-2,133	2,243	-790
Venezuela										
Current account	2,170	257	351	4,731	4,000	-3,999	4,427	5,418	3,086	-2,177
Capital account, net	136	-2,424	3,251	164	-1,882	-1,657	-4,098	-3,848	-1,104	-1,697
Change in reserves[b]	-2,692	15	-4,098	-3,764	20	7,693	-337	-1,878	-1,707	3,814

Source: Inter-American Development Bank, *Economic and Social Progress in Latin America, 1987 Report.*

[a]Estimate.

[b]The minus sign indicates an increase in international reserve holdings.

Table A-5 Indices of Total Industrial Production, 1976–1986 (1980 = 100)

Region/Country	1976	1977	1978	1979	1980	1981	1982	1983	1984	1985	1986
Latin America & Caribbean	80	84	88	96	100	98	96	94	105	—	—
Argentina[a]	102	104	93	103	100	85	81	90	94	87	98
Brazil[b]	79	81	87	93	100	81	81	76	81	87	97
Chile*[a]	74	81	87	94	100	101	85	89	98	98	106
Colombia[c]	83	86	93	97	100	100	100	101	108	110	118
Mexico[a]	72	74	82	91	100	109	107	97	102	107	102
Venezuela*[c]	59	67	76	87	100	111	121	119	124	127	131

Source: United Nations, Industrial Statistics Yearbook, 1984, vol. 1: General Industrial Statistics (1986).
*Manufacturing only.
[a]Estimates by the author for 1985 and 1986 are based on IMF, International Financial Statistics.
[b]Estimates by the author for 1985 and 1986 are based on data supplied by the Getulio Vargas Foundation.
[c]Inter-American Development Bank.

Table A-6 Indices of Total Agricultural Production, 1977–1986 (1976–1978 = 100)

Region/Country	1977	1978	1979	1980	1981	1982	1983	1984	1985	1986
Latin America & Caribbean	101	104	107	112	116	116	115	122	127	122
Argentina	97	106	110	99	103	112	114	123	120	112
Brazil	104	101	107	118	124	120	120	130	145	132
Chile	105	97	92	106	112	113	110	117	121	128
Colombia	96	107	114	120	123	121	120	122	122	124
Mexico	101	107	107	118	120	114	119	118	118	122
Peru	102	94	98	90	98	96	94	105	103	101
Venezuela	103	107	106	112	110	118	117	120	129	136

Source: U.S. Department of Agriculture, Economic Research Service, World Indices of Agricultural and Food Production, 1977–1986 (September 1987).

Table A-7 Latin American Integration Association (ALADI) Intraregional Trade, 1975–1986 (in Millions of U.S. Dollars)

	1975		1979		1984		1985		1986	
	Amount	% of Total	Amount	% of Total	Amount	% of Total	Amount	% of Total	Amount	% of Total
Intraregional trade	5,244	100.0	10,308	100.0	8,108	100.0	7,050	100.0	7,556	100.0
Percentage of total regional exports	14.2		14.5		8.0		7.4		9.4	
Argentina										
Imports from region	*	*	*	*	1,576	19.4	1,192	16.9	1,600	21.2
Exports to region	*	*	2,050	19.9	1,383	17.1	1,485	21.1	1,462	19.4
Brazil										
Imports	*	*	*	*	1,994	24.6	1,521	21.6	1,674	22.2
Exports	1,350	25.7	2,608	25.3	2,829	34.9	2,234	31.7	2,439	32.3
Mexico										
Imports	*	*	*	*	505	6.2	562	8.0	337	4.5
Exports	378	7.2	590	5.7	823	10.2	597	8.5	608	8.1
Venezuela										
Imports	*	*	*	*	639	7.9	637	9.0	729	9.7
Exports	1,106	21.1	1,666	16.2	1,077	13.3	711	10.1	377	5.0

Source: Inter-American Development Bank, Economic and Social Progress in Latin America, 1987 Report, and earlier years.
Note: Member countries of ALADI are Argentina, Brazil, Chile, Mexico, Paraguay, Uruguay, and Bolivia; and Colombia, Ecuador, Peru, and Venezuela (Andean Group).
*Not applicable or not available.

Table A-8 Growth of Bank Exposure (Total Claims) to Latin America and the Caribbean, 1981–1986 (in Millions of U.S. Dollars at Year-End)

	1981	1982	1983	1984	1985	1986
BIS reporting banks, total[a]	196,646	214,210	225,216	227,258	236,531	240,070
United States banks, total[b]	80,541	82,873	85,011	87,165	82,394	78,945
9 money center banks	n.a.	49,942	51,440	54,195	53,042	50,953
14 next largest banks[c]	n.a.	16,465	17,361	17,450	14,649	14,160
Germany, Fed. Rep. DM, million	9,624	11,308	13,213	14,376	17,391	17,858
Converted into US$	4,268	4,758	4,851	4,567	7,066	9,201
United Kingdom, US$	39,760	35,100	36,200	38,200	40,100	40,200
Japan, total to LDCs,[d] US$	n.a.	n.a.	38,000	45,400	49,900	65,500

Sources: BIS, *The Maturity Distribution of International Bank Lending;* United States—Federal Financial Institutions Examination Council, *Country Exposure Lending Survey of U.S. Banks;* United Kingdom—*Bank of England Quarterly Bulletin;* Germany—Deutsche Bundesbank, *Statistische Beihefte zu den Monatsberichten;* Japan—Ministry of Finance.

[a]Including the United States. Data compiled by BIS prior to 1985 are not strictly comparable with those for later years because of change in statistical coverage.

[b]Total of 183 reporting U.S. banks at year-end 1986. All data are on a fully consolidated basis, but cover only cross-border and nonlocal currency lending.

[c]15 reporting banks prior to 1986.

[d]All developing countries.

Table A-9   Estimated Lending in International Cross-Border Markets,
1984–1986 (Net Flow of Disbursements Less Amortizations, in Millions of
U.S. Dollars)

	1984	1985	1986
Net international bank lending, total	90.0	105.0	165.0
Of which to:			
Industrial countries	76.5	77.0	139.7
Eastern Europe	—	5.7	4.2
OPEC	−1.9	0.2	0.2
Other LDCs	10.0	11.1	0.2
Of which: Latin America	5.4	1.7	−0.9
Other countries	5.4	11.0	20.7
Net external bonds	83.0	125.0	156.0
Minus double counting*	28.0	55.0	76.0
Net new bank and bond lending	145.0	175.0	245.0
Euro-notes held outside the banking system	—	5.0	15.0
New international equities	—	2.0	8.0
Total	145.0	182.0	268.0

Sources: BIS, *International Banking and Financial Market Developments* (October
1987), and OECD, *Financial Market Trends,* no. 37 (November 1987).
    *Statistical adjustment to allow for overlaps between individual statistical series
and lack of comprehensiveness in the coverage.

Table A-10   Latin America and the Caribbean: IMF Stand-by Arrangements Approved, January 1, 1979–April 30, 1986 (in Millions of SDRs)

Member	Date of Inception	Amount of Arrangement
Argentina	January 24, 1983	1,500.00
	December 28, 1984	1,419.00[a]
Barbados	October 1, 1982	31.88
Belize	December 3, 1984	7.13
Bolivia	February 1, 1980	66.38
Chile	January 10, 1983	500.00
Costa Rica	March 12, 1980	60.50
	December 20, 1982	92.25
	March 13, 1985	54.00
Dominica	July 18, 1984	1.40
Dominican Republic	April 15, 1985	78.50
Ecuador	July 25, 1983	157.50
	March 11, 1985	105.50
El Salvador	June 23, 1980	10.75
	July 16, 1982	43.00
Grenada	November 6, 1979	0.65
	May 11, 1981	3.43

Table A-10 *(continued)*

Member	Date of Inception	Amount of Arrangement
Guatemala	November 13, 1981	19.10
	August 31, 1983	114.75
Haiti	August 9, 1982	34.50
	November 7, 1983	60.00
Honduras	November 5, 1982	76.50
Jamaica	June 22, 1984	64.00
	July 17, 1985	115.00
Nicaragua	May 14, 1979	34.00
Panama	March 23, 1979	30.00
	April 18, 1980	90.00
	April 28, 1982	29.70
	June 24, 1983	150.00
	July 15, 1985	90.00
Peru	August 10, 1979	285.00
	April 26, 1984	250.00
Uruguay	March 16, 1979	21.00
	May 14, 1980	21.00
	July 15, 1981	31.50
	April 22, 1983	378.00
	September 27, 1985	122.85

Source: Margaret Garritsen de Vries, *Balance of Payments Adjustment, 1945 to 1986, the IMF Experience* (International Monetary Fund, 1987).

Note: As of July 1987, one SDR was equivalent to US$1.269. The value has fluctuated between US$1.317 in 1979 and US$.980 in 1984.

[a]Amount of arrangement later reduced to SDR 1,182.50 million.

Table A-11   Extended Fund Facility Arrangements for Member Countries in Latin America and the Caribbean, July 7, 1975–April 30, 1986 (in Millions of SDRs)

Member	Date of Inception	Date of Expiration	Total Amount of Arrangement	Amount Not Purchased at Expiration or Cancellation
Brazil	3/1/83	2/28/86	4,239.38	1,496.25
Chile	8/15/85	8/14/88	750.00	—
Costa Rica	6/17/81	6/16/84	276.75[a]	254.25
Dominica	2/6/81	2/5/84	8.55	—
Dominican Republic	1/21/83	1/20/86	371.25[b]	247.50
Grenada	8/24/83	8/23/86	13.50[c]	12.37
Guyana	6/25/79	6/24/82	62.75[d]	52.75
	7/25/80	7/24/83	150.00[e]	98.27

Member	Date of Inception	Date of Expiration	Total Amount of Arrangement	Amount Not Purchased at Expiration or Cancellation
Haiti	10/25/78	10/24/81	32.20	21.40
Honduras	6/28/79	6/27/82	47.60	23.70
Jamaica	6/9/78	6/8/81	200.00[f]	130.00
	6/11/79	6/10/81	260.00[g]	175.00
	4/13/81	4/12/84	477.70[h]	74.90
Mexico	1/1/77	12/31/79	518.00[i]	518.00
	1/1/83	12/31/85	3,410.63	907.95
Peru	6/7/82	6/6/85	650.00[j]	385.00

Source: Margaret Garritsen de Vries, *Balance of Payments Adjustment, 1945 to 1986, the IMF Experience* (International Monetary Fund, 1987).

[a]Canceled as of December 20, 1982, and replaced by a stand-by arrangement.

[b]Arrangement canceled as of January 17, 1985.

[c]Arrangement canceled as of January 23, 1984.

[d]Canceled as of June 24, 1980.

[e]Arrangement augmented by SDR 50.00 million in July 1981 to a total of SDR 150.00 million. Arrangement canceled as of July 22, 1982.

[f]Canceled as of June 10, 1979.

[g]Canceled as of April 12, 1981.

[h]Arrangement augmented by SDR 241.30 million in June 1981 to a total of SDR 477.70 million.

[i]Includes augmentation by repurchase equivalent to SDR 100.00 million.

[j]Arrangement canceled as of April 24, 1984, and replaced by a stand-by arrangement.

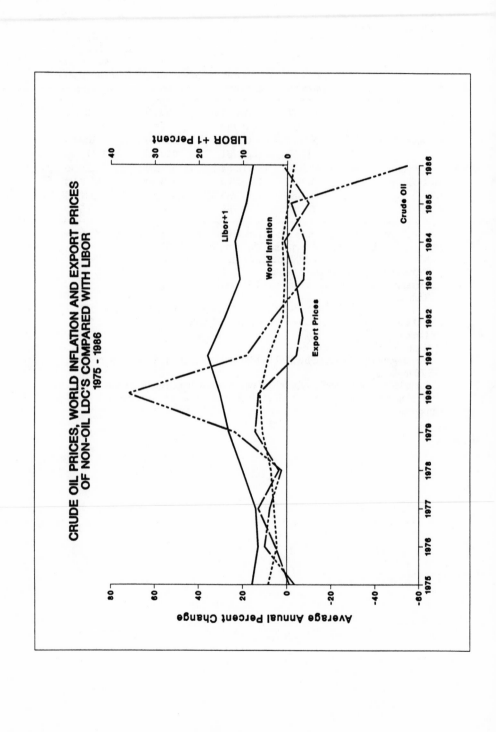

CRUDE OIL PRICES, WORLD INFLATION AND EXPORT PRICES
OF NON-OIL LDC'S COMPARED WITH LIBOR
1975 - 1986

LIBOR +1 Percent

Average Annual Percent Change

Libor+1

World Inflation

Export Prices

Crude Oil

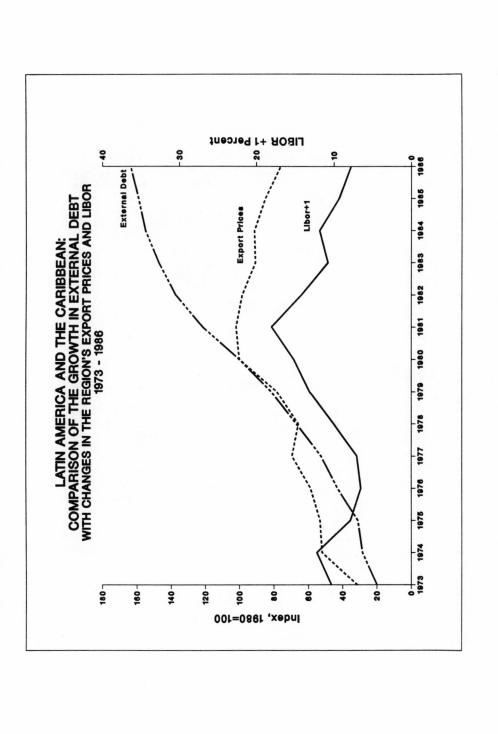

LATIN AMERICA AND THE CARIBBEAN:
COMPARISON OF THE GROWTH IN EXTERNAL DEBT
WITH CHANGES IN THE REGION'S EXPORT PRICES AND LIBOR
1973 - 1986

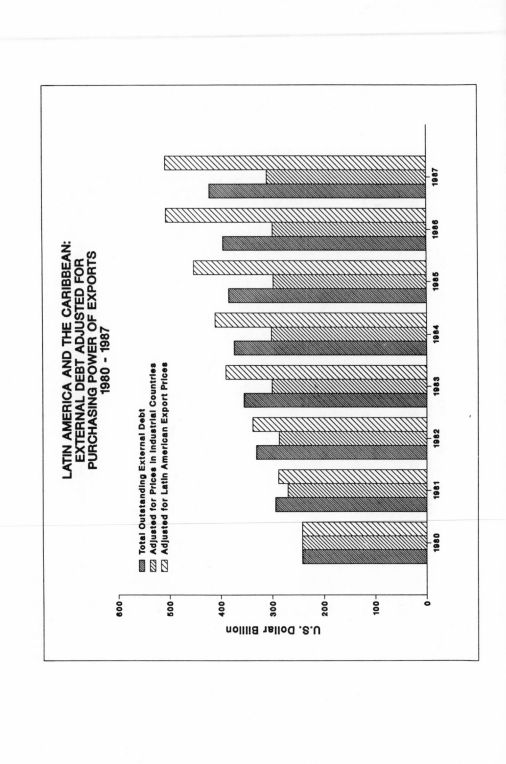

LATIN AMERICA AND THE CARIBBEAN:
EXTERNAL DEBT ADJUSTED FOR
PURCHASING POWER OF EXPORTS
1980 - 1987

Notes

---

1. A Latin American Problem

1. Walter B. Wriston, *Risk and Other Four Letter Words* (New York: Harper & Row, 1986), p. 151.

2. A systematic study of these past debt cases can be found in Irving S. Friedman, *The World Debt Dilemma: Managing Country Risk* (Philadelphia: Robert Morris Associates, 1983).

3. See the account by Lee Iacocca in *Iacocca: An Autobiography* (New York: Bantam Books, 1984), p. 240, on how banks kept lending to Chrysler and then abruptly cut off when there were clouds on the horizon.

4. "Latin America" refers to Latin America and the Caribbean as a whole, even though most of the smaller Caribbean islands are not directly involved in the debt problems discussed here.

5. See, for example, Organization for Economic Cooperation and Development (OECD), *External Debt of Developing Countries: 1983 Survey* (Paris: OECD, 1984), and successive annual issues of the *World Development Report* from the World Bank. While the level of industrial development is indeed a useful measure of economic development, it is not particularly useful in the analysis of external debt. Such a classification puts into the same category countries as diverse as Brazil, Mexico, and Argentina, on the one hand, and South Korea, Taiwan, and Thailand, on the other; the former are countries that have a high external debt and modest export earnings, while the latter rely on export-led growth and a more modest external indebtedness. Moreover, measuring average industrialization against gross national product (GNP) may conceal major regional differences; for example, in relation to GNP, India may not look very industrialized because of the huge weight of its peasant economy, but its industrial sector was already one of the largest in the world in the late nineteenth century.

6. Technically, it would be more nearly accurate to compare debt and debt service to exports of goods and services, which include income from services such as tourism and workers' remittances, for example. In practice, however,

central banks have difficulty collecting foreign exchange from services, and it is therefore not generally available to them for meeting external payments. Furthermore, the balance of the service account in Latin America is almost always negative because of interest payments and profit remittances, so that it is not a net provider of foreign exchange. It is therefore practical to use only merchandise exports as the standard of comparison for debt statistics, although obviously any comparison suffers from limitations.

7. The famous book sponsored by the Club of Rome, *The Limits to Growth,* by Dennis Meadows et al. (New York: Universe Books, 1972), was the most prescient and representative example of the fear, ushered in by the rise in the price of oil, that the world would face shortages of key raw materials.

8. Commercial paper consists of short-term bills issued by first-class corporations, typically representing future receivables. The paper is bought by other corporations and institutional investors with temporary surpluses of cash. It is placed directly or through agents such as investment banks. The paper is cheaper than borrowing from a bank because it avoids the cost of reserves, which banks have to keep for the safety of their depositors; it also keeps overhead cost to a bare minimum (normally 0.10 to 0.25 percent). Given the quality of the issuer and its short-term maturity, the paper is highly liquid. There is about $300 billion worth of such paper outstanding in the United States, compared to $700 billion of all corporate loans outstanding by U.S. banks.

9. As noted in Chapter 2, however, the International Monetary Fund was consistently cautious in its views on recycling. See Chapter 2, note 11.

10. See Bibliography for several relevant pieces by William R. Cline of the Institute for International Economics, the staff of the Federal Reserve Bank of New York, and others.

11. See, for example, Wassily Leontieff, *Essays in Economics,* essay 17 (Oxford: Oxford University Press, 1966). For a discussion of the basic concepts of development, see Sir W. Arthur Lewis, *The Evolution of the International Economic Order* (Princeton: Princeton University Press, 1977), as well as his *The Theory of Economic Growth* (Homewood, Ill.: Homewood Publishers, 1955); and W. W. Rostow, *The Process of Economic Growth* (New York: Norton, 1952).

2. Development in the 1960s and 1970s

1. Besides the usual statistical and conceptual caveats involved in such data (see, for example, the famous work by Oskar Morgenstern, *On the Accuracy of Economic Observations* [Princeton: Princeton University Press, 1963]), statistics in developing countries are, in large degree, estimated. A few examples: foreign trade data may include large "guesstimates" for smuggling or drugs; farm production is often not known accurately because of the large output for personal use by small farmers; price statistics may be distorted by out-of-date consumer baskets and by the desire of governments to keep published inflation figures low.

2. Because of the difficulty of measuring the distribution of personal incomes accurately, there is much debate regarding the facts and causes of uneven distribution. Brazil is probably the most controversial case, with a debate between those who argue that the growth in the period 1964–80 led to increasingly uneven incomes and those who argue that growth improved income distribution. See, for example, Albert Fishlow, *Brazilian Size Distribution of*

Income, American Economics Association, Papers and Proceedings (Washington, D.C., May 1972), and subsequent writings; and G. P. Pfeffermann and R. Webb, *Poverty and Income Distribution in Brazil,* World Bank Staff Working Paper 356 (Washington, D.C., September 1979).

3. Inter-American Development Bank, *Economic and Social Progress in Latin America,* 1982 Report (Washington, D.C., 1982). Other sources show less growth in regional trade.

4. See two recent comprehensive analytical studies: Angus Maddison, *Two Crises: Latin America and Asia, 1929–38 and 1973–83* (Paris: OECD, 1985); and Jeffrey D. Sachs, *External Debt and Macroeconomic Performance in Latin America and East Asia,* Brookings Papers on Economic Activity, 2 (Washington, D.C., 1985).

5. See, for example, the following United Nations ECLA (now ECLAC because of the addition of the Caribbean to its title) publications: *The Economic Development of Latin America in the Post-War Period* (New York: United Nations, 1964); *The Process of Industrial Development in Latin America* (New York: United Nations, 1966); *Development Problems in Latin America: An Analysis by the United Nations Economic Commission for Latin America* (Austin: University of Texas Press, 1970); and Raúl Prebisch, *Change and Development: Latin America's Greatest Task,* also available in Spanish: (*Transformación y Desarrollo: La Gran Tarea de America Latina*) (Washington, D.C.: Inter-American Development Bank, 1971).

6. For a discussion of Latin American trade and exchange rate policies, see Morgan Guaranty Trust, *World Financial Markets,* May 1985; and G. P. Pfeffermann, *Latin America and the Caribbean: Economic Performance and Policies,* World Bank Reprint Series no. 228 (Washington, D.C., 1983).

7. Prebisch, *Change and Development.*

8. *Fortune,* November 26, 1984.

9. Pedro-Pablo Kuczynski, "The Peruvian External Debt: Problem and Prospect," *Journal of Interamerican Studies* 23, no. 1 (February 1981): 3–27.

10. See the annual *World Debt Tables* and the *Annual Report* of the World Bank.

11. The IMF annual reports are an exception to the praises of recycling. The IMF repeatedly warned against too much borrowing and not enough "adjustment" by borrowers. See, for example, *1977 Annual Report.*

12. Carlos F. Díaz-Alejandro, *Latin American Debt: I Don't Think We Are in Kansas Anymore,* Brookings Papers on Economic Activity, 2 (Washington, D.C., 1984).

13. Morgan Guaranty Trust devoted part of its March 1986 issue of *World Financial Markets* to the subject of "LDC Capital Flight." Despite some caveats about the difficulties of estimation, the piece concludes that if there had been no "capital flight," Argentina and Mexico would have negligible foreign debts, and Venezuela would actually have a negative debt. These are interesting arithmetical calculations but may fail to take account of the fact that part of the capital flight could in fact have been unregistered imports (smuggling) because of import prohibitions and high tariffs (a major problem in most Latin American countries), and that the existence of dual exchange markets in several countries makes basic balance-of-payments statistics somewhat untrustworthy. The more important point, however, is that large external borrowing made possible overvalued exchange rates, which in turn encouraged capital flight. The bank lenders appeared little concerned with capital flight in the heyday of lending (1975–82).

14. See Morgan Guaranty Trust, *World Financial Markets,* March 1986.

3. The Role of the State and State Enterprise

1. The Institute for Liberty and Democracy in Peru has done a number of sample surveys which show that the informal sector of the economy is much larger than originally thought. See Hernando de Soto Polar, *El Otro Sendero* (Lima: Instituto Libertad y Democracia, 1986).

2. See Pedro-Pablo Kuczynski, *Peruvian Democracy under Economic Stress: An Account of the Belaúnde Administration, 1963–1968* (Princeton: Princeton University Press, 1975), p. 83, where I calculated that the taxes lost in order to encourage assembly plants would have enabled each worker employed in the plants to receive an annual state subsidy of $10,000, several times the industrial wage in the mid-1960s.

3. See, for example, *Towards Full Employment: A Program for Colombia* (Geneva: International Labor Office, 1970); report of a team led by Professor Dudley Seers.

4. International Monetary Fund, *Government Finance Statistics Yearbook 1985* (Washington, D.C., 1986).

5. Cited in G. P. Pfeffermann, *Latin America and the Caribbean: Economic Performance and Policies,* World Bank Reprint Series no. 228 (Washington, D.C., 1983).

6. International Monetary Fund, *Government Finance Statistics Yearbook 1985.*

7. See, for example, G. P. Pfeffermann, "The Social Cost of Recession—Brazil" (World Bank, Washington, D.C., 1985, unpublished paper). Pfeffermann was chief economist of the World Bank for Latin America and the Caribbean.

8. See Pfeffermann, *Latin America and the Caribbean.*

4. Mexico, Latin America, and the International Economy, 1980–1982

1. See, for example, Mario Henrique Simonsen, "The Developing Country Debt Problem," in *International Debt and the Developing Countries: A World Bank Symposium,* ed. Gordon W. Smith and John T. Cuddington (Washington, D.C.: World Bank, 1985).

2. For a long-term comparison of real interest rates, see Milton Friedman and Anne Jacobson Schwartz, *A Monetary History of the United States, 1957–1960* (Washington, D.C.: National Bureau of Economic Research, 1963).

3. Despite some hesitancy, this was assumed in the annual report of the World Bank in 1982 (see Chap. 2) and World Bank, *World Development Report 1982,* both of which came out in July 1982. The annual report of the International Monetary Fund in 1982 (see pp. 31–40) is far more cautionary. However, the IMF data on p. 36 substantially underestimate the medium- and long-term debt of Latin America.

4. Malvinas is the Spanish name, just as Malouines (derived from the French port of Saint-Malo) is the French name. President Fernando Belaúnde Terry of Peru played an important role in May 1982, attempting a reconciliation between the two warring sides through then-Secretary of State Alexander Haig as a conduit to Britain and directly to President Galtieri of Argentina. The effort was doomed when, on May 2, a British torpedo sank the Argentine cruiser

Belgrano, with over one thousand men aboard, when it was clearly outside the war zone limits set by the British.

5. See Jeffrey D. Sachs, *External Debt and Macroeconomic Performance in Latin America and East Asia,* Brookings Papers on Economic Activity, 2 (Washington, D.C., 1985).

6. Pedro-Pablo Kuczynski, "Latin American Debt," *Foreign Affairs* (Winter 1982/83): 344–64.

7. U.N. Economic Commission for Latin America and the Caribbean (ECLAC), *Preliminary Overview of the Latin American Economy, 1985* (Santiago, Chile, December 1985). It has been argued that drug exports kept Colombia away from debt: other countries had drug exports but still faced a debt problem. The key factor in Colombia was the low level of debt to banks.

8. Data from The First Boston Corporation, 1985.

9. Morgan Guaranty Trust, *World Financial Markets,* various issues.

10. The rate quoted in newspapers and financial information services is, of course, an indicative average. Actual transactions and the actual rates applicable to individual loans usually differ by some small margin.

11. The U.S. prime lending rate, which is not directly market-determined, has usually been higher than LIBOR, a deposit rate.

12. See Pascual García Alba and Jaime Serra Puche, *Causas y Efectos de la Crisis Económica en México* (Mexico City: El Colegio de México, 1984), p. 39.

13. See Chapter 2, table 2-5.

14. The late Joseph Kraft's brilliant and entertaining account, *The Mexican Rescue* (New York: Group of Thirty, 1984), is required reading for anyone interested in the debt question. It covers the subject of this section in detail.

15. See Kuczynski, "Latin American Debt."

16. "Can Brazil Make It?" *Euromoney,* November 1982.

17. See speech by Carlos Geraldo Langoni, president of the Central Bank of Brazil, New York, December 20, 1982, reported in the *New York Times,* December 21, 1982.

18. See, for instance, *Time*'s cover story, "The Debt Bomb—The World-wide Peril of Go-Go Lending," January 10, 1983.

19. Kraft, *Mexican Rescue,* p. 48.

20. One percent, one-time fee on the $20 billion refinancing, and 1.25 percent on the $5 billion new loan. The fees came out of the new loan.

21. As noted, these were mostly European equipment credits that had been in the making for some time.

22. This cost was eventually partly offset by the Fideicomiso para la Cobertura de Riesgos Cambiarios—Exchange Risk Trust Fund of the Banco de Mexico. In synthesis, companies that adhered to a payment schedule in pesos were deemed to discharge their foreign exchange obligation at an exchange rate prearranged in advance and much more favorable than the present and likely future exchange rates. The cost of such schemes, which were also adopted by Argentina and Venezuela, is the implicit credit and monetary expansion that they create.

23. See M. S. Mendelsohn, *Commercial Banks and the Restructuring of Cross Border Debt* (New York: Group of Thirty, 1983), pp. 20–30.

5. Lenders and Debtors, 1982–1985

1. See, in particular, William R. Cline, *International Debt: Systemic Risk and Policy Response* (Washington, D.C.: Institute for International Economics, 1984): Morgan Guaranty Trust, *World Financial Markets,* particularly February, June,

and September 1983, as well as October/November 1984; International Monetary Fund, *World Economic Outlook,* April 1984 and April 1986.

2. President de la Madrid was a senior career officer in the Central Bank before he became director of public credit in the Finance Ministry, a path that had also been followed by Finance Minister Silva Herzog. In a number of Latin American countries, the Central Bank has been the training ground for many economists.

3. See, for example, Morgan Guaranty Trust, *World Financial Markets,* March/April, May, and August 1985.

4. An especially useful analysis of each country is found in Esperanza Durán, ed., *Latin America and the World Recession* (Cambridge: Cambridge University Press, 1985), which includes, among others, case studies on Brazil (by Julian Chacel), Mexico (George Philip), Chile (Tim Congdon), and Venezuela (Ramón Escovar Salom).

5. The author, as minister of energy and mines, pushed through the elimination in 1980 of a 17 percent ad valorem tax on traditional exports, but in 1983, with the support of the IMF, export taxes began to be reintroduced by a new cabinet in order to generate short-term fiscal revenue.

6. See, for example, Morgan Guaranty Trust, *World Financial Markets,* October 1982.

7. International Monetary Fund, *World Economic Outlook,* April 1986.

8. Inter-American Development Bank, *Economic and Social Progress in Latin America,* 1985 Report (Washington, D.C., 1985).

9. See, for example, U.N. Economic Commission for Latin America and the Caribbean, successive annual preliminary reviews of the Latin American economy.

10. See, for example, World Bank, *Poverty in Latin America: The Impact of Depression,* report prepared by G. P. Pfeffermann (Washington, D.C., August 1986).

11. Regulatory practices vary from country to country.

12. Public Law 98-181 of November 30, 1983: Domestic Housing and International Recovery and Financial Stability Act.

13. See, for example, Allan H. Meltzer, "A Way to Defuse the World Debt Bomb," *Fortune,* November 28, 1983, pp. 137–43, and Larry A. Sjaastad, "The International Debt Quagmire: To Whom Do We Owe It?" *World Economy* (September 1983): 305–24.

14. Anatole Kaletsky, *The Costs of Default* (New York: Twentieth Century Fund, 1985), p. 114.

15. Speech by Paul Volcker to the Bankers Association for Foreign Trade in Boca Raton, Florida, May 13, 1985.

16. Wassily Leontieff, *Essays in Economics,* essay 17 (Oxford: Oxford University Press, 1966), is an example of the theoretical foundation for this argument.

17. Present value assuming a discount rate of 8.5 percent.

18. Fideicomiso para la Cobertura de Riesgos Cambiarios (FICORCA), a fund in the Banco de Mexico specially created to manage the service of the foreign debt of the private sector.

19. These buyers of cheap companies were a new generation of entrepreneurs known as the "pirañas."

20. For example, Samper, a major Colombian cement producer, exchanged $130 billion of debt to banks (75 percent of the total) for a 75 percent equity

interest of the lenders in the company, including valuable real estate that had not been part of the $180 billion investment that the banks had financed.

21. Alexis Rieffel, *The Role of the Paris Club in Managing Debt Problems,* Princeton Essays in International Finance (December 1985), is a good recent account of the Paris Club.

6. The Role of the IMF and the Multilateral Agencies

1. See, for example, Marcilio Marques Moreira, *The Brazilian Quandary* (New York: Twentieth Century Fund, 1986), p. 31. Fundamental reading on the IMF and Brazil is Carlos Geraldo Langoni, *A Crise do Desenvolvimiento— Uma Estrategia Para O Futuro* (Rio de Janeiro: Jose Olympio Editora, 1985).

2. Schweitzer, who came from a distinguished Alsatian family that included his uncle Albert Schweitzer and his cousin Jean-Paul Sartre, had been head of the French Treasury (as was Jacques de Larosière subsequently).

3. Spoken by British Member of Parliament Stuart Holland at the International Conference on Exchange Rates in Zurich, June 1986. The conference was organized by Senator Bill Bradley (D., N.J.) and Representative Jack Kemp (R., N.Y.).

4. International Monetary Fund, *Government Finance Statistics Yearbook,* 1985, and *World Economic Outlook, 1986,* p. 56.

5. See Chapter 5, table 5-4. A recent systematic study of the effect of IMF programs on output is Thorvaldur Gylfeson, *Credit Policy and Economic Activity in Developing Countries with IMF Stabilization Programs,* Princeton Studies in International Finance, no. 60 (1987). The countries covered are mostly smaller economies with active programs in the period 1977–79. Gylfeson concludes from that group that the impact on growth is not major.

6. This model is essentially a monetary balance sheet approach, under which the more the resources of the banking system (such as capital and deposits) grow compared with the credit or asset side, the more foreign reserves increase, or decline if credit grows faster than resources. This is, of course, an ex-post accounting identity that helps to clarify variables but does not necessarily explain what makes them move.

7. A number of economists (e.g., William R. Cline) have argued that the indexation component of the deficit should be subtracted to arrive at the real deficit, which exerts demand pressure on real resources. This is true if the indexation component is saved (as was the case in Brazil), but it may well be spent, for example, on buying foreign exchange, if there is no confidence and if there is a high preference for foreign exchange. This is what happened in Mexico during much of 1985 and early 1986. The "real deficit" concept can thus sometimes be misleading and can be applied to promote inflationary economic prescriptions.

8. See, for example, Persio Arida and André Lara-Resende in *Inflation and Indexation: Argentina, Brazil, and Israel,* ed. John Williamson (Washington, D.C.: Institute for International Economics, 1985). An expanded and modified version is the Portuguese language edition, *Brasil, Argentina, Israel: Inflaçao Zero,* ed. Persio Arida (Rio de Janeiro: Paz e Terra, 1986). The book includes an evaluation of the Plan Austral by Argentine economist Guillermo Rozenwurcel and an appraisal of the Israeli price stabilization program by Prof. Michael Bruno, who became governor of the Bank of Israel in mid-1986.

9. Venezuela was one of the few countries to employ outside financial

advisers in 1983–84, despite strong objections from the Advisory Committee of Commercial Banks.

10. After Stanley Please, a former World Bank economist, who demonstrated that additional revenue generally creates additional expenditure.

11. Ragnar Nurkse, *Conditions of International Monetary Equilibrium,* Princeton Essays in International Finance, no. 4 (Spring 1945).

12. Technically, the IMF does not extend credit; a country "purchases" foreign currency from the IMF with its own currency and repays the credit by "repurchasing" its own currency with foreign currency. The IMF operates in Special Drawing Rights (SDR), a weighted unit of account comprising the U.S. dollar, the Deutsche mark, the yen, the pound sterling, and the franc. The value of the SDR thus fluctuates. In the period shown, it ranged from $1.10 per SDR to $1.02. During the period shown, "repurchases" were not significant.

13. Proposed by the Mexican authorities in 1982, according to Carlos Massad in "Debt: An Overview," in *The Debt Problem: Acute and Chronic Aspects* (special issue), *Journal of Development Studies,* no. 16 (1985): 3–24. There are, of course, many other references to the idea; some are cited in the Bibliography.

14. International Monetary Fund, *International Financial Statistics,* monthly, several issues.

15. The Compensatory Financing Facility (CFF) of the IMF was created in 1963 mainly to help commodity exporters suffering shortfalls beyond the control of the country. The shortfall for the previously elapsed twelve-month period is compared with the trend of what exports would otherwise have been over five years (two back, the shortfall year, and two projected years) so that actual drawing of funds from the Facility can be slow. Opponents of the CFF, the U.S. copper mining industry in particular, have argued that it has been used by Chile to sustain production and depress world prices beyond what would otherwise have been the case. Altogether, between the CFF and other forms of credit from the IMF, a member can in theory draw up to about 400 percent of its quota over a period of three years.

16. Citicorp, Public Affairs Department, New York, December 1983. A more cautious view is that of Rimmer de Vries, chief international economist of Morgan Guaranty Trust, in "International Debt: A Play in Three Acts," in Massad, *The Debt Problem,* pp. 185–94.

17. This system gives the lenders control over the proper use of funds, avoiding corruption and other forms of misuse.

18. At the end of fiscal year 1985, for example, the World Bank had reasonably liquid investments of $19.8 billion against likely disbursements in the following fiscal year of about $10 million. See World Bank, Annual Reports for 1985 and 1986. A recent analysis of the role of the World Bank toward the debtor country is Richard E. Feinberg, ed., *Between Two Worlds: The World Bank's Next Decade* (Washington, D.C.: Overseas Development Council, 1986).

19. World Bank, *Annual Report,* 1986, p. 21.

20. The IMF agreed to monitor the Colombian financial program each quarter, but, since there was no IMF money involved, the disbursements of the bank credits were not directly tied to IMF credit.

21. See, for example, Allan H. Meltzer, ed., *International Lending and the IMF* (Washington, D.C.: Heritage Foundation, 1983).

22. International Monetary Fund, *World Economic Outlook, 1984,* chap. 4; *1985,* chap. 2; and *1986,* chap. 5.

23. For example, Ronald Leven and David L. Roberts, "Latin America's

Prospects for Recovery," *Federal Reserve Bank of N.Y. Quarterly Review* 8 (Autumn 1983): 6–13; Rimmer de Vries, "International Debt"; "Third World Debt and Global Recovery," 1983 Jodidi Lecture at Harvard by World Bank President A. W. Clausen; speech by William Rhodes at the Financial Times Banking Conference, December 6, 1983.

24. George Soros, "The International Debt Problem" (Morgan Stanley, New York, 1983, Research paper). See also his *The Alchemy of Finance: Reading the Mind of the Market* (New York: Simon & Schuster, 1987).

25. International Monetary Fund, *World Economic Outlook,* yearly.

26. See, for example, United Nations Conference on Trade and Development (UNCTAD), *Trade and Development Report* (New York, 1986). Annex tables 11–13 give data on increases in developing countries' production for export of commodities.

27. A recent description of the problem is, for example, "Farm Subsidies Have Global Impact," *Washington Post,* July 13, 1986.

7. The Political Economy of External Debt

1. This projection assumes a marginal propensity to import of 1.25–1.50 (i.e., for every 1 percent increase in GDP, imports grow 1.25–1.50 percent) and world inflation of 3 percent, both rather conservative assumptions.

2. This figure is based on the assumption that approximately $30,000 of export value creates or maintains one job per year, a similar ratio to that used in several other estimates.

3. The most comprehensive attempt is by the World Bank, *Poverty in Latin America: The Impact of Depression,* report prepared by G. P. Pfeffermann, former chief economist of the Latin America and Caribbean Region (Washington, D.C., August 1986).

4. The Venezuelan authorities suspended the service on about $6 billion of private sector debt in 1983 and 1984, with a gradual easing in 1985 as most debts were registered and checked by RECADI, the office in the Finance Ministry specially created for that purpose. In June 1986 the Venezuelan Congress unilaterally limited interest on the private external debt to 5 percent annually and set a minimum maturity of 15 years. Under pressure from the U.S. Federal Reserve and creditor banks, in September 1986 Finance Minister Manuel Azpurua obtained a reversal of the legislation.

5. *New York Times,* June 16, 1986.

6. William R. Cline, *International Debt: Systemic Risk and Policy Response* (Washington, D.C.: Institute for International Economics, 1984), pp. 86–93; Anatole Kaletsky, *The Costs of Default* (New York: Twentieth Century Fund, 1985), pp. 13–20.

7. See, for example, poll in Peru conducted in January 1986 by *Peru Económico* and published in February 1986. Only 2.8 percent of low-income respondents were in favor of not paying, versus 8.3 percent for middle-income respondents; 29 percent of the poorest also said an effort should be made to pay at the original terms, the highest proportion of any group.

8. Carlos Rodríguez-Pastor had been director-general of the Central Reserve Bank of Peru in 1968–69. At that point, in March 1969, a few months after the coup of Gen. Juan Velasco Alvarado, he and his deputy—the author of this book—were forced to resign by the military. Rodríguez-Pastor became a senior officer of the Wells Fargo Bank from 1969 to 1982 and head of its international group for most of that period.

9. For example, at a U.N. ECLAC meeting in Bogotá, in 1983, Carlos Rafael Rodríguez, vice-president of Cuba, lauded Cuba's orderly servicing of its external commercial debt.

10. The idea of linking debt service to a percentage of export earnings is at first sight logically attractive. However, the ability to service debt depends of course on the whole of the balance of payments, including capital inflows. It is difficult logically to set a particular percentage of export earnings for debt service: Haiti had trouble with debt service of about 2 percent of exports in the sixties, while South Korea has no difficulty with 15 percent.

11. The members of the Cartagena Group are Argentina, Bolivia, Brazil, Chile, Colombia, Dominican Republic, Mexico, Peru, Uruguay, and Venezuela.

12. See Chapter 5, table 5-1.

13. See, for example, Cline, *International Debt,* chap. 8; and Thomas O. Enders and Richard P. Mattione, *Latin America: The Crisis of Debt and Growth* (Washington, D.C.: Brookings Institution, 1984). Both in retrospect overestimated export growth.

14. See Chapter 2, table 2-4.

15. An analysis in depth of this point is in Rudiger Dornbusch, *Policy Performance Links between LDC Debtors and Industrial Nations,* Brookings Papers on Economic Activity, 2 (Washington, D.C., 1985).

16. I am indebted to Prof. Larry Sjaastad on this point. His preliminary findings, reported to the July 1986 Wingspread meeting on International Debt organized by the University of Chicago, are that the terms of trade of major Latin American debtors rose by about 40 percent from 1973 to 1980, or by about the same percentage as the U.S. dollar depreciated against other major currencies, while since 1980 the reverse is true. Floating exchange rates are thus a key background element in the debt problem.

17. See, for example, Bela Balassa, *Change and Challenge in the World Economy,* pt. 6 (New York: Macmillan, 1985); also Bela Balassa, Gerardo M. Bueno, Pedro-Pablo Kuczynski, and Mario Henrique Simonsen, *Towards Renewed Economic Growth in Latin America* (Washington, D.C.: Institute for International Economics, 1986), chap. 2 and bibliography.

18. See Balassa, *Change and Challenge,* pp. 415–17.

19. SELA was formed in 1975 at the urging of President Echeverría of Mexico. See SELA, *The Renegotiation of Latin America's External Debt* (Quito, Ecuador: January 1984).

20. Felix G. Rohatyn, *The Twenty-Year Century* (New York: Random House, 1983), pp. 59–64.

21. Peter B. Kenen, "A Bailout Plan for the Banks," *New York Times,* March 6, 1983.

22. Minos Zombanakis, "The International Debt Threat—A Way to Avoid a Crash," *Economist,* April 30, 1983, pp. 11–14.

23. George Soros, "The International Debt Problem—A Prescription" (Morgan Stanley, New York, May 1984 Paper), and "The Debt Crisis—Why System-Wide Reform Is Critical," *New York Times,* August 19, 1984.

24. Harold Lever and Christopher Huhne, *Debt and Danger: The World Financial Crisis* (Boston: Atlantic Monthly Press, 1986), pp. 131–36.

25. See *Frankfurter Allgemeine Zeitung,* November 6, 1986. Another proposal was made by Henry Kissinger, "Solving the Debt Crisis: What's Needed Is Statesmanship," *International Herald Tribune,* June 25, 1984. And Adalbert Krieger Vasena, former economy minister of Argentina, has, along with others, proposed that Japan invest its surpluses through an IMF trust fund to help debtors in Latin America and elsewhere.

26. The author has made several proposals to various major debtors to swap floating rate debt into fixed rate obligations. All have foundered on the political objection of having to pay a higher immediate interest cost, even though governments recognize that in the long run a fixed rate obligation might well be cheaper.

27. John H. Makin, "How to Defuse the Mexican Debt Crisis," *Financial Times,* May 14, 1986.

28. Senator Bill Bradley, "A Proposal for Third World Debt Management" (Speech delivered in Zurich, June 29, 1986, reported in the *New York Times, International Herald Tribune,* and others, June 30, 1986).

29. The total U.S. subscription to the World Bank is about US$17 billion, of which $1.5 billion has actually been paid in cash since 1945.

30. *New York Times,* May 13, 1984.

31. Leonard Silk in the *New York Times,* May 9, 1984.

32. See, for example, op-ed editorial by the author, "Real Relief for World Debt," *New York Times,* August 24, 1986. In the summer of 1986 the First Boston Corporation pioneered two such issues, one for Standard Oil of Ohio ($375 million) and one for USX (formerly US Steel, $250 million).

33. See the study by Richard A. Debs, David L. Roberts, and Eli M. Remolona, *Finance for Developing Countries: Alternative Sources of Finance, Debt Swaps* (New York: Group of Thirty, 1987).

34. Among the market-based ideas that have been presented to Latin American borrowers in recent years is the system of "zero coupon" bonds, which exists in the United States and also in the Euromarket. Interest accumulates but does not get paid until final maturity. For example, when interest rates were high in 1984, a Latin American debtor could have bought a 30-year "zero" for about 12 cents on the dollar and thus guaranteed the full repayment of principal 30 years later. However, since the interest matters far more than the principal, a stream of "zeros" would also have to be purchased to guarantee the various interest payments. The transaction would then become prohibitively costly. The idea of "zeros" was a red herring for developing country debtors. See Chapter 9 for Mexico's offer in 1988.

Another technique was introduced in the Mexican multiyear reschedulings. It gave banks with a non-U.S. dollar deposit base the right to convert part of their loans into their home currency, which usually had a lower interest rate than in U.S. dollars. The potential saving, however, would have been more than offset in 1985–86 by the gain in value of nondollar currencies, a burden for debtors whose exports are usually priced in dollars. Fortunately, the potential amounts are small, and the options have apparently not been exercised so far.

35. On July 28, 1986, his first anniversary in office, President García of Peru announced a two-year cut-off of profit remittances abroad by foreign-owned corporations in Peru and the suspension of external debt service by all private companies. The idea is to "save" $500 million in foreign exchange in the period. The long-term cost in foreign investment inflows, taxes, and jobs lost is likely to be far higher. One year later, on July 25, 1987, he proposed the state takeover of all domestic commercial banks.

36. Since most of the interest paid is due to indexing to reflect inflation, and interest is about 15 percent of public outlays, eliminating the indexing component from the deficit calculation leaves a small public sector surplus. The theory is that the inflation component of interest is saved, which is true enough in a normal situation. However, in Mexico the central bank holds about 40 percent of the domestic debt and, given the slide of the peso, holders of the rest of the debt may not hold their interest earnings in pesos but may instead buy

dollars with them, putting even more downward pressure on the exchange rate and thus exacerbating inflationary pressures on the side of costs. The theory, which the IMF reluctantly accepted for the sake of expediency, is thus debatable.

37. No doubt Uruguay participated because of the active role of its foreign minister, Enrique Iglesias, as secretary of the Cartagena Group. Iglesias, as head of U.N. ECLAC until 1984, took a very active role in providing countries with up-to-date economic information relevant to the debt question.

38. See, for example, *International Herald Tribune,* June 30, 1986; also *New York Times,* op-ed editorial by the author, "Real Relief for World Debt," August 24, 1986.

8. *Is Development Dead?*

1. See, for example, William R. Cline, *International Debt: Systemic Risk and Policy Response* (Washington, D.C.: Institute for International Economics, 1984), chap. 4.

2. As of late July 1987, 50 U.S. banks had reported reserve additions totaling $16.7 billion and second-quarter net losses totaling $12.9 billion. See the *Wall Street Journal,* July 20, 1987.

3. The "exit bond" idea is not yet a marketable option: only a very few of the 360 banks in the Argentina syndicate availed themselves of the option. The discount on the exit bond was too large, and small lenders felt they could do better on their own. For a description and analysis of various possible components of the "menu," see William R. Cline, *Mobilizing Bank Lending to Debtor Countries* (Washington, D.C.: Institute for International Economics, 1987).

4. See George Moore, "LDC Debt Woes and the Banks," *Journal of Commerce,* June 12, 1987.

5. An increase of about 80 percent was endorsed in principle early in 1988 by major countries.

6. See article by the author, "Development Bank Stalemate Impedes Latin Recovery," *Wall Street Journal,* June 29, 1987.

7. See Eileen Marie Doherty, "Japan's Response to the Latin American Debt Crisis" (Paper prepared for the Japan Economic Institute, Tokyo, August 1987). Early in 1987 Prime Minister Nakasone announced a $30 billion recycling plan, but many of the details remained to be worked out, and the funds are not necessarily intended for the highly indebted countries in Latin America.

8. Bela Balassa, Gerardo M. Bueno, Pedro-Pablo Kuczynski, and Mario Henrique Simonsen, *Towards Renewed Economic Growth in Latin America* (Washington, D.C.: Institute for International Economics, 1986), p. 176. Obviously, such estimates are subject to all sorts of caveats, especially assumptions about world economic growth and commodity prices.

9. *Postscript and Update*

1. A major proposal to purchase LDC debts at a discount by a new international institution and to transfer part of the relief to the debtors—a scheme similar in nature to those advocated by George Moore and others—was made by James Robinson, chairman of American Express, at the end of February 1988. Despite its sophisticated financial features, the initiative is likely to encounter opposition from creditors and their governments.

Select Bibliography

General Books

Avramovic, Dragoslav, et al. *Economic Growth and External Debt.* Baltimore: Johns Hopkins Press, 1964. The economics of external borrowing and growth in developing countries. Basic text.

Balassa, Bela, Gerardo M. Bueno, Pedro-Pablo Kuczynski, and Mario Henrique Simonsen. *Towards Renewed Economic Growth in Latin America.* Washington, D.C.: Institute for International Economics, 1986. An analysis of policy reform in the debtor countries.

Cline, William R. *International Debt: Systemic Risk and Policy Response.* Washington, D.C.: Institute for International Economics, 1984. Comprehensive analysis and projections.

Delamaide, Darrell. *Debt Shock: The Full Story of the World Credit Crisis.* New York: Doubleday, 1984. A journalist's historical account.

Dornbusch, Rudiger. *Dollars, Debts, and Deficits.* Cambridge: MIT Press, 1987. Includes a wide-ranging analysis of the LDC debt question.

Friedman, Irving S. *The World Debt Dilemma: Managing Country Risk.* Philadelphia: Robert Morris Associates, 1983. Textbook; focuses on 1970s.

Inter-American Development Bank. *La Deuda Externa y el Desarrollo Económico de America Latina: Antecedentes y Perspectives.* Washington, D.C., 1984.

———.*Deuda Externa: Crisis y Ajuste* (1985 issue of the annual report on Economic and Social Progress in Latin America). Washington, D.C., 1985. Both indispensable reports; also available in English.

Lever, Harold, and Christopher Huhne. *Debt and Danger: The World Financial Crisis.* Boston: Atlantic Monthly Press, 1985. Brief and provocative account and proposals.

Lomax, David F. *The Developing Country Debt Crisis.* New York: St. Martin's Press, 1986. Systemic textbook analysis.

Lowenthal, Abraham F. *Partners in Conflict: The United States and Latin America.* Baltimore: Johns Hopkins University Press, 1987. The political perspective.

Makin, John H. *The Global Debt Crisis: America's Growing Involvement.* New York: Basic Books, 1984. Historical account and proposals.

Mayer, Emilio. *International Lending: Country Risk Analysis.* Reston, Va.: Reston Publishing, 1985. Account of past analytical mistakes and proposals for improvement.

Miller, Morris. *Coping Is Not Enough! The International Debt Crisis and the Roles of the World Bank and the International Monetary Fund.* Homewood, Ill.: Dow Jones-Irwin, 1986.

Collections of Articles and Essays

Durán, Esperanza, ed. *Latin America and the World Recession.* Cambridge: Cambridge University Press, 1985. Articles by David Stephen, Jonathan Hakim, John Williamson, Gustav Ranis and Louise Orrock, Julian M. Chacel, George Philip, Tim Congdon, Ramón Escovar Salom, and Victor Bulmer-Thomas.

Federal Reserve Bank of Boston. *Key Issues in International Banking.* Proceedings of a Conference, October 1977. Articles by Frank E. Morris, Henry S. Terrell and Sidney Key, Henry C. Wallich, Christopher W. McMahon, Irving S. Friedman, and Rudiger Dornbusch.

———. *The International Monetary System: Forty Years after Bretton Woods.* Proceedings of a Conference, May 1984. Articles by Jeffrey H. Bergstrand, Edward M. Bernstein, Richard N. Cooper, John Williamson, Pedro-Pablo Kuczynski, Robert V. Roosa, Robert Triffin, Henry C. Wallich, Otmar Emminger, Adolfo C. Diz, and Jacques J. Polak.

Feinberg, Richard E., ed. *Between Two Worlds: The World Bank's Next Decade.* Washington, D.C.: Overseas Development Council, 1986. Articles by Gerald K. Helleiner, Joan M. Nelson, Sheldon Annis, John F. M. Purcell, Michelle B. Miller, Charles R. Blitzer, and Howard Pack.

Feinberg, Richard E., and Valeriana Kallab, eds. *Adjustment Crisis in The Third World.* Washington, D.C.: Overseas Development Council, 1984. Articles by Albert Fishlow, Tony Killick, Graham Bird, Jennifer Sharpley, Mary Sutton, Stanley Please, Joan M. Nelson, Colin I. Bradford, Riordan Roett, Lance Taylor, and DeLisle Worrell.

———. *Uncertain Future: Commercial Banks and The Third World.* Washington, D.C.: Overseas Development Council, 1986. Articles by Lawrence J. Brainard, Karin Lissakers, Christine A. Bogdanowicz-Bindert, Paul M. Sacks, George J. Clarke, Catherine Gwin, and Benjamin J. Cohen.

Journal Of Interamerican Studies and World Affairs 27, no. 4 (Winter 1985–86). Devoted to the Latin American debt question. Articles by M. J. Mamalakis, J. C. Baena Soares, J. R. Behrman, I. L. Horowitz, F.

Pazos, F. E. Thoumi, H. Schwartz, H. C. Wallich, R. Z. Aliber, P. L. Brock, J. H. Street, and W. R. Cline.

Massad, Carlos, ed. *The Debt Problem: Acute and Chronic Aspects* (special issue). *Journal of Development Studies,* no. 16 (1985). Articles by C. Massad, W. R. Cline, R. Dornbusch and S. Fischer, D. Avramovic, A. Ferrer, P. Malen, A. B. Taylor, P.-P. Kuczynski, R. Prebisch, W. Robichek, A. M. Solomon, R. de Vries, L. Taylor, and F. Ffrench-Davis and S. Moline.

———. *Latin America: International Monetary System and External Financing.* Santiago de Chile: United Nations Commission for Latin America and the Caribbean, 1986. Articles by C. Massad, R. Arriazu, Mohsin Khan, and Roberto Zahler.

Meltzer, Allan H., ed. *International Lending and the IMF: A Conference in Memory of Wilson E. Schmidt.* Washington, D.C., 1983. Articles by A. H. Meltzer, W. A. Wallis, B. W. Sprinkel, J. Lewis, P. T. Bauer, M. B. Krauss, R. Vaubel, and A. B. Mandelstamm.

Myers, Robert J., ed. *The Political Morality of the International Monetary Fund.* New York: Carnegie Council on Ethics and International Affairs, 1987. Articles by John Williamson, Irving S. Friedman, Lance Taylor, Henry B. Schechter, Pedro-Pablo Kuczynski, Robert S. Browne, I. L. Horowitz, G. von Furstenberg, D. Gale Johnson, A. Robushka, L. J. Brainard, and Sally Shelton-Colby.

Smith, Gordon W., and John T. Cuddington, eds. *International Debt and the Developing Countries: A World Bank Symposium.* Washington, D.C.: World Bank, 1985. Articles by Richard N. Cooper and Jeffrey D. Sachs, Mark Gersovitz, Paul Krugman, Mario Henrique Simonsen, Jack M. McFadden, Richard Eckhaus, Gershon Feder, Vassilis Hajivassiliov, Stephen O'Connell, Rudiger Dornbusch, Arnold C. Harberger, Leopoldo Solis and Ernesto Zedillo, Yung Chul Park, D. J. Wood, and Anne O. Krueger.

Williamson, John, ed. *Prospects for Adjustment in Argentina, Brazil, and Mexico: Responding to the Debt Crisis.* Washington, D.C.: Institute for International Economics, 1983. Articles by Edmar Bacha, J. M. Dagnino Pastore, and Ariel Buira.

Country Studies

ARGENTINA

Dagnino Pastore, José Maria. *Progress and Prospects for the Adjustment Program in Argentina,* with comment by Miguel Kiguel. In John Williamson, ed., *Prospects for Adjustment in Argentina, Brazil, and Mexico: Responding to the Debt Crisis.* Washington, D.C.: Institute for International Economics, 1983.

Morgan Guaranty Trust. "Argentina." *World Financial Markets,* February 1985.

Prebisch, Raúl. *La Crisis del Desarrollo Argentino—de la Frustración al Crecimiento Vigoroso.* Buenos Aires: El Ateneo, 1986.

BOLIVIA

Baptista Gumucio, Fernando. *Estrategia Nacional para La Deuda Externa.* La Paz, Bolivia: 1984.

BRAZIL, ARGENTINA, ISRAEL

Arida, Persio, ed., with André Lara-Resende, Guillermo Rozenwurcel, and Michael Bruno. *Inflaçao Zero.* Rio de Janeiro: Editora Paz e Terra, 1986.

BRAZIL

Bacha, Edmar L. *The IMF and the Prospects for Adjustments in Brazil,* with comment by Rudiger Dornbusch. In John Williamson, ed., *Prospects for Adjustment in Argentina, Brazil, and Mexico: Responding to the Debt Crisis.* Washington, D.C.: Institute for International Economics, 1983.
Chacel, Julian M. *Brazil's Foreign Debt: The National Debate.* In Esperanza Durán, ed., *Latin America and the World Recession.* Cambridge: Cambridge University Press, 1985.
Dupas, Gilberto. *Crise e Transicao Democratica: 83/86—A Delicade Trajetoria Brasileira.* São Paulo: Editora Klaxon, 1987.
Fraga, Arminio. *German Reparations and Brazilian Debt: A Comparative Study.* Princeton Essays in International Finance, no. 163. Princeton, N.J.: Princeton University Department of Economics, 1984.
Geraldo Langoni, Carlos. *A Crise de Desenvolvimento, uma Estrategia para o Futuro.* Rio de Janeiro: José Olympio Editora, 1985.
Marques Moreira, Marcilio. *The Brazilian Quandary.* New York: Twentieth Century Fund, 1986.
Morgan Guaranty Trust. "Stabilization Policies in Brazil." *World Financial Markets,* July 1984.
———. "Brazil: Beyond the Cruzado Plan." *World Financial Markets,* August 1986.

CHILE

Congdon, Tim. *The Rise and Fall of the Chilean Economic Miracle.* In Esperanza Durán, ed., *Latin America and the World Recession.* Cambridge: Cambridge University Press, 1985.

COSTA RICA

Sanders, Sol W. *The Costa Rican Laboratory.* New York: Twentieth Century Fund, 1986.

MEXICO

Bailey, Norman A., and Richard Cohen. *The Mexican Time Bomb.* New York: Twentieth Century Fund, 1987.
Buira, Ariel. *The Exchange Crisis and Adjustment Program in Mexico.* In John Williamson, ed., *Prospects for Adjustment in Argentina, Brazil, and Mexico: Responding to the Debt Crisis.* Washington, D.C.: Institute for International Economics, 1983.
Freymond, Jean, and Alexandre Swoboda, eds., *The Mexican Debt and*

Payments Crisis. Geneva: International Center for Monetary and Banking Studies, 1983. Articles by R. Auberjonois, N. Bailey, M. Dealtry, J. Freymond, F. Garza, N. Krul, F. Leutwiler, J. J. de Olloqui, C. Segré, and Victor Urquidi.

García Alba, Pascual, and Jaime Serra Puche. *Causas y Efectos de la Crisis Económica en México.* Mexico City: El Colegio de México, 1984.

Kraft, Joseph. *The Mexican Rescue.* New York: Group of Thirty, 1984.

Morgan Guaranty Trust. "Mexico: Progress and Prospects." *World Financial Markets,* May 1984.

Newell, Roberto, and Luis Rubio. *Mexico's Dilemma: The Political Origins of Economic Crisis.* Boulder, Colo.: Westview Press, 1984.

Philip, George. *Mexico: Learning to Live with the Crisis.* In Esperanza Durán, ed., *Latin America and the World Recession.* Cambridge: Cambridge University Press, 1985.

Rubio, Luis, and Francisco Gil-Diaz. *A Mexican Response.* New York: Twentieth Century Fund, 1987.

PERU

Ortiz de Zevallos, Felipe, and Guillermo Thornberry, *Hipoteca y Rescate: Algunas Reflexiones sobre la Deuda Externa.* Lima: Mosca Azul Editores, Apoyo S. A., 1985.

VENEZUELA

Echeverría, Oscar A. *Deuda ... Crisis Cambiaria: Causas y Correctivos.* Caracas: Universidad Católica Andrés Bello, 1986.

Institutional Reports and Analyses

Bank for International Settlements. Annual reports, 1982–1987.

International Bank for Reconstruction and Development (World Bank). *World Development Report 1985.* New York: Oxford University Press, 1985.

International Monetary Fund (IMF). Annual issues of *World Economic Outlook,* 1983–1987.

Morgan Guaranty Trust. *World Financial Markets.* Monthly Publication. Issues of:

"International Lending." *World Financial Markets,* October 1982.

"Global Debt: Assessment and Prescriptions." *World Financial Markets,* February 1983.

"Global Debt: Assessment and Long-term Strategy." *World Financial Markets,* June 1983.

International Debt: Progress Report and the Task Ahead." *World Financial Markets,* September 1983.

"Currency Diversification for LDC/External Debt." *World Financial Markets,* August 1984.

"The LDC Debt Problem—At the Midpoint?" *World Financial Markets,* October/November 1984.

"Latin America's Trade Policies." *World Financial Markets,* May 1985.

"Strengthening the LDC Debt Strategy." *World Financial Markets,* September/October 1985.

"The Baker Initiative: The Perspective of the Banks." *World Financial Markets,* February 1986.

"LDC Capital Flight." *World Financial Markets,* March 1986.

"Growth and Financial Market Reform in Latin America." *World Financial Markets,* April/May 1986.

"LDC Debt: Debt Relief or Market Solutions?" *World Financial Markets,* September 1986.

"LDC Debt Realities," *World Financial Markets,* June/July 1987.

Organization for Economic Cooperation and Development (OECD). *External Debt of Developing Countries, 1983 Survey.* Paris, 1984.

United Nations Economic Commission for Latin America and the Caribbean. *Preliminary Overview of the Latin American Economy,* annual, 1982–1986, and *Panorama Económico de America Latina,* annual, 1982–1986.

Major Monographs and Articles

Bergsten, C. Fred, William R. Cline, and John Williamson. *Bank Lending to Developing Countries: The Policy Alternatives.* Washington, D.C.: Institute for International Economics, 1985.

Bogdanowicz-Bindert, Christine A. "World Debt: The United States Reconsiders." *Foreign Affairs* (Winter 1985/86).

Cline, William R. *Mobilizing Bank Lending to Debtor Countries.* Washington, D.C.: Institute for International Economics, 1987.

Debs, Richard A., David L. Roberts, and Eli M. Remolona. *Finance for Developing Countries: Alternative Sources of Finance, Debt Swaps.* New York: Group of Thirty, 1987.

Díaz-Alejandro, Carlos F. *Latin American Debt: I Don't Think We Are in Kansas Anymore.* Brookings Papers on Economic Activity, 2 (Washington, D.C., 1984).

———. "Goodbye Financial Repression, Hello Financial Crash." *Journal of Development Economics* 19, no. 1/2 (1985).

Dornbusch, Rudiger. *Policy and Performance Links between LDC Debtors and Industrial Nations.* Brookings Papers on Economic Activity, 2 (Washington, D.C., 1985).

Enders, Thomas O., and Richard P. Mattione. *Latin America: The Crisis of Debt and Growth.* Washington, D.C.: Brookings Institution, 1984.

Feldstein, Martin, Herve de Carmoy, Koei Narusawa, and Paul R. Krugman. *Restoring Growth in the Debt-Laden Third World.* Report to the Trilateral Commission, no. 33. New York: Trilateral Commission, 1987.

Fishlow, Albert. *The State of Latin American Economics,* in Inter-American Development Bank, *External Debt: Crisis and Adjustment.* Washington, D.C., 1985.

Guttentag, Jack M., and Richard J. Herring. *The Current Crisis in International Lending.* Washington, D.C.: Brookings Institution, 1985.

———. *Disaster Myopia in International Banking.* Princeton Essays in International Finance, no. 164. Princeton, N.J.: Princeton University Department of Economics, 1986.

Kaletsky, Anatole. *The Costs of Default.* New York: Twentieth Century Fund, 1985.

Kraft, Joseph. *The Mexican Rescue.* New York: Group of Thirty, 1984. Also covers non-Mexican aspects. Basic reading.

Kuczynski, Pedro-Pablo. "Action Steps after Cancún." *Foreign Affairs* (Spring 1982).

———. "Latin American Debt." *Foreign Affairs* (Winter 1982/83).

———. "Latin American Debt: Act Two." *Foreign Affairs* (Summer 1983).

———. *Debt and Latin America.* University of Geneva, International Center of Monetary and Banking Studies, 1984.

———. "The Outlook for Latin American Debt." *Foreign Affairs* (Fall 1987).

de Lattre, André. *L'Endettement International et les Pays en Voie de Developpement.* University of Geneva, International Center for Monetary and Banking Studies, 1983.

Lessard, Donald R., and John Williamson. *Financial Intermediation beyond the Debt Crisis.* Washington, D.C.: Institute for International Economics, 1985.

Maddison, Angus. *Two Crises: Latin America and Asia, 1929–38 and 1973–83.* Paris: Development Center of the OECD, 1985.

Mendelsohn, M. S. *Commercial Banks and the Restructuring of the Cross-Border Debt.* New York: Group of Thirty, 1983.

———. *The Debt of Nations.* New York: Twentieth Century Fund, 1984.

Pfeffermann, Guy Pierre. "Latin America and the Caribbean: Economic Performance and Policies." *Southwestern Review of Management and Economics* (Winter 1982).

———. *Poverty in Latin America: The Impact of Depression.* Washington, D.C.: World Bank, August 1986.

Roberts, David L., and Ronald Leven. "Latin America's Prospects for Recovery." *Federal Reserve Bank of New York Quarterly Review* 8, no. 3 (Autumn 1983): 6–13.

Sachs, Jeffrey D. *External Debt and Macroeconomic Performance in Latin America and East Asia.* Brookings Papers on Economic Activity, 2 (Washington, D.C., 1985).

———. *Managing the LDC Debt Crisis.* Brookings Papers on Economic Activity, 2 (Washington, D.C., 1987).

Sachs, Jeffrey D., and Harry Huizinga. *U.S. Commercial Banks and the Developing Country Debt Crisis.* Brookings Papers on Economic Activity, 2 (Washington, D.C., 1987).

Sjaastad, Larry A. "The International Debt Quagmire: To Whom Do We Owe It?" *World Economy* (September 1983).

Soros, George. *The Alchemy of Finance: Reading the Mind of the Market,* chaps. 5 and 18. New York: Simon & Schuster, 1987.

Index

Interest rates, 23, 34, 38, 47, 156, 169, 202; and commodity export prices, 14; and external debt, 12, 19, 31, 41, 42, 81–82, 112, 118, 161; and loans, 40, 79, 82, 143, 162. *See also* Fixed interest rates; Floating interest rates; Inflation, and interest rates; Real interest rates

Interest relief. *See* Debt relief

International financial institutions, 43, 122, 183. *See also* Multilateral development banks

International Harvester, 9

International Monetary Fund (IMF), 8, 108, 119–20, 162, 180, 206; and Brazil, 92–93, 96, 97, 152, 173, 176, 201; and Colombia, 130; debt information by, 43, 80, 123, 124, 199; and Latin America, 95, 123–24, 132–33; and Mexico, 84, 88, 89–90, 91, 122, 171–72, 205; and Peru, 150; policies, 124–31; programs, 5, 88, 89–90, 96, 97, 102, 117–18, 120, 121–22, 178, 189; special facilities, 41, 124, 132, 134, 164, 189, 190

Investment cost, 63, 64

Investments, 16, 48, 69, 102, 128–29, 142, 153, 191, 192, 198. *See also* Capital investment; Foreign investment; Public expenditures; Savings, and investment

Involuntary loans, 90, 93, 112, 114, 116, 119, 121, 179, 205–6

Jamaica, 25, 36, 86, 146

Japan, 45, 47, 193, 199; loans by, 117, 136, 194; loans to Mexico, 39, 87, 162, 172

Kaletsky, Anatole, 110–11

Kenen, Peter, 162

Kuhn Loeb Lehman Brothers, 7, 39

Labor force, 16, 25–26, 103, 105, 198, 207. *See also* Employment; Trade unions

Langoni, Carlos, 97

Latin America, 44; economic growth, 5, 14, 15–17, 21–22, 29–36, 146, 155–56; economic policy, 56, 70; economy, 94, 96, 198; external debt, 11–12, 13–

14, 36–38, 42, 52, 112, 133, 198–99; external debt payments, 18–19, 67, 114, 201–2; loans to, 2, 3, 7, 14–16, 35, 111, 123

Lazard Frères, 7

Leutwiler, Fritz, 92

Lever, Lord Harold, 162

LIBOR. *See* London Interbank Offered Rate

London Interbank Offered Rate (LIBOR), 40, 77, 79, 113, 163, 168

Long-term debt, 30, 74, 76, 80, 86, 163

López Portillo, José, 83, 84, 88

Lower income groups, 16, 105, 149

McNamar, R. T., 88, 91

McNamara, Robert S., 41, 136

Makin, John, 164

Mancera, Miguel, 82, 84

Manufactures, 16, 27, 64, 65, 158, 183–84, 187. *See also* Brazil, manufactures

Martin, Preston, 112–13

Martínez de Hoz, José, 40

Mexico, 45; economic growth, 25, 87, 175, 198; economic policy, 65, 68, 88–89, 94, 98, 177, 186, 195; economy, 50, 95, 96–97, 102, 134, 138, 145–47, 187, 194; external debt, 7, 11, 22, 36, 42–43, 74, 79, 118, 166, 168, 169, 182, 192, 203, 204–5; external debt payments, 1, 71, 81, 86–90, 92, 110, 113, 116, 124, 148, 164, 175; GNP, 20, 89, 122, 171, 172; industrialization, 15, 32; inflation, 96, 97, 122, 175, 177, 201, 202; loans to, 39, 73, 74, 76–77, 81, 87–88, 89–90, 114, 126, 131, 162, 171–72, 180, 204; monetary policy, 35, 37, 45, 47, 81, 83, 84, 88, 105; politics, 21, 105–6, 147–48; population, 2, 25; state enterprises, 39, 60, 63, 64, 83, 84, 88, 172; taxation, 60

Middle income groups, 16, 67, 105, 149

Mining, 60, 61, 65, 184. *See also* Copper

Mistry, Percy, 162

Moctezuma Cid, Julio, 83–84

Monetary policy, 32, 34, 125. *See also* Devaluation; Exchange controls; Interest rate controls; Monetary policy under countries, e.g. Venezuela, monetary policy

LATIN AMERICAN DEBT

Designed by Martha Farlow.
Composed by BG Composition, Inc., in Century Old Style.
Printed by R. R. Donnelly & Sons Company on 50-lb. Cream White Sebago
and bound in Holliston Roxite A cloth.